The Critical I

The Critical I

Norman N. Holland

NEW YORK

● Columbia University Press

COLUMBIA UNIVERSITY PRESS
NEW YORK   OXFORD

Copyright © 1992 by Norman Holland
All rights reserved

Library of Congress Cataloging-in-Publication Data
Holland, Norman Norwood, 1927–
    The critical I / Norman N. Holland
        p.   cm.
    Includes bibliographical references and index.
    ISBN 0–231–07650–9
    1. Criticism.   2. Literature—20th century—History and criticism.
    3. Saussure, Ferdinand de, 1857–1913.   4. Literature—Psychology.
    I. Title.
    PN94.H64   1991
    801′.95′0904—dc20   91–27851
                                                                                          CIP

♾

Casebound editions of Columbia University Press books
are Smyth-sewn and printed
on permanent and durable acid-free paper

Book design: Teresa Bonner
Printed in the United States of America

c 10 9 8 7 6 5 4 3 2 1

To Jane,
the I for this I

Contents

I[ai] *pron.* The first person singular pronoun in the nominative case. Used to represent the speaker or writer. —*n.* The pronoun I regarded as a word or represented as a person; *metaphorically* the self; ego. —*n. pl.* I's. Persons. —*v. neologism.* To consider ideas or writings from the standpoint of what they say about the I or self. —to I. —I-ing.

Preface

The Critical I. You can take my title in at least eighteen different ways. Please note that I do not say it has at least eighteen different meanings. My not saying that is the very core of this book.

I is defined on the preceding page in three different ways. As a pronoun or noun, it can refer to me specifically or to the idea of the subject generally. But it is also a verb, and you will find me using *I-ing* from time to time. In my title, I intend all three: pronoun, noun, and verb. This book is an "I-ing" (pun intended) of some contemporary practices in literary criticism.

As for *critical,* the trusty *Oxford English Dictionary* offers six senses. "Given to judging, *esp.* to adverse or unfavourable criticism." Yes. I's in general do judge and often adversely, and this I does a lot of that both in and out of this book. "Involving or exercising careful judgment." I'd like to think so. "Occupied with or skillful in criticism." The degree of skill you will have to judge for yourself, but "occupied with"—oh, yes! This book is much occupied with current literary, filmic, and other forms of criticism. "*Med.* Relating to the crisis or turning point of a disease." Sure. You could think of this book as addressing a disease, a disease of the intellect. "Of the nature of, or constituting, a crisis." That seems a bit dramatic for something that has so removed itself from the real world as literary criticism today, but still, it fits. "*Math.* and *Physics.* Constituting or relating to the point at which some action, property, or condition passes over into another." Now, wouldn't that be nice! If only this critical I marked the point at which there was a change in the actions of critics. It hardly seems likely, though, given the professorial investment in today's practice.

The Critical I is an I-ing of current criticism, its practice and theory. I-ing means two things to me. First, I look at today's critical practice to see what some of the practitioners assume about the I, the person engaged in the literary transaction. Second, I compare what critical practice and theory say about that I to a model of the I based in psychology and linguistics.

Part one establishes a baseline, my I-ing of an actual audience, three people seeing a porn movie. Surely, if any text should determine a response, a pornographic one should. But it doesn't. Their three responses have some things in common yet remain, finally, individual. From their comments on the movie, I derive a model of how they see the same movie but see it differently. This is an update of the model in *The I*, 1985, and *The Brain of Robert Frost*, 1988. I test the model against the famous Kuleshov experiment—yes, it will explain the Kuleshov effect. The analysis of response yields a picture of the I that we can use to think coherently about literature, even in all kinds of postmodern ways.

In part two a group of critics—a New Critic, three deconstructionists, two Lacanians, two psychoanalytic critics, and a generic postmodernist—read "Thirty days hath September." The question is, What do they assume about the I who reads and writes? The answers show profound differences between the psychological critics and the others—and profound confusions.

In part three I challenge today's literary "theory." The whole elaborate structure rests on a disproven linguistics and a dubious psychology. That is, most of today's "theory" carries on as though Chomsky's 1957 revolution in linguistics never took place. Most literary "theory" proceeds as though the only psychology were a crude stimulus-response behaviorism. The argument applies to a wide range of contemporary theorists: Barthes, de Man, Eco, Derrida, Foucault, Lacan, Miller, and others. These leading theorists criticize the old New Critics for mistaken linguistic and psychological assumptions—and they are right to do so. Yet they often draw on those same assumptions themselves.

What is needed today is literary theory that, one, acknowledges the human beings who create literature and literary experiences and, two, rests on a firm foundation in current linguistics and psychology. That is the promise this book holds out.

Speaking of human beings, I owe much in this book to a great many of them. I am thinking particularly of the students, colleagues, and friends who have helped me develop the ideas in this book. Some provided the responses discussed in parts one and two. Others provided criticism of the manuscript or consultation. Still others aided with research. All have helped make this a better book than it would otherwise have been, and to all I am deeply grateful. Let me thank specifically Robert de Beaugrand, Theodore Bickford, Alistair Duckworth, Gerald Graff, Deborah Hooker, Arthur Samuel Kimball, John Leavey, Brenda Marshall, Kimberley McSherry, Daniel Moors, Bernard Paris, Ellie Ragland-Sullivan, Robert Ray, Craig Saper, Murray Schwartz, Robert Silhol, Henry Sullivan, Gregory Ulmer, and Agnes Webb. To John Perlette in English and Gary Miller in classics at the University of Florida, I owe especial and large appreciation for their careful readings of part three and their detailed help in matters of literary and linguistic theory. Both went far beyond the basics of collegiality. Both took the time to teach me a great deal. The book and I have profited much, and I am more grateful for what they did for this book and its author than I can say.

Some of the chapters that follow have appeared in earlier forms as articles and lectures. The sections of part one that deal with *The Story of O* first appeared as "I-ing Film" in *Critical Inquiry* (1986), 12: 654–71. The parts that deal with the Kuleshov experiment appeared as "Film Response from Eye to I: The Kuleshov Experiment" in *South Atlantic Quarterly* (1989), 88.2: 416–442. They appeared in a still earlier form as "Psychoanalyse und Film: das Kuleschow-Experiment," *Phantasie und Deutung: Psychologisches Verstehen von Literatur und Film,* herausgeben von Wolfram Mauser, Ursula Renner, und Walter Schönau (Würzburg: Königshausen und Neumann, 1986), pp. 282–298. Some of part two appeared as "Twenty-Five Years and Thirty Days" in *Psychoanalytic Quarterly* (1986), 55: 23–52. Part three began as the keynote address, "Speaking Figuratively, I . . ." for the University of Louisville's Fourteenth Annual Twentieth-Century Literature Conference on Self and Other (February 22, 1985). Let me thank Professor Harriette Seiler here for both invitation and hospitality. Versions of what I say in chapter thirty about Lacan have appeared as an article-review of *The Works of Jacques Lacan: An Introduction*, by Bice Benvenuto and Roger Kennedy in *Psychoanalytic Psychology* (1990), 7.1: 139–149, and as "I-ing Lacan" in *Criticism and Lacan: Essays and Dialogue on Language, Structure, and the Unconscious*, edited by Patrick Colm Hogan and Lalita Pandit (Athens and London: University of Georgia Press, 1990), pp. 87–108. Most recently, I have discussed the matter as "The Trouble(s) with Lacan" at the Seventh International Conference on Literature and Psychology at Urbino, July 6–9, 1990. I am grateful to the editors of *Critical Inquiry*, the University of Georgia Press, *New Literary History*, *Psychoanalytic Psychology*, *Psychoanalytic Quarterly*, and *South Atlantic Quarterly* for permission to adapt here materials that first appeared under their aegis.

In addition I appreciate the help I have received from Stuart Krichevsky of Sterling Lord Literistics and Jennifer Crewe and Leslie Bialler of Columbia University Press in achieving publication. Most of all, though, I am grateful to the lady of the dedication—for everything.

The Critical I

I-ing an Audience

1

Kim's Case Study

Kimberley McSherry was a graduate student at the Center for the Psychological Study of the Arts at the State University of New York at Buffalo when I was teaching there. Kim had taught high school, and she was returning to the university for a master's degree. For a research project for that degree, she wanted to compare men's and women's responses to a pornographic movie. Accordingly, she led Agnes, Ted, and Norm (me) to a suburban art theater to see Just Jaeckin's well-known film, *The Story of O*, which was based on the anonymous novel of that name.

We were all involved in the literature-and-psychology Ph.D. program. Agnes had also taught school but was now embarked on a Ph.D. in education. Unlike Kim, she was a mother as well as a teacher and student. Ted, recently married, was trying to decide that spring between going into the family business and becoming a professor of English. Norm was—is—a professor of English, in his mid-forties at the time of Kim's case study, husband, father, and the student of reader-response with whom Kim was working.

After we had viewed this soft-porn, sadomasochistic

movie, Kim asked us to tell how we interpreted the movie and to talk about how we felt as we watched it. She asked us to narrate the story in our own words and to say how we felt toward the several characters—standard questions for this kind of reader-response case study. She tape recorded and transcribed these interviews, which approximated free associations. In doing so, she achieved something rare in the world of film studies: a record in considerable detail of what some real spectators said in response to a real film. She was I-ing an audience.

Kim and I were testing the proposition that people respond to texts, in this instance a movie, in determinate ways. We thought Kim's study would shed light on the various theories people set out so enthusiastically these days to account for such patterns. Surely if any film can dictate a standardized response, a pornographic film would. Kim expected *The Story of O* to stimulate desire in the men watching it, and she thought it might stimulate in women exactly the opposite response.

But it didn't. Kim did not find any pattern of differences between male and female responses to *The Story of O*. That is an even more interesting result than the predicted one, and Kim did indeed get her M.A. Kim's results show, I think, that we need to balance theory against fact. To that end, I would like to explore here in some detail what the three of us, Agnes, Norm, and Ted, said about *The Story of O*.

For those of you who have not seen it, the movie begins when O's lover, René, takes her to a castle where she submits to whippings and degrading sexual experiences at the hands of René and other men to whom he gives her. O obeys with apparent pleasure, and her accepting all this abuse initiates her into a sort of secret society, whose rules she continues to obey when she "graduates" from the castle. Soon René turns her over to his great friend, Sir Stephen. He too whips her, gives her to other men, uses her to lure women for René, and even has her branded. O submits to all this proudly and happily. She regards these experiences (and Sir Stephen does too) as evidence of a sublime kind of love. The film ends as they vaunt their relationship before a party of admiring guests, she wearing an owl headdress, but otherwise naked and chained to Sir Stephen.

None of us reported being sexually aroused by the film. That, you might think, was to be expected, given the anaesthetic tone of Kim's case study. I am not so sure. We had all four of us just participated, the previous semester, in an unusually open "Delphi seminar," in which we said a great many frank things about ourselves and one another. Indeed that was why Kim felt free to ask the three of us to watch this porn movie. Had any one of us found the film purely and simply sexy, I am sure we would have had no inhibitions about saying so. Also, since Kim was working with free associations, I would have expected them to reveal any suppressed arousals.

In any case, what I would like to address is a more general question about reponse. The three subjects, Agnes, Ted, and Norm, did sometimes feel and think about the film more or less alike. At other times, though, we squarely contradicted one another. I want to ask, therefore, two questions of the responses Kim taped. First, we three saw the same film, but responded differently. How can one relate the variety of responses to the singleness of the film? Second, we were about equally skilled in seeing and analyzing movies. How can one relate the variety of our responses to our having roughly the same skills with which to see this film? In general, then, the question I want to ask is, What is the relation, in our seeing this movie, between what we three shared in seeing *The Story of O* and what was quite individual and unique to each one of us?

Customarily, critics and theorists say that the film caused or controlled our responses, and then each of the three of us added some individual variation to the general response dictated by the movie. Viewers and film "interact." I think we can find a much more precise answer and one closer to what we know in the 1990s about human psychology. To do so, however, you and I will need to look almost microscopically at key words, phrasings, and recurrences in what the three viewers said. You and I need to do that, rather than paraphrase, because, as in a psychoanalysis, what counts is the exact wording. To understand the viewers' unconscious reactions as well as their conscious statements, the surface of their language is as important as the people or events referred to "through" their language. Our particular phrasings of our thoughts are what reveal patterns of repetition and contrast that will in turn show how we three were making an experience of the film.

For example, the film opens oddly. The opening scene shows O's lover René undressing her in a taxi as he takes her to the castle where she will undergo her sexual instruction. Having done the scene once, a voice over announces that they will do the scene again. Each of us "made sense of" that replay differently—as we shall see.

Agnes

This is how Agnes began to talk about the repetition of the opening scene: "I had a sort of snotty view. I was going to sit there and watch what they were doing wrong in the movie. They said the trees were dark, and I thought, they're not dark; they're light." (As I hear her, by this opening move, Agnes is establishing her own control over the film.) A few sentences later, on noticing that the film "sort of revised the fantasy," "Then I thought, this is somebody's fantasy, and then I relaxed. Since it's a fantasy, I don't have to do anything about it, just watch it." She relaxed, yet the theme of control—doing something about it—remained strong. "I thought about the revising of it, because I revise my fantasies. I start them out, and if I don't like the direction the story is taking, I start them over again. See if you can make it work differently."

She said she associated the castle where O trains in perversity with

> girls' schools that I had gone to and taught in. The silly little things—walking in line, attention to clothes, costume, furniture, the kind of dainty, precise eating they

were doing at the table, downcast eyes. We were trained in high school to keep our eyes down, like postulants in a convent, plus all the physical restraints. I keep thinking of high school.

Agnes associated control with schools she herself went to, with the school O goes to, and later, with the place where O is branded. She commented on it, "You could fly. You could leave." On the other hand, if you are in a certain place, that limits your choices. Thus, "Once you accept going to the castle—well, going into that place is of your own free will, but once you're there and have committed yourself to bearing this, there isn't any free will to individual acts. You've accepted the whole thing."

She went on to associate the castle of pain with her own dominance, as a high school teacher, over students. "Just being in the school and being a student with a teacher, you can say you have the freedom not to answer, and then you ask them a question, well, there really isn't freedom not to answer." Agnes recalled her own high school: "the no running, no laughing, no talking, no running around, no physical exuberance at all." She remembered a retreat at which a friend got hysterical on the stone floor.

Agnes went on to imagine herself in the castle:

> I remember thinking, after a few days, if that had happened to me, I would have been so disoriented I wouldn't remember what day it was, or what time of the day it was. And I thought that just before the comment she made, that she didn't know what day it was or where she was, and at that point I felt sympathy for her, and I suppose at that point I accepted the reasons that she was there—really believed those reasons.

A place can disorient you, and, because she saw O as being victimized by a place, Agnes sympathized with her and believed her.

In this part of Agnes' response, we are seeing one of her major themes: we are controlled by the places we are in. We are also seeing the process critics loosely term "identification," but now we can see how it really works. Agnes has taken O's feelings into herself, making them her own. Notice, though, that to do this, she first picked out of the stream of the film something O said and shaped it into something that mattered to her, Agnes. She decided that O was disoriented *because* of the place she was in. *Then* Agnes could say, "At that point I felt sympathy." "At that point I accepted the reasons . . . really believed." At that point she was not judging or controlling O. Agnes was feeling as O felt (or, more precisely, as she imagined O felt). Agnes "identified" to the extent she had fitted O to her own psychological themes.

In Agnes' world, place controls you, and escape from that place means freedom. In another example of her spatial mode of thinking, Agnes thought "connection" important. Connection to her means purpose, the opposite of isolation, self-centeredness, or indifference. Thus she could read pain in the movie in two different ways, depending on connection. Bad pain is "where you become turned in on yourself. Suffering becomes a way of life, rather than a means to something." The bad thing about the pain in this movie was that "I didn't see anything creative coming out of, or anything generated out of all the accepting of pain and suffering and humiliation. She [O] became predatory."

Agnes (herself a mother) contrasted that kind of pain with childbearing, the pain of which, she said (citing Helene Deutsch), resolves childhood fantasies for a woman. "Not that suffering is good for you, but suffering has a resolving effect."

> It was that hysterical seeking of pain I think is so horrible. . . . That's what I thought was in the movie. I thought it was the unregenerative type. I thought it had become seeking of pain for pain's sake, rather than the healthier aspect of pain—the joy of pain, as funny as that sounds—when pain is actively connected to something of worth to it.

"Actively connected." That phrase says to me something about Agnes' sense of place as a way to be active and in charge. Suffering "enables them [women] to go on to another stage of development—one where the suffering isn't dwelt on or lulled over," another place. The opposite—isolation, self-containedness— Agnes associated with not controlling your circumstances and with pain for pain's sake.

Thus at the beginning of the movie she read O this way:

> When the film started, in the car, I remember not liking O. She had no expression on her face. She was taking off her clothes and looking at the driver. I think she said at one point, the driver will hear or is looking, and other than that, she seemed to have no reaction on her face. Her face was blank. And I remember thinking at that

point, you don't have to do this. You could react somewhat and not be like a dream-walker.

Agnes wondered in the early part of the movie, "Why are you so dumb to do this and to go through all this pain?" "She kept telling us over and over, it was to prove her love for him [René]," and Agnes had trouble believing that. At the end of the film, "I remember thinking she had become predatory. As predatory as all the people were in that spa, or pain factory. But beautiful in all her cold, aloof predatoriness. I think it was the aloofness and coldness that bothered me. Very calculated."

It was the lack of connection ("aloofness") that put Agnes off. It was "coldness" that she read as "predatory." Conversely, the only motive she, with her values, could hear was one of connection: O was suffering pain to prove her love for her first lover, René. "I suppose at that point I accepted the reasons that she was there—really believed those reasons. She was there out of love for René, and I thought that was a pretty odd way to work it out."

Again, in a spatial mode, when Agnes disapproved of René, "I wrote him out of it." "I just considered he wasn't an important part of it." She simply moved him out of the film. She ended his connection to it. Conversely, when she liked Sir Stephen, O's second lover, she placed him: "The only time I liked Stephen was in the scene where they were talking outdoors. There was a colonnade, and she was holding his arm . . ." Connection established is good. "But then he tells her he will give her to someone else, and I thought, 'Ugh! I don't like that.'" Connection broken is bad.

Norm

Agnes saw *The Story of* O through her belief in the power of place and connection. To hear Agnes' patterns *as* a pattern, it helps if you contrast another response, say, Norm's—mine (although here I will write of my long-ago self in the third person). Agnes had used the replay of the opening episode as a chance to relax her controls. Norm, however, found it an occasion to intellectualize the film. "There are a lot of puzzles for me in this movie. One is that opening scene in the cab. They run that scene, and then they say, Well here is another version, and then they do it again. I couldn't figure out what was going on there."

In general, Norm treated the film as something to be figured out.

> I was struck by all the Os. That is . . . starting with her underwear in the very first scene, where he [René] undresses her in the cab, you get a whole lot of circles. Like the necklace—that leather thing she wears around her neck—or the various chains, the garter-type corset—Os of all kinds. I just had a sense of circular openings of one kind or another. The manacles, handcuffs that she

wears—all kinds of stuff like that. And this kept running through the movie. . . . There are many others—the way her eyes are circles when she's dressed up like the bird at the end, the many different kinds of rings—the one on her hand, the one on her genitals— many, many circles around.

Norm's interpretation of the Os suggests why he converted the movie to an intellectual puzzle.

I kept hearing or thinking about the Os as simply the initial for "obey," which would be the way I would do it [i.e., work the movie out critically], and that holds in French too, and also a . . . zero in the sense that she becomes a kind of nullity—a no-person—at the end, and the O as in the chains, a kind of bondage.

Although Norm is a psychoanalytic critic, supposedly alert to sexual symbolism, it seems not to have occurred to him to talk about these enclosing Os as possible symbols for a vagina. Rather, he read those Os as ethical rules to be obeyed by O (but implicitly, perhaps also by himself). "She has to learn all this stuff and these are the rules of the game—the rules of *this* world. And so I felt the O and the circles were all kinds of constraints."

Norm did something very similar with the opening "retake":

I couldn't figure out what was going on there. And I thought to myself, 'Well, perhaps it's like a fable. We're not supposed to take this story as true, but only like a fairy story,' which indeed makes perfect sense, because it seems like a very unreal, impossible place— the castle or wherever it was—so that . . . it becomes a tale with a moral, like an Aesop's fable, but a longer version, and you begin to wonder what the moral is.

In other words, by Norm's effort to make "perfect sense" of it, to convert this sexy film into a puzzle he could solve intellectually, he was trying to put the film into an ethical framework. Just as Norm read O as having to learn the rules of this world, he felt he had to find an Aesopian moral to the story. He was using rules for interpretation to generate rules for conduct.

When Norm talked about O's branding Sir Stephen with the hot round end of his cigarette holder, he hinted at what he was trying to puzzle through. "Finally, of course, when she marks him with her O, she indicates in some way that she isn't a nullity, that she has, in some way, taken possession of him." If you can mark the film as your own, as by your skilled interpretation of it, you are not a nullity. You have taken possession of it. It does not master you—you master it.

By interpreting, Norm would learn "the rules of the game, the rules of *this* world." That suggests to me now, thinking about Norm then, that he was hoping by his puzzling to find the rules of the much bigger, realer world you and Norm and O and I inhabit. Hence, like Agnes, Norm gave a religious reading of the film:

> It's as though people were in the service of an exotic kind of cult. The rules in many ways were as strict as they might be for a monastery or a nunnery, or something like that. There were these confessions you had to make, tasks you had to perform, ordeals you had to go through, and you became initiated into a group of believers who had these rules.

Norm converted the bizarre, perverse practices of "this world" into religious and moral rules.

Further, Norm seems to have felt that this sadomasochistic pattern of either ruling or being ruled represented an almost desirable mode of human society, even if the rules are perverse. "I don't know what in the film was saying that to me, but something was saying that very much: that everybody would be doing this if they had any real guts—if they were really able to go with their unconscious desire." (In 1991, it occurs to me that it may have been the solemn, almost liturgical music.) "It's as though these [sadomasochistic] people are the really courageous ones—the heroes."

This heroism and these rules have a lot to do with possession in Norm's interpretation.

> Part of the specialness of this group was, I think, the sense of possession. I remember a line that I jotted down, that you can't give something away unless you truly own it. And one of the rules of the group is that the women are all common property. If another guy says, "Well, I'd like to go to bed with her," well, you just hand your girlfriend right over.

This, Norm said, was "so sick and so lousy."

At the same time, he thought there was something ennobling about this possession.

> This is that sort of total possession, which is at the same time total nonpossession, because you don't have any right to her, and in that sense, it's like all those paradoxes that you read in the New Testament . . . . In order to find your soul, you have to lose your soul—or whatever. It's as though to really own a girl, you have to not own her. It's all sort of paradoxical.

He was also saying that to be possessed or controlled is to be a fool or a dupe or a slave. The second lover, Sir Stephen, therefore fitted his values better: "There seemed to be much more to him." "He seemed to be much the master of both René and of O, and just really on top of the whole situation." "A much more interesting character, and a man who was much more in tune with all these religious possibilities—the spiritual discipline quality." René, by contrast, Norm saw as driven to obey this cult. Hence his "giving her over to other men really struck me as so sick and so lousy."

To be active, possessing, or controlling is the opposite of sick and lousy. Indeed, Norm thought Sir Stephen so sophisticated a possessor that he could risk being the possessee. "He learned something at the end. To some slight extent, he became her servant, as she was his, at the end—in a way that never happened with René." If you are "really on top of the whole situation," if you learn something, if you know the rules of this "spiritual discipline," then you can relax and become the woman's servant, and it's all right, even "imposing."

Norm's attitude toward O was by no means this equitable. "I responded to O as a body all the time. Very little response to her as a person." By responding to O as a mere body or possession, he freed the attractive sexy world of the senses from the world of ethical standards. His phrasing, however, suggests that he thought he *ought* to respond to O as a person, not as (in his phrase) "just a lady with her clothes off." By his word "lady" he suggested an upper-class woman subjected to a series of restricting and degrading rules, some of which make her naked to the sexual demands of men.

In sum, if Agnes shaped the movie through place and connection, Norm re-created the film around the idea of a person's achieving domination by possessing rules. He could possess or master this movie or woman or world by solving abstract, intellectual puzzles of the kind he felt comfortable with. They yield the rules of "this world," which turn out to be, in his view, moral, even religious. It is as though one could rid oneself of guilt by looking literarily for patterns of repetition and contrast. By recognizing the themes, you can master the strangest, most disturbing things, making them ethically coherent.

Norm's need to possess by means of this skill at generalizing themes fends off what is a real danger for him: the loss of possession and being controlled by another. A Sir Stephen who is master is so superior he can risk being possessed or controlled. In effect, pain, loss of possession, and subjection to the control of another are *so* dangerous for Norm that to risk them constitutes a bravery that is, for all its perversity, admirable, even holy.

In writing about this film, I—and now I mean the 1991 Norm—have seen it again and again. I'm not sure my feelings now are the same as they were then, but they are surely similar. My interpretation of the characters and events is virtually the same, however. I have the curious sensation, as I reread the associations of this earlier Norm, that they feel comfortable to me. I would not use the same words today, but these words feel right somehow. To borrow a term from Freud, they are *heimlich*.

Ted

Ted shaped the film quite differently from either Agnes or Norm. For Agnes, it was domination by place, for Norm, domination by rule. For Ted, it was domination by one's growing up:

> I felt as though I was actually seeing the fantasies which underlie submission in women and aggression in men. We can't help it because that's a part of our lives, because that's the way men and women are brought up to be. And I thought it was fascinating that we were actually seeing the fantasies associated with these attitudes. I think they were all of our fantasies.

When Ted says these "were all of our fantasies," I hear him telling me something about himself. *He* feels he was brought up to believe that being aggressive and controlling was being manly and being submissive was womanly.

Just moments before, he had been talking about the sadomasochistic college as a place where the women learned to submit: "I don't think they [the women] have to learn in there. I think they learn it naturally as they grow up." And he went on about assertiveness and sadism. "Obey, obey, obey. I'm your master and all that—I lost my train of thought."

In the same way, he broke off talking about a submissive woman he and his wife knew.

> We've just had an experience with some friends up in Toronto, and we've been criticizing this girl that we know because she's so submissive, and she's going out with this business executive type who completely controls her life and tells her exactly what to do and she seems to love it. That seems to be exactly what she wants.
>
> I still feel that microphone. I suppose after a while I'll get used to it. This is a new experience for me. I can't just free associate under these conditions.

I find his response at this moment fascinating. In talking about women's being forced to submit, he seems to cast himself in that role. He feels the microphone as coercion, and he loses his ability to think freely. In effect, he and his wife have been saying to the woman in Toronto, "You don't have control, but *we* do." In the interview situation, however, he felt he might not have control, and that threatened Ted. "My fear was that I was going to see victims in this movie, and I didn't want to see victims."

Agnes thought O's consent illusory, but Ted found it a reassurance: she really *did* keep control. "Obviously, she consented to it, so she must have been getting some satisfaction out of it." The opposite possibility, "that made me nervous, at first. I didn't like that. I was afraid that she was going to be a victim, and she was going to go into that against her will, but then when she consented to it all, that sort of put me to ease a bit. Then I could be interested in it."

Notice, by the way, how Ted's interpretation serves him as a defense. He allayed his anxiety by the way he read O's consent as really reflecting her will. Then he could enjoy the movie. A successful defense allows a (perhaps illicit) pleasure in fantasy. Often, when we are in a movie or theater audience, we can "borrow" a defense from the others around us. We think to ourselves, "If they are laughing and enjoying it, I can too," or "If the people around me are crying, it's all right for me to cry." Here, Ted borrowed a defense from the characters. If they are consenting, he can "be interested in it." Like Agnes, he could identify to the

extent he read the characters as having his own characteristic defenses.

Throughout the movie, people's consenting or having the
possibility of not consenting reassured Ted: "There were no victims because everyone consented to it. There was no one screaming, 'No, no, no,' except with obvious ambivalence, because they
had consented right beforehand. They knew what they were getting into, even so far as the branding." A refusal of consent therefore served Ted as a reassurance. "I liked it when the girl ran
screaming from the branding [of O] scene. I liked that. I was
happy to see that there was some sanity in the movie." For Ted,
the ability to consent or refuse equals "sanity."

Thus, when Sir Stephen lets O brand him, that showed he had
completed his own development as a masochistic personality,
"because he accepted the brand. The brand was a test. There was
a choice: Would he leave his hand there or pull it away? He left
his hand there. I still feel as though I'm talking into that microphone." As before, talking about the issue of keeping control reminded Ted, uncomfortably, that he was not wholly in control of
his own situation in the interview.

One way Ted kept control in the movie was to dichotomize
its situations. Then *he* would choose between the alternatives. For
example, he described O as both "submissive" and "ruthless." "I
was excited at first . . . but then . . . I felt myself getting cold toward her." He felt pity at first, but no pity when she consented.
Well, a little: "I pitied the human part of her at those moments
she was getting hurt, even if she did seem to enjoy it."

He singled out the moment when O did some whipping herself. "The sadistic side of her personality was bound to come out
sooner or later. She had such a high degree of the masochistic, it
was just a matter of time before the complementary aspect of it
was revealed." (Another way Ted kept control was by using his
psychoanalytic knowledge.)

Later, approving of Ivan (who wants to marry O), he said,
"There was gentleness instead of these guys unzipping their pants
and going to it." That, I thought, was the ultimate dichotomy for
Ted: being offered a choice ("gentleness") or having the choice
made by others for their own pleasure. And I thought, too, he

saw the choice as being made by a man (himself), choosing either to be gentle or brutally sexual. For Ted, more than for Agnes or Norm, the issue in the film was submission or domination, but the ultimate question was whether he, Ted, was dominated or not, by the film, the microphone, or his own growing up.

5

Feedback

When we set out three responses this way, we can see substantial differences among them. Agnes, Norm, and Ted "read" the same things in the movie rather differently, although they did see the "same *things*." All three remarked on the doubling of the first scene, the training castle, and the brandings. All three used the same codes of crosscut or flashback to read the film.

Agnes took the doubling of the first scene to mean that the scene represented someone's fantasy. Norm assumed it meant that he could interpret the story as a fable or fairy story.

Ted read the castle where O learns her perversion in terms of what he took to be universal gender patterns of submission and obedience. The same castle reminded Agnes of the prohibitions in her own conservative Catholic girls' high school.

Agnes decided that, when O was branded, she was not, really, doing these things of her own free will, only because she was committed to a certain place. Ted felt that she "obviously" consented to it.

Late in the film, O burns an "O" into Sir Stephen's hand, and Ted saw this as the completion of her develment, sadism now accompanying masochism. Norm interpreted it as one in a pattern of Os throughout the film.

Agnes related pain in the movie to the pain she thought her own religious upbringing encouraged and rewarded. Norm also thought the film had a religious dimension, but because of the rules and paradoxes he read in the film.

The biggest differences came in the responses to characters. For example, Agnes thought O was like a sleepwalker, cold, aloof, and (finally) predatory. For Norm, however, she was just a naked body, while Ted felt cold toward her, because she submitted and consented to pain.

As for O's first lover, René, Agnes dismissed him as a repellent procurer, while Norm disliked him, calling him sick and lousy. Agnes just wanted Sir Stephen, O's second lover, to make O happy, while Norm thought him the most interesting character in the film: imposing, masterful, perhaps even a spiritual adept. Ivan, the boy who wanted to marry O, Norm thought lacking in courage, while Ted thought him normal and gentle.

The point of all this is that we three spectators saw the same images on the screen, but we saw them differently. The movie itself was, of course, simply "there." The same beady reflections bounced from the screen to the eyes of all of us looking at Jaeckin's film. Everybody saw sadomasochism, whips, panties, leather, René, and Sir Stephen. Everybody agreed that René's name was not Algernon. These perceptions at least were relatively fixed. Each of us, however, read the characters of René and Stephen differently. Each of us toned the undressings or the trainings differently. The film we saw was the same—but different. How can one understand the multiplicity of our responses alongside the singleness of the film? How can one understand our variety within the generality of the codes for understanding movies that we all shared? To answer, I propose to read Kim's case study in the light of a much larger and far more rigorous experimental tradition, namely, contemporary cognitive and perceptual psychology.

We have learned a great deal since 1950 about human perception. Today psychologists of perception say the way we see and hear is like a dialogue. The world does not simply shove itself through our senses into our minds in a stimulus-response way.

Rather, we *propose* hypotheses to reality, and reality *disposes* of them. We perceive by trying out constructions on the world. The world confirms and rewards these hypotheses or gives back nothing, chaos, or painful correction. In other words, the mere seeing or hearing something, to say nothing of interpreting a character or theme, proceeds by feedback.

To get at the idea of feedback, think of a familiar mechanical example, the cruise control on a big American car. Suppose that we have set the desired speed at sixty-five. The speedometer senses that the car is going sixty or sixty-eight or sixty-five—whatever. Somewhere in its innards, the cruise control compares the speed the speedometer senses with the speed set by the driver. If the car is going at sixty instead of sixty-five, the cruise control feeds more gas to the carburetor. If the car is going at sixty-eight, it feeds less. If the car is going at sixty-five, the control does nothing.

One can think of such a control system as asking questions of the world it senses: Are we moving at more or less than sixty-five miles per hour? The system of car and road then answers that question. If the answer is "No," the control system feeds the appropriate amount of gas. It does something physical to the car so the cruise control will perceive the correct value. In effect, the system's behavior controls the system's perception of speed.

We can analogize from the car's feedback system to the feedback systems we humans use to meet the world. The control system is like a rudimentary brain. In effect, the cruise control constantly tests its world, limited to the speed of the car. It asks, What is the difference between what I see and what I want to see (the reference level or standard that has been set in me from outside)? I will act so as to minimize that difference. The control system uses sensors and valves to change the speed of the car, so that the cruise control will get a yes answer to the value of sixty-five set by the driver from outside the loop.

In such a control network, there has to be something outside the feedback loop to set the standard for the loop the way the driver sets the cruise control. Outside the loop, the human driver compares what is happening with what he or she wants to happen and the driver sets the cruise control faster or slower accordingly. In other words, the human driver behaves much as the cruise control does: testing the environment, being satisfied or dissatisfied with the results, acting accordingly, testing again, and so on, round and round. The driver is another loop setting the standard for the lower loop which is the cruise control.

Notice that stimulus-response makes an inadequate model for such a cybernetic or feedback process. A gust of headwind might slow the car down and cause the cruise control to feed more gas to the engine. But then again, it might not—if, for example, the road simultaneously went downhill. The stimulus does not just cause a response. The stimulus enters an ongoing system of testing for error and then correcting for error. The cruise control takes in a stimulus from outside like wind or a hill. Speed is all the control senses, however. Therefore the stimulus gets lumped into all the other information the cruise control is processing about speed. The cruise control then compares the speed that it senses is happening with the speed that is programmed to happen, and it accelerates or decelerates accordingly. The higher-level feedback loop, the driver, sets the standard for the lower-level loop, the cruise control.

Whether running in steady-state or dealing with a new stimulus, the cruise control functions, as we say, automatically. If the car starts running at sixty-eight miles an hour (because, say, it is going down a hill), the feedback within the system reduces the gasoline fed to the engine so as to slow the car down to the sixty-five set as its standard. That is, if the car is "on automatic," the smaller networks of the system keep cycling round the loop. These lower-level loops sustain the more encompassing standard. At least they do *unless*—and this is where Agnes and Ted and Norm come in—unless the human driver outside the loop resets the standard for the low-level control system inside the loop.

The higher-level human loop controls another lower-level loop—and this is the key to Agnes', Ted's, and Norm's response to the film. At higher levels at least, *The Story of O* does not "stimulate" or even "dominate" or "control" Agnes' experience. Agnes and the movie make an experience together. More exactly, she uses the film to make an experience. She tests what she is seeing by codes at different levels. Is this a hand? A face? A garter? Does this castle place O? Is this a crosscut? A flashback? Notice how the "replaying" of the opening scene did not fit that test for her. "Is this a flashback?" she asked herself. The sequence of scenes didn't fit her usual notions of a flashback. She had to work out a new way of coping with it.

In general, the spectator of a film brings to it a construction or hypothesis ("Is this a flashback?"). The film confirms or denies the hypothesis. The spectator supplies a new construction or hypothesis. The film gives its next response. That leads to a next construction from the spectator, and so on round and round the loop, over and over again. The system is circular—hence the term *feedback loop*. To begin, continue, and regulate that questioning, each spectator looks to the physical film, the reflections from the beady screen. The whole process thus rests on the physical film, but the film "controls" our responses only *reactively*. The film controls Agnes' response only as it answers questions posed by Agnes from her repertoire of hypotheses. What Agnes gets from the film depends on what Agnes asks the film. It is Agnes who begins, continues, and regulates the loop that determines what the film can say to her.

It is Agnes, moreover, who determines whether the feedback is satisfactory, and hence, whether a given construction has worked. It is Agnes who hears the answers fed back, and she hears them in the same distinctive style in which she posed the questions. In other words, the film "controls" her responses only reactively, and even that control takes place within Agnes' individual style. That is, she colors both the hypotheses she poses to the film and the answers she sees and hears from it.

Outside the cruise control built into the car is the human who sets the speed. The standard so set comes from the values and concerns of the driver. Agnes, in watching *The Story of O,* cared about themes of connection and intimacy. Ted developed themes of submission and dominance. Norm talked about rules, interpretations, and morality. Out of these large concerns, our three spectators (probably unconsciously) set their three different standards for the way they interpreted smaller elements: a leather halter, a grimace, the branding of Sir Stephen, or the character of René.

The film met the concerns of Agnes or Ted—or it didn't. The physical film made their constructions easy or hard, and so confirmed or denied their hypotheses. They then tried new readings of the film or clung to old ones. They may have strained the film to get what they wanted, or they may simply have rejected it. However they did it, though, they saw the film through the lenses of their particular values and concerns. Our state of mind shapes the hypotheses we bring to the film, and those hypotheses then determine how we see it.

6

Identity

Agnes', Ted's, and Norm's values and concerns shaped the way they saw the film. To relate an individual response like Agnes' to the film, then, we need to have a way of talking fairly precisely about her individuality. I propose, as I have before, *identity*. Basically, we use the word to refer to the continuity we see between a self at one moment and a self at another moment years later. Of the many ideas of personal identity, I have found the psychoanalyst, Heinz Lichtenstein's, the most useful. We can think of a person's identity as a theme and variations, as in music. We can try to read humans as though they were works of art, because, in a way, they are.

As I watch that other work of art, *The Story of O*, at any given moment, I am seeing something different from what I was seeing a moment before. Late in the film, O first enjoys a dinner deluxe. Then, on that very table, she suffers a degrading, but desired, sexual assault. I can phrase a relation between those two events by seeing them as variations on one theme: obedience, perhaps, or nullifying the self through appetite or being the subject of appetite. I can read other events of the film as variations on other themes. I can relate those several themes to one another. Ultimately, then, I can relate any two events in the film. The similarity I see between them comes from my perception that they share a theme. The difference comes simply because they *are* different. The similarities restate themes. The differences I can read as variations on the themes.

So I can use the concept of identity to read Agnes, Ted, and Norm thematically. At any given moment, I see Agnes or Ted doing something new. The very name Agnes or Ted, however, shows that I sense a continuity between the Agnes and Ted I see at this present moment and the Agnes and Ted that I have seen up to now. I can use themes, as I use their names, to describe these continuities. Even if I say, "That's not like Ted," I am assuming that there is a like-Ted (a set of Ted-themes) that I must now modify to include this new and surprising act. I can think of the sameness that I call "Ted" as a theme or style that I perceive as persisting through the variations. I can understand changes and growth in this "Ted" as variations on one or several such identity themes. In the case of Norm, we have seen a continuity of moralism and intellectualizing over a dozen years.

"I can think . . . " "I can understand . . . " An identity is not something "in" a person, but a way to think about that person. Identity is a construct, a way to represent the continuities we see in someone. Identity is a representation, a way of using words to explore and inquire into the interactions between one self and other selves. Identity is thus decentered, imperfectly known, systematically elusive, not simply "in" the person being interpreted, but "between" interpreter and interpretee. In other words, I can only construct Ted's identity from within my own identity. I phrase an identity for Ted or Agnes by the very same feedback processes of testing with which I saw the film or by which I see anything, according to modern psychology. I cannot know someone's identity—I cannot know anything at all (as we shall see)—except through my own identity.

Identity is somebody's representation of an identity, but, because of feedback, it is also an agency and a consequence in feedback loops. In this aspect, we can think of it as "in" Ted. His identity both acts and is a consequence of its own acts, like the speed of the car under cruise control. Indeed we can think of identity as like the cruise control, in that identity is what governs the various loops by which Ted perceives. At the same time Ted is created as a result of those loops, like the speed of the car.

Like the cruise control, an identity deals with a stimulus that impinges upon it by bringing to bear on that stimulus tests (or hypotheses or guesses). Is that cigarette holder hot enough to burn Sir Stephen? Does that nod of the head mean yes? Does that eight-sided red sign mean "Stop"? Does this set of free associations have a theme? Does the causality in this movie make sense? You pose a hypothesis, and you get back an answer that may or may not meet your standards for satisfying that hypothesis. If unsatisfied, you will try a new hypothesis. If satisfied, you will subside. Yes, Ted thought, that nod of the head does mean yes. She is consenting. I can go on to think about the next thing. But suppose Ted had thought, No, that nod can't mean yes. She can't want them to do these things to her. Then Ted would have wanted (probably) to try other questions. If it doesn't mean yes, what does it mean? I have to come up with some other hypotheses.

Through this testing, an identity experiences the stimuli that come from the world on its own terms, so to speak. If our tests make sense, that is, if we feel coherence or satisfaction in terms of our particular identity, we accept what we are testing. If our tests give us unsatisfactory (or incoherent or painful) feelings, we defend against what is coming from outside. We have to try some other line of inquiry or deal otherwise with the stimulus.

Agnes, Ted, and Norm experienced the movie as they experience the world—by testing it. Their identities governed, and were governed by, feedback loops of hypothesis and response. Because they perceived through this testing, their identities experienced the movie on their own terms. Yet they also experienced the movie with similarities to the experiences others have—because Agnes, Ted, and Norm were using tests that others also use. Hence they saw *The Story of O* both as others do and differently from others. Agnes', Ted's, and Norm's readings are each unique and all similar, because a unique identity tries out similar guesses about the movie. We can account for the uniqueness as individual identity. We can account for the sameness by the sameness of the hypotheses they brought to the movie. Some were hypotheses

Do these change from "interpretive community"? to "i.e."

(see p. 30)
(see p. 35)

about real things like, Is this a garter? Some were hypotheses about movies like, Is this a flashback?

Incidentally, it is these shared hypotheses that enable separate identities to cohere as the collective, *audience.* Because many of the people in the theater with Agnes, Ted, and Norm shared some of their hypotheses, they had somewhat similar experiences of the film. Accordingly they were hushed or restless, laughing or crying. When people in the audience manifest their experiences this way, even just by quietly watching, they have a multiplier effect. They make their behavior available to other members of the audience to use as a license. More precisely, we can use the responses of others as a (probably) unconscious defense. One can think, These people are taking this movie seriously. I can too. Indeed it would be embarrassing if I didn't. In an unruly audience, one might think, These noisy, jeering people think this is junk. I am free to reject and attack it, too. Or, These laughing people think this is funny. I am entitled to laugh, too. The presence of others in the theater watching this sexual movie no doubt eased some of the guilt Agnes, Ted, and Norm might otherwise have felt.

The audience's supplying defenses, however, does not change the basic process. The behavior of the other people in the theater simply becomes one more fact to be processed by the identity in question. Identity governs feedback loops that test hypotheses against the physical film, the surrounding audience, and every other physical aspect of the film, the theater, the advertising, and so on.

Identity is not, therefore, something separate, autonomous, or finite. Rather, to think of identity at all, I have to think of it "always already" governing a repertoire of feedback loops. My I includes the various schemata my human body and my culture have supplied me for testing, and so perceiving, my world. My I is inseparably coupled to these loops, which come from my culture, but they are also part and parcel of my personal history. From the point of view of cognitive science, Ulric Neisser writes, "Every person's possibilities for perceiving and acting are entirely unique, because no one else occupies exactly his position in the world or has had exactly his history."

set of metaphors

We thus arrive at a way of modeling how Agnes', Ted's, and Norm's responses are the same but different, individual but collective. One's identity-themes may be unique, but the loops they govern are certainly not. Hypotheses about garters and flashbacks are widely shared in our culture. The history, however, of the individual I that combines loops and identity and the I that results are unique (since no two people can have exactly the same experiences).

The feedbacks that an identity governs go on in a hierarchy of higher and lower feedbacks. The spectator begins, continues, and regulates these trials, to be sure, but not always directly. In this hierarchy of feedbacks, a higher feedback can set the standard for a lower (as the driver sets the cruise control).

An individual identity has experiences by using widely shared hypotheses. Higher levels tell lower levels what will feel satisfying or unsatisfying. My notion of what makes sense in a movie requires that when it shows an eight-sided red sign, it means "Stop." If that familiar lower-level loop does not work, I have to try a more complex reading of the red octagon before I can get about the larger business of reading the scene it is in.

Agnes set standards of commitment and connection at the highest level. At this high level, she expressed her identity most directly. She also had a repertoire of tests to apply to *The Story of O,* tests about flashback and motivation that were not unique to her but would be shared by any competent moviegoer. Her concerns and values set standards for these lower or more automatic processes that seem less personal to her, like perceiving a garter as a garter or a crosscut as a crosscut. As Sir Frederic Bartlett wrote in his classic *Remembering* a half century ago: perception "is directed by interest and feeling."

Higher, more individual concerns direct lower-level processes like memory or perception that are physiologically about the same for all of us. What results, therefore, is a perception of the film that is both uniquely different from the perceptions of other members of the audience and somewhat the same. Agnes' need for commitment led her to see a repeated scene as the revision of a fantasy, but she did see that the scene was repeated, and so did we all. Her experience of a Catholic girls' school drove her perception of the castle, but she saw a castle just as the rest of us did.

Once we admit the role of what Bartlett calls the "appetites, instincts, interests, and ideals peculiar to any given subject," we can sort out how her response is both shared and individual, both the same as Ted's or Norm's, and different. We can then go on to model the way her individual experience of the film combines shared culture with her individual identity.

7

Codes and Canons

Once we have the idea of an identity governing a repertoire of feedbacks in a hierarchy, we can use it to think about the kinds of codes Agnes, Ted, and Norm must have used for perceiving *The Story of O*. If I analogize from the more familiar case of reading, it seems to me their identities must be governing at least one physical and two cultural levels of schemata.

We can, that is, draw distinctions within the hierarchy we suppose for Agnes, Ted, and Norm. One, surely, would be between mental testing and physical. The physical level is controlled by the mental, as the speed of the cruise control is set by the driver. In that sense, we can speak of "lower," controlled loops and "higher," controlling loops.

In these lower loops, physical perception uses the body's hard-wired circuits or to use a currently popular term, *transducers*. Our retinas translate edges into neuronal impulses just the way a phonograph cartridge (another "transducer") translates the hills and valleys of a long-playing record into electrical impulses. At the most immediate level of perception, the physical systems of our eyes or ears or noses make brightnesses and tones and edges and tastes into electrochemical changes in our neurons and finally in our minds.

Dr. Johnson gleefully kicked a stone. He was proving to Boswell how solid and "there" the world is and how wrong Bishop Berkeley was to claim that that solidity depends upon our perceptions. In fact, he was proving precisely Berkeley's position. The solidity of the stone depends precisely upon his physical method of perception, a kick. By newer modes of perception, we now "know" that the stone is made up of quarks and other unkickable entities.

Nevertheless, in a larger sense, Dr. Johnson was right. We do rely totally upon the solidity of the world we physically sense. As we have seen with *The Story of O,* all our feedbacks, no matter how abstract, rest finally on our physical connection to the physical world.

Reading provides an example as obvious as Dr. Johnson's rock. We can't read at all if there is not enough light—why? Because as we put our hypotheses into the text (Is this a *g*? a *t*?), there is no feedback with which to say yea or nay. Likewise, if the bulb in the projector burns out, there is no way one can ask of the image, Is this Sir Stephen? Is this a garter?, and get feedback. Perception, at its most basic, takes place at a relatively low physiological level.

Once we distinguish mental feedbacks from these physiological transductions, however, we can draw further distinctions. Mostly our physiological schemata are built into our bodies. We were born with them. By contrast, a surprising proportion of the hypotheses we live by are learned. (That is one major difference between us and our primate relatives.) Imagine, for a moment, how much of your daily experience rests on perceptual hypotheses you had to learn: aromas, art, cause-and-effect, clothing, colors, flavors, gender, manufactured objects (natural objects too), money, music, numbers, pain, reading, relationships, rules for conduct, rules for safety, shapes, spatial relations, time—the list could go on and on. Most of these we learned as children, either very early from our parents or later in school.

We internalize these higher feedbacks from our culture. Then these mental, cultural loops use the lower, physiological loops we were born with. We edit a clustering of tones into a scream or an

aria, or we understand a jumble of tastes and smells as "soup."
We convert curves into letter *a*. We understand the pink and grey
and tan reflections from the screen as O's face. We recognize a bra
as a bra, a bath as a bath, and so on throughout the movie. At
higher levels of inference, we surmise that O works as a photog-
rapher, that Sir Stephen is very rich, and that the woman wearing
a black uniform and a white apron is a maid. We are constantly
processing the raw sensations we get from the screen into "facts"
or "story" or "event." To do so, we test by means of the hypotheses that we internalized from our culture. We use these hypotheses to convert immediate, low-level sensations from transducers
into higher-level things and events and persons. At least this is a
rough approximation of familiar psychological processes.

The first distinction that we can draw in our hierarchy, then,
is between physiological feedback loops, close to raw, unmediated, unprocessed sensations, mere transductions, and "internalized culture." Among the cultural loops, we can then draw a
second useful distinction. Some of the schemata we apply to the
world are very loose, others very tight, so tight as to constitute a
normality. For example, one cannot normally, in our culture, read
an eight-sided red sign at an intersection as other than a stop sign.
You break the law if you do. "Normally" has unfortunate con-
notations of health and sickness, but it is the only word I know
to say what I want to say. "Customarily" or "typically" almost
serve, but cultures are more coercive than those neutral terms suggest. One cannot "normally" interpret a certain configuration of
stars and stripes as anything but an American flag. Someone who
announced it was the Brazilian flag we would think mad or
strangely ignorant. "In a department store, you are given goods
in exchange for money or a debt." No member of our culture
would normally believe that department stores give their wares
away. Someone who behaved as though they did would quickly
find themselves in trouble. Such schemata constitute cultural
norms, and in that strict sense they are "norm-al."

Other schemata we hold quite loosely. "That's not art!"
shouts the politician at the new sculpture in City Hall. "That's
not music!" wails the irate neighbor at the teenager's rock-and-
roll. "That's rank injustice!" grumble the well-to-do at a new tax.

It is customary, it is even "norm-al" for people to disagree in our culture about political, aesthetic, and even factual matters.

We can separate loose from tight cultural feedbacks by the shibboleth, "No member of this culture would normally say the rule is otherwise." "Not otherwise" rules are mostly conventions: the flag; uniforms; money; units of time, and so on. Red means stop and green means go. "Otherwise" rules are all the things we normally differ about, including many things we assert are "facts." Like the "facts" about welfare or capitalism or the Arabs or AIDS.

"Not otherwise" cultural codes depend upon the culture to which we belong. "Otherwise" cultural codes depend on the "interpretive communities" we belong to within that culture. Lots of normal members of our culture would have trouble saying what distinguishes a Burgundy from a Bordeaux, something that would be automatic for most winegrowers. Lots of normal members of our culture might feel a diminished seventh called for some subsequent tonality—but lots of normal people wouldn't, including some avant-garde musicians. Within the American grain, I can read as a liberal or a rightwinger, a postmodern critic or a structuralist, a theist or a humanist, depending on the opinions I hold, depending on the political or intellectual community to which I belong. All these are "could be otherwise" rules.

Language provides our most familiar sets of "otherwise" and "not otherwise" schemata. No member of our culture would normally hear the sound [red] as a form of the verb "to go." In reading, no member of our culture would normally read r other than as r , as g , for example, or n . No member of our culture would normally think that 4 really means five.

If we think simply of reading one letter, we realize that we cannot read otherwise than as the code prescribes. I cannot see g as something other than g . The process is: I see (via physiological feedback) some printer's ink on a page. I try out on my partially processed sensation the hypotheses I learned as a child in this culture for reading letters. From the hypotheses for g , I get positive feedback, and the loop closes tightly, no longer admitting the possibility of f or z . Further, the code I used is common to everyone in my alphabetic culture. No normal mem-

ber of my culture could see g other than as g or *ing* other
than as ing or *gaping* as other than   gaping . These perceptions are culture-bound. These are positive. On the negative side,
I can make no sense at all of Arabic or Japanese characters. Why?
Because I never internalized the hypotheses for them.

Reading letters or single words provides one example of testing a physical reality by means of "not otherwise" cultural codes.
Other "not otherwise" codes in reading would be understanding
the relationship of an adjective to its noun or a subject to its predicate in a sentence. "This house is red." No normal person in my
syntactic culture could think I was saying the house was not red
or that "this house" was part of some other sentence. By this kind
of "not otherwise" code, we recognize objects. There are probably peoples to whom O's garter belt has no meaning at all, but
for most of Western culture, garter belts respond to a "not otherwise" code. So do traffic lights, toaster ovens, and all the thousands of other artifacts of our culture. Conversely we would have
great difficulty in recognizing or using the objects in a Bushman's
hut or an Eskimo's igloo.

Obviously, even though the code itself may be "not otherwise," there may be "otherwises"—ambiguities—in its application. "This house is red, also this color." Is the house two colors
or is "this color" red? I claim only that the code is unambiguous.
The rule we would apply is shared by all normal members of a
certain culture, and it would be difficult, if not impossible, to vary
it, although we might very well differ about how to apply the rule.
That is why the rules are also hypotheses or, conversely, we derive
the hypotheses to apply from the rules we know.

In reading both books and movies, however, we also use a
second, looser kind of rule, rules that can be otherwise. I am
thinking, for example, of the kind of code by which we read a
facial expression. Does that curve of her mouth mean O is enjoying whipping this other woman? Do Sir Stephen's quick speech
and half-shut eyes mean he really disapproves of O when he is
first alone with her? Similarly, we have loose codes for interpreting motivation. Does Sir Stephen hate and contemn O at first? Or
is he just saying those awful things to cause her pain? Or both?
Does René really love her? If so, then how can I reconcile his
giving her to Sir Stephen with my ideas of love? Or is he using her

to get at Sir Stephen? Since it causes her pain, why does O continue to do what she is doing? Even looser are the ideas by which we formulate character. Is René a masochist? A sadist? I could read him via Freud, Jung, Horney, or your generic social psychologist. Does Ivan love O or just wish to own her as Sir Stephen does? Is Sir Stephen a good man? Honest? Loving and caring? Movies aside, we need to interpret in order to get along in the world, yet our interpretations necessarily differ from our fellow human beings' because, at this level of interpretation, the rules "could be otherwise."

Perhaps the most pervasive example of "could be otherwise" rules is the meanings of words. Words look as though they mean according to a one-to-one code as recorded in a dictionary, but the actual process is more complicated. *Film* might refer to a movie or to the stock on which it was shot or to something entirely different, the grime on a windowpane or what forms on top of boiling milk, or some complicated combination of these. Words do not simply "mean" or "signify." Rather, we *make* them mean by bringing to bear some set of tests. When I hear "film" in the context of movies, am I hearing about *The Story of O,* 35 mm. stock, or dirt on the lens? Which works in the context? I have to construe to find out. I have to hypothesize.

Lots of people in our culture might normally read "whip" otherwise than we viewers of *The Story of O.* A chef might think of a whisk for whipping cream. A Member of Parliament might think of a party leader. Lots of normal members of American culture, on hearing [red] might try as a first meaning, neither a color nor the past participle of "to read," but a political epithet. We differ about the meanings of words, and it is normal to do so.

So with sentences. When I told Kim McSherry, "I was struck by all the O's," I used the physical sentence (via codes) to express and confirm something in my own mind. The sentence did not deliver a meaning like a pipeline, however. I did not put a meaning into one end of the sentence which she then took out at the other. She used the same physical sentence but to confirm what was probably a quite different hypothesis in her mind. I might have been saying to myself, Does "was struck" express my feeling of puzzlement? She might have been, as the psychoanalysts say, listening with the third ear. She might well have asked herself,

How does an O strike? What fantasy about Os is he expressing in this sadomasochistic context? Her higher-level interpretations took for granted the lower-level, fixed codes she and I shared. These are the codes by which I said and she recognized "O" or "struck." But we did not arrive at the same meanings for the words "O" or "struck." By "O's," was I saying the heroine's name or referring to circles or nullities? Did my "struck" hint at the whippings in the movie?

I suggest the terms "codes" and "canons" to divide rules according to this "otherwise" shibboleth. By this definition, codes cannot, if you are functioning as a normal member of the culture, be otherwise. We all use codes to know that a g is a g or a garter belt a garter belt. "Canons" can be otherwise, depending on which interpretive community you belong to within a given culture.

The meanings we supply to words are canons. You can read "whip" as a chef or a politician or a masochist would. Even if we cannot get loose from a or 4, you and I, at this higher level of "could be otherwise," can and do differ. In particular, we can differ as to what theme runs through a set of free associations, indeed as to whether it is right to talk of themes at all. We will read identities differently, and we may disagree as to whether there are such things. As in the lower levels, we try these hypotheses on the "out there," but we hold the hypotheses themselves as a matter of belief, perhaps, or efficiency. We may think of "whip" as prune whip or as persuasive legislator in order to communicate with the particular person we are talking to. Or we continue to try out ideas of human perfection or conservative reluctance because they have worked for us in the past. Or we may use the language of deconstructionism, Lacan, psychoanalysis, or Marx because we believe in a certain set of ideas.

We have distinguished physiological codes from cultural codes, and cultural codes from canons. A third distinction we can draw is between personal concerns and cultural, between identity and canon. It is the difference between Norm's moralistic concerns about *The Story of O* and the widely shared but by no means universal view that the movie is "pornographic." Concerns and values that are relatively rare and personal (identity themes) can parallel concerns that are widely shared in the culture although they "can be otherwise" (canons).

Many people, in today's America, seeing *The Story of O,* would be outraged. Many, no doubt, would proclaim widely shared religious or "family" values. Yet the deeper reasons for the outrage (and for the values) will be as various as Agnes' need for commitment, Norm's for rules, or Ted's for submission-dominance. These deeper needs may be unconscious in a psychoanalytic sense. Certainly their roots will be.

One can be a rightwinger or a liberal, and those are culturally shared canons. Yet the deeper needs that those overt political stances satisfy may be quite personal, having no cultural backing. It is useful to keep in mind that identical opinions (canons) can reflect—*must reflect*—different identities. In this respect, canon and identity blur into each other, because the unconscious needs that lead someone to choose some particular repertoire of canons also shape identity. This model does not force a choice between conscious and unconscious response. Rather, unconscious response finds expression in conscious comment.

It is we who *use* codes and canons to serve our conscious and unconscious wishes. Hence, the distinction between code and canon overlaps the psychoanalytic distinction between what is conscious and what is unconscious. We will be aware of our canons and some of our codes, but canons and codes alike will draw on unconscious roots. It is through codes and canons that our needs, both conscious and unconscious, express themselves, determining our perceptions.

Oftentimes literary critics and philosophers polarize conscious and unconscious or the individual and the culture. Either a response is individual or it is cultural. But that much oversimplifies the matter. Identity fulfills itself by acting on the world through cultural canons, cultural codes, and physique. Even the most rigid cultural codes serve personal needs. Codes enlarge us.

Conversely, codes can limit us. I can read 4 as four , but by the same token it is well-nigh impossible for me to see 4 as anything but four . It is very hard for me to drive on the left as you have to do in Japan.

In this way, these hypothesizing loops both enable and limit their users. Hence this cognitive-psychoanalytic model does not force a choice between a response to a film determined by codes, canons, culture, or the film itself and a response that an autonomous individual chooses. In this model Agnes, Ted, and Norm are not simply "free" or "autonomous" (in the nineteenth-century sense). Neither are they simply the products of their culture (as some twentieth-century thinkers imagine). Nor are they constrained by the film. Rather they are both free and determined. They see the movie both in uniquely personal and in shared and culturally dictated ways. By using the idea of an identity governing codes and canons, it is possible to explore in some detail how culture and personality, determinism and freedom, combine.

We are dealing with a spectrum, moreover. Large "otherwise" hypotheses (like beliefs or ideology) do not limit us as strictly as do smaller "otherwise" hypotheses like the meanings of words or images. And none of the "otherwise" canons have the consequences of the "not otherwise" codes like the shapes of letters and numbers or the "not otherwise" physical and physiological constraints. We can change our canons, but we would have great difficulty changing our codes. We can add codes, as when we learn a language, but the codes themselves are givens. As for the physical world, it is as hard as Dr. Johnson's rock. The distinctions I am drawing are by no means that hard. They do, however, let us sort out the different ways we are "free" to act individually and constrained to act culturally when we respond to a movie or language or anything, really.

The Kuleshov Effect

For cinema, the classic investigation of codes and canons was the Kuleshov experiment. In 1929 the Russian director and theorist, V. I. Pudovkin, described an experiment that has since passed into the mythology of film as "the Kuleshov effect." I say the "mythology" of film because it is not clear exactly what happened in the experiment. Indeed it's not clear that the experiment ever took place at all. Nevertheless, people have written as though some experiment had in fact taken place, and, as so often, that is enough to constitute "research" in the humanities. The experiment has become something of an inkblot into which to project all kinds of theories, and now I suppose I am about to do the same. I propose to re-read the experiment in the light of the distinctions I am drawing between codes and canons. In doing so, I am bringing to bear on the Kuleshov experiment, as on McSherry's case study, contemporary cognitive and perceptual psychology.

Pudovkin described the experiment this way:

> Kuleshov ["a young painter and theoretician of the film"] and I made an interesting experiment. We took

from some film or other several close-ups of the well-known Russian actor Mosjukhin. We chose close-ups which were static and which did not express any feeling at all—quiet close-ups. We joined these close-ups, which were all similar, with other bits of film in three different combinations. In the first combination the close-up of Mosjukhin was immediately followed by a shot of a plate of soup standing on a table. It was obvious and certain that Mosjukhin was looking at this soup. In the second combination the face of Mosjukhin was joined to shots showing a coffin in which lay a dead woman. In the third the close-up was followed by a shot of a little girl playing with a funny toy bear. When we showed the three combinations to an audience which had not been let into the secret the result was terrific. The public raved about the acting of the artist. They pointed out the heavy pensiveness of his mood over the forgotten soup, were touched and moved by the deep sorrow with which he looked on the dead woman, and admired the light, happy smile with which he surveyed the girl at play. But we knew that in all three cases the face was exactly the same.

Kuleshov himself, in an interview published when he was sixty-eight, recalled that they had kept their experimentally edited films around for years, looking at them repeatedly, until they were destroyed during World War II. He remembered the experiment somewhat differently from Pudovkin, mixing it up with a second experiment involving the actor's intention. The film was never shown to a theater audience, he said. Only the experimenters looked at it. (If that were true, of course, it would be the same as the experiment's never having taken place at all, since the whole thing depends on an audience "which had not been let into the secret.") Kuleshov also remembered the shot of the dead woman differently, as a half-naked woman lying seductively on a sofa, but perhaps that is the memory of an old man thinking of half-naked actresses.

We can supplement Kuleshov's cuts, though, with a more modern, more sophisticated example of montage, the time-flow segment in Mike Nichols' *The Graduate* (1967). Nichols' editing plays off Benjamin's trysts with Mrs. Robinson against his summer by the swimming pool at home. Benjamin walks through a door at home—and into the hotel room where he meets Mrs. Robinson. He gets out of bed with Mrs. Robinson, and he is in the living room at home. In the living room at home, sipping a beer, he is lying on the bed in the hotel room as Mrs. Robinson walks back and forth in front of him, getting dressed. He dives into the pool, pulls himself up onto a rubber float, and finds himself on top of Mrs. Robinson.

When I watch that sequence, I also interpret it. The thought occurs to me that rolling over onto Mrs. Robinson has become routine. She has become as empty as an inflatable sex doll or as idle as a rubber raft in the summer sun. Perhaps she is full of hot air. When he opens the door, I think of the doors and windows that occur throughout this film all the way to the climax which takes the form of barring the doors to the wedding. From doors, I go to transitions, again, all through the film from the moving sidewalk in the airport at the opening of the film to his frantic driving to and from Berkeley to the bus in which the lovers escape at the end. For me *The Graduate* is a film very much about transitions, notably Benjamin as a young man in transition from university to career, from sex to love, from his parents' program to his own.

My interpretation of the sequence in *The Graduate* illustrates the same phenomenon as the three responses to *The Story of O*. A personal reading uses "normal" readings that everybody shares. That is, everybody sees the door as a door, Benjamin as a young man, and Mrs. Robinson as an older woman. I think everybody in our culture must also interpret Nichols' cuts from the pool to the hotel room as showing two aspects of Benjamin's life. We all interpret Nichols' images and cuts by means of feedbacks from very basic "not otherwise" codes for seeing movies, codes that we learned early in life.

Different people, however, will interpret differently the putting of Benjamin on top of, first, the raft, second, Mrs. Robinson. Not everybody will think of Mrs. Robinson as full of hot air. That interpretation might be "otherwise." Not everybody, moreover, will think of that summer as tedious or Benjamin as guilty. These readings reveal canons at work, the same way the readings of Mosjukhin's face did.

Then, when I go even further and read from Nichols' jump cuts to a whole film about transitions, I am showing my critical beliefs in pattern and wholeness. You might read the film from a feminist or a psychoanalytic perspective. Someone else might develop a Christian or Marxist meaning. Each of us would use Nichols' cuts in the service of our high-level canons in different ways. Each of us would be using codes so as to work out our various canons.

I mention this film because I can use my own reading as an example of a personal reading overlaid onto other readings that everybody shares. When I unpack my reading of Nichols's cuts, I can see it involves two stages and two kinds of cultural hypotheses. It involves hypotheses that I consciously choose or that less consciously simply "feel right" to me and other hypotheses that my culture inscribed in my perceptual modes. My reading involves, in short, hypotheses that could be otherwise and hypotheses that could not be otherwise. In exactly the same way, the Kuleshov experiment cuts between "otherwise" and "not otherwise" cultural loops, between codes and canons.

The Kuleshov audience's canon-plus-code reading of Mosjukhin's face also demonstrates how high-level canons use low-level codes. "That expression on Mosjukhin's face means something, but what? Ah. The other shot shows a bowl of soup. He has forgotten his soup. What would make a man forget his soup? Heavy pensiveness. Yes, his face does look as though he is thinking hard." All this, of course, very fast, quite unconscious, and almost automatic.

That automaticity is why, if we consider the process by introspection alone, it *feels* as though we are being physically controlled by the film. These lower-level feedbacks happen willy-nilly, without our being aware of them. They feel as though they are happening to us without any action on our part. We cannot do otherwise. Everybody gets the same results. We feel as though we are being caused, simply responding in some behaviorist way to a stimulus.

But we aren't. The cognitive scientists tell us that, even at the very lowest levels of perception, we are applying hypotheses to what the world supplies us. In school, I was told that the eye is like a camera. Light passes through the lens and falls on the retina, where it stimulates nerves that send images to the brain along what amounts to a one-way street from outside to inside. That picture, according to modern perceptual psychology, is false. The eye has to scan the world, and if the movements of the eyeball are canceled out, we see nothing. We see colors, not because a certain frequency of light falls on the retina, but because the blue-green and the red peaks in our retinas process the light into a certain sensation. We use the same kinds of feedbacks at the lowest, physiological level that we do at the highest interpretive level. Norwood Hanson put it neatly: "People, not their eyes, see. Cameras and eyeballs are blind."

Lower-level, automatic perceptions do not model higher-level interpretations. The psychology of perception suggests it is the other way round. The higher-level processes provide the model for the lower-level processes. It is by lower-level processes that we see sixteen or twenty-four frames a second as motion or a cut from a bowl of soup to a man's face as different angles on one event. When one begins reading modern perceptual psychology, one learns that these lower-level processes work the same way as the higher-level processes by which I understand *The Graduate* as a film about transitions. That is, the feedbacks we can sense ourselves using as we try out complicated hypotheses on a film are also operating unconsciously, automatically, and quickly in our small perceptions of a door, a bowl of soup, or even the seeing of sixteen and twenty-four still pictures a second as motion. The feedbacks by which I read Mosjukhin's expression continue and build on the feedbacks by which I see a cut from a bowl of soup to a man's face as different angles on one event. To interpret the character of Sir Stephen or the state of O's mind, Ted and Agnes and Norm needed to be able to build on the lower-level, syntactic codes of film. We had to be able to take for granted things like crosscutting, establishing shots, the look of a bra or a garter, or the sufficient brightness of the projector bulb.

At higher levels we were very much on our own. Our assertions about characters, facial expressions, motivations, themes, all the things interpreters disagree about, by that very fact, show that they come from our applying canons.

We can read back from the answers that people get to see what kinds of questions they were asking, that is, what kinds of hypotheses they were trying out. If everybody in the audience gets similar results, they are using a low-level feedback, either a physical-physiological loop or a "not otherwise" cultural code. This is the way we all see twenty-four frames a second as motion or we all see Mrs. Robinson as Mrs. Robinson and the rubber raft as a rubber raft. When different people get different results, that is the sign of a "could be otherwise" canon. We may well differ as to whether the cuts represent Benjamin's sexual fantasies, his guilt, or his boredom. Readings of this kind represent the feedback from canons that I (consciously or unconsciously) choose and hold. By contrast, the "not otherwise" readings result from applying codes "inscribed" (consciously or unconsciously) in my perceptual modes by my culture.

The Kuleshov experiment cut precisely between canon and code, between the "otherwise" and the "not otherwise" kinds of cultural loops. In interpreting the juxtaposition of Mosjukhin's face with a bowl of soup or a playing child—that is, in reading the montage—everybody responded the same. "It was obvious and certain that Mosjukhin was looking at this soup." Evidently, no person in the Kuleshov interpretive community would normally see two shots, one after the other, as unrelated. They were using a "not otherwise" code, but one for interpreting the juxtaposition of shots rather than the image of a face or a bowl of soup. We are seeing some filmic syntax in action.

Reading the expression on the actor's face, however, was evidently like supplying a meaning for "whip" or "red." It could be otherwise. The audience could read the same image on the screen as heavy pensiveness, deep sorrow, or a light, happy smile. The hypotheses about Mosjukhin's expressions are canons, since a given image accepts a variety of interpretations. In other words, it is not a matter of stimulus-response at all, but of projection.

Our canons for interpreting a relatively neutral facial expression vary widely from interpreter to interpreter and situation to situation. When Kuleshov's audience projected the emotion appropriate to the soup, woman, or child onto Mosjukhin's face, the uniformity of their response shows they were using codes, but not codes for reading neutral facial expressions. (Those are canons.) They were using two codes. One related the first shot to the second. The second code had to do with the images. Our codes relate coffins to death and (usually) sorrow. Our codes relate soup to hunger. Kuleshov's audience used these codes to project an emotion onto the face which they then imagined (as we do when we project) that they read it "from" the face.

Then, although Pudovkin had no reason to mention them, we are also seeing a number of other lower-level "not otherwise" loops at work in the Kuleshov experiment. Some were cultural. The spectators all saw the soup as soup and Mosjukhin as a man. They all treated the blacks and whites and greys on the screen as representations of reality. Other low-level, "not otherwise" loops were physiological. The audience all saw sixteen frames a second as motion. They all were able to discern whites, blacks, greys, and the edges of the images.

In short, we have drawn distinctions between identity, canon, code, and physiological feedback. These distinctions let us sort out a classic problem in cinema theory. We have an explanatory model.

9

The Model

We have a combination of two case studies and one (perhaps) experiment. No one of them is as rigorous as a proper psychologist would like, but perhaps they do not need to be. We can interpret them in the light of a vast body of highly rigorous experimental work, namely, the remarkable developments since 1950 in cognitive and perceptual psychology. The model I have been developing in chapters five, six, and seven rests on a huge body of experimental work by others. Except for the role of a psychoanalytic idea of identity— that is my contribution—the model states in minimal form the picture of the mind developed in the burgeoning field of "cognitive science" or in the title of Howard Gardner's strong summary, "the mind's new science." Applied to movies, the theory is best known in the works of David Bordwell and Edward Branigan. Applied to the visual arts, Ernst Gombrich is the most widely read spokesman. Applied to literature, I have been developing the model in earlier works, and it pervades the standard textbooks on the psychology of reading (although these seem not to be known by literary critics).

"The literature on cognitivism in psychology, philosophy, social theory, linguistics, anthropology, and even aesthetics," writes Bordwell, "has become so vast that no introduction can do justice to it. Indeed nobody can keep track of it." That is not my purpose. I want to suggest here a minimal statement of the idea of the human being that cognitive science has developed. My own contribution is simply to suggest that it is an identity (as developed in psychoanalytic thought) that governs the feedback loops described by cognitive scientists.

This combination of a theme-and-variations identity with "constructivism" allows us to draw a coherent picture of an individual's response to a text or, indeed, to anything. That is, we can state this model of an I in a very general form. An identity governs a hierarchy of feedback loops, each providing the standard for the loop below it. We can think of this model as having three levels—

at the highest level, a unique identity interpreted as a theme and variations;

at intermediate levels, loops internalized from culture, of two kinds:

canon-loops, rules about which different "interpretive communities" regularly differ;

code-loops: "No member of this culture would normally believe the rule is otherwise."

at the lowest level, physiological loops the human species shares.

We respond to movies and other things through this hierarchy.

At lower and intermediate levels, we test what is before us, as the cruise control of chapter five tested the speed of the car. The lowest, most basic level consists of the physiological tests we make of the physical film: its brightness, loudness, contrast, edges, and so on. This testing process converts that physical film reflected from the screen in front of us into impulses along our neurons, impulses that correspond to brightness, loudness, speed, or sequence. These lowest-level tests elicit a physiological feedback that can be as decisive and coercive as a wall or a flash of light.

Above these physiological feedback loops, we can distinguish two kinds of psychological loops or codes, higher and lower. The lower limits us in a manner almost physical. This is the syntax of film and of objects. It involves tests based on hypotheses or rules that "cannot be otherwise." A garter has to be a garter, a flashback a flashback. Then other, higher codes use these lower physical and syntactic codes in the service of different modes of interpretation and different interpretive communities. We test the film to see if it embodies our ideas about the gaze or the suture or the female body. Monitoring all these lower levels is an identity with emotions. Does this *feel* right to me, to my especial sensibility? Can I read this film in such a way as to express my own identity? And that is what Agnes, Ted, and Norm did.

This model, an identity governing canons, codes, and physiological tests, enables me, finally, to do what I set out to do. I can understand the relation between Agnes', Ted's, and Norm's individual responses and the aspects of those responses they shared with others in the theater: the physical film, the codes for seeing that film; moral and social values.

I can relate their personal responses to what they shared with most other human beings: the physical film, the various lights and shadows and colors reflected from the screen. I can relate their responses to the codes they shared with all members of their moviegoing culture: the objects they saw on the screen; the syntax of film editing; the spatial relations they inferred from close-up and long shot. Most important, and that is the question with which we began, I can put into words a comparison among Agnes' and Ted's and Norm's responses. I can see what they are doing as the setting of very individual standards for culturally shared feedback processes of perception. The various reference levels in their feedbacks—their interrogations of the film—I can phrase as functions of their different identities.

As I formulate Ted, he was the kind of person who divides the world into those who dominate and those who submit. His concern for control colored his perceptions of men and women, parents and children, microphones—and *The Story of O*. As I read myself now, some years after the event, I see a Norm who tried to master the film by figuring out rules by means of which the characters could live and enjoy living. (I think I am doing the same thing in the paragraphs you are reading.) Agnes, as I represent her, was the kind of person for whom commitment and connection are the most important values, often represented by places, and she controlled the characters and the situations to reflect her themes. Each of our identities used methods of interpretation that fitted the concerns of that identity.

Each of our identities used methods of interpretation, but these methods in turn used—built on—lower-level interpretations. At the most basic level, there was the physical film. "They [the voice over] said the trees were dark," said Agnes, "and I thought, they're not dark. They're light." Even Agnes' rejection of what the voice said rested on a still lower level of perception, her hearing of the sound track.

"They were in the car taking off her panties and cutting her bra, and she said that it didn't work that way sometimes, and then she sort of revised the fantasy." No one in our culture could read that bra as a man's undershirt or her panties as a hat. Using the codes for the physical images she was seeing, Agnes had to see O being stripped, and having seen that she had to find a way of dealing with it.

"Her face was blank," said Agnes. "And I remember thinking at that point, you don't have to do this." "I thought it was O's fantasy. I thought about the revising of it, because I revise my fantasies. I start them out, and if I don't like the direction the story is taking, I start them over again." Agnes felt freed of restraint—an important issue for her—because she interpreted O's voice as describing a fantasy. Then she could revise the fantasy and assure O, "You don't have to do this."

Finally, an identity like Agnes', Ted's, or Norm's uses theories about this film (and film in general) to create a personal experience of *The Story of O*. Each of their identities is an agency that sets the reference levels for the feedback loops it governs. It is not only the identity that gives rise to each of their experiences of this film, but also the identity that results from it, and this circularity is the essence of feedback or, if you prefer, inquiry leading to dialogue.

Norm seeks to master the world by knowing patterns and unities. Hence he reads the re-run of the opening sequence as legitimating his search for a moral in the picture. Agnes wants to establish connections and intimacies, so she reads that opening re-run as some person's fantasy, to be revised like her own.

Ted was working out themes of submission and dominance.

Hence, for him, the important thing about O's branding Sir Stephen was Ted's perception of Sir Stephen's consent. Norm, however, wanted to find unity and pattern, and he focused on the "O" on Sir Stephen's hand, one O among many Os.

Ted saw the castle where O is trained as a symbol of universal human patterns of submission and obedience. Agnes, with her sense of connection through place, thought of her own Catholic girls' high school. Again, Agnes saw O's branding in terms of connection: she submitted to it only because she was committed to a certain place. Ted felt that she "obviously" consented to it.

Agnes related the pain in the movie to the pain she thought her own religious upbringing encouraged—she established a connection. Norm also thought of religion, but rules and paradoxes, not pain.

Agnes just wanted Sir Stephen, O's second lover, to make O happy—connections again—while Norm thought him impressively dominant, perhaps even a magus or guru—someone who had mastered the system. Ivan, the boy who wanted to marry O, Norm thought lacking somehow, a bit spineless, because he was unwilling to undergo the spiritual discipline Norm saw in Sir Stephen. Ted thought him normal and gentle, because he and O were able temporarily to escape the submission-dominance polarity.

In short, by understanding Agnes', Ted's, and Norm's identities as themes, I can understand their different readings of the same scene, event, or character as variations on those themes. At the same time that they were interpeting differently, however, they were also building similar intepretations on shared canons and codes. All saw whips, bras, and a castle. Thus, I can understand how each saw a different movie and each saw the same movie.

Most film theories have the film dictating or controlling the response. Typical is the "suture" theory of film response. It says that the film creates gaps, offscreen spaces, and the next shot fills them. The spectator is, so to speak, sewed or sealed into the film so that the spectator sees events as the camera does. Such theories are, in psychological jargon, stimulus-response theories or, in the language of reader-response, text-active theories. Some are bi-active. That is, they explain the commonalities in Agnes', Ted's, or Norm's response by saying the film controls those. Then

Agnes, Ted, and Norm can add their individual variations to "the" standard response.

Both these kinds of theories, text-active and bi-active, seem weak to me. There are, I think, several reasons to prefer a spectator-active or reader-active model.

One you have just seen. You can explain with it. In a complex set of responses, like Agnes', Ted's, and Norm's, there are two things to be explained. Why are they alike in the ways that they are alike? Why are they different in the ways they are different? Most people assume that the likenesses are caused somehow by the film—the text. The film "guides" or "controls" or "constrains" its audience. One can better explain the similarities in reponse, however, by saying that they come about because Agnes, Ted, and Norm are using similar hypotheses on the film, similar notions of garters, whips, flashbacks, and cross-cutting. This is the model the psychologists of reading have arrived at in their experiments, although they do not pay much attention to individual differences. Why is it better? Because it rests on the psychologists' experimental evidence. Because it provides a psychological account of the way we perceive texts. There is no explanatory power, no psychology really, in statements that the film guides, controls, or constrains its viewers. How does such guiding come about? Nobody says.

Naturally, the identity-governing-feedbacks picture explains the second matter, why the individual responses are different, because that is what it was designed to do. By contrast a bi-active model requires two kinds of explanations, one for the likenesses, another for the differences. (And it is as mute on the details of the psychology of difference as it is of likeness.)

Positing two modes of response introduces another difficulty. If there are two modes by which we apprehend texts, what determines which mode is in action at any given moment? Why does the one model cease functioning and the other come into play? People agree that O wears tight garters—that, says the text-active model, the film controls. People disagree about what the rewriting of the opening fantasy means. In the rewriting, the text does not control, and individuals decide. But why did the text suddenly lose control? And when? By contrast a reader-active model explains *both* the sharing of basic features (garters) *and* the differences about other basic features (like the rewriting). Similarly, a reader-active model explains differences arising from gender, age, education, or class with one model. By contrast, the idea that some things are text-active and some reader-active, usually expressed as "interaction," again requires two different models. Again the question arises, When and why does text-control stop and control from the viewer's gender, age, education, or class take over?

In short, the reader-active picture of an identity governing a hierarchy of feedbacks has advantages of precision and parsimony. Using it, I can understand how a complex series of responses, like Agnes', Ted's, and Norm's, can be simultaneously very personal to each of them but have elements shared by other viewers of the film. I can see how they could read the images of the film, its conventions, and its sequence as other filmgoers would and yet derive from those same shared responses highly individual interpretations of O's actions. I can understand how Kuleshov's audience could all agree about the meaning of the cuts (when there was no "meaning" in them). I can understand how they could all see the actor's face as having different expressions, when the expressions were in fact the same. I can understand how my reading of Benjamin Braddock's summer builds upon and uses Mike Nichols' radical experiments in cutting.

By contrast, a text-active model has considerable difficulty with the Kuleshov effect. The text or stimulus is just one piece of film, a montage of shots. If we assume the Kuleshov cuts were the stimulus, the audience all responded the same way. All agreed the face was being put in a certain context. Reading the actor's face, however, the audience did different things with the same stimulus. Because the audience saw that one stimulus (Mosjukhin's face) differently in different contexts, a stimulus-response model requires us to assume that the individual shot is one stimulus but the juxtaposition of face and context, the cuts, another. I find the idea that one thing is two different stimuli very confusing. I find it much easier to imagine one individual using two different codes on one thing.

A second reason I prefer this model is that it fits what the great majority of modern psychologists tell us about perception.

We perceive in a continuing dialogue, in which we pose a question to the "out there," and that question elicits an answer which affects the next question. This question-and-answer or feedback model corresponds precisely (even quantitatively) to the processes that the psychologists of perception tell us are the way we perceive all kinds of things, not just movies. Hence, this model provides a continuity between the way we see a certain set of pinks and yellows as a flesh tone, the way we see the twenty-four frames a second into continuous motion, the way we perceive a pair of panties as a pair of panties, the way we know how to interpret a certain kind of cut as a flashback, and the way we find the relation between René and O interesting or sick and lousy. We can see why, given a cut from a bowl of soup to a man's face, we interpret the facial expression as hunger. Our high-level conclusions are our own, but we built those high-level conclusions from the most immediate questions that we made the physical film answer yea or nay to. By contrast, a text-active model gives us no way to explain why responses are variable in some respects and fixed in others.

I have a third reason for preferring this model to suture or other text-active theories. This hierarchy of feedbacks in which the deepest and most far-reaching concerns of an Agnes or a Norm set the reference levels for particular perceptions fits what the physiologists of the brain tell us about that mysterious architecture. Obviously, there is much they do not know, and this feedback metaphor drastically simplifies what we do know about the brain. On the other hand, the metaphor does open the possibility of exploring the ways we read films with some attention to what we know about the way the human body works.

Even identity, we now know, may be a psychic structure. The human brain, like the brain of all higher mammals, goes through a process of growing and losing neurons and synapses (the gaps between neurons where the action is). In the first few years of our life we sprout synapses at an astonishing rate. The six-year-old child has a brain that is as big as an adult's and uses twice the energy—as those of us who have parented six-year-olds had suspected. From the age of eleven on, however, only the fittest of these neurons and synapses survive. That is, only if we use them do neurons and synapses get the neurochemicals they need.

Furthermore, that has been true *from birth*. Only the neurons and synapses that we used got the necessary chemicals to survive. The child who grew up in New York developed neurons for blocks and subways. The child who grew up in Kansas got a brain for big skies and fields of grain, quite a different kind of space. The child whose mother over-controlled developed patterns of mind and action to fit her pattern. In this way, the patterns of relationship to people and things that we established from earliest infancy to adolescence became inscribed in the very structure of our brains. That inscribed structure is, it seems to me, the physiological basis for psychoanalysis' sayings about the importance of early childhood. That inscribed structure is what we call identity.

A fourth reason I adopted this model is that it combines traditional and poststructuralist views of persons and texts. An identity governing feedbacks not only makes sense of the old idea of persons and texts as organic unities, but it also fits our late twentieth-century skepticism about such certainties or essences. If we follow psychoanalysts, psychologists, and biologists (I am thinking here of Maturana and Varela), we imagine identity as an organic unity. We imagine an "originary" identity in the language of today's deconstructionists, and they would say we err in doing so. Yet perhaps we are not so old-fashioned as it seems. The model also says our imagining is necessarily "off." Identity is decentered because identity is always somebody's representation of an identity, and the somebody can only do that through the somebody's own identity. Agnes, Ted, and Norm are always somebody's Agnes, somebody's Ted, somebody's Norm. In this essay, each of their identities is a product of my interpretation through a hierarchy of feedback loops that I use for reading identities. These and all identities, therefore, are decentered and systematically elusive. This model uses, but avoids being trapped by, essentialism.

Even if I try to read my own identity, I can only read it by splitting myself. That is why, at those points in this book, I have referred to myself in the third person, as "Norm." The part of me that (consciously and unconsciously) interprets my I is not quite the same as the identity being interpreted, "Norm." The identity that exists after a given act is not quite the same as the identity that (consciously and unconsciously) performed that act. Hence, even if it is "in" our own brains, identity is necessarily imperfect, elusive, decentered, deconstructed, because identity can only be one identity's reading of the psychic structure underlying another's identity.

To summarize, we can relate three things. One, a real individual response. Two, the text that evoked it. Three, the feedbacks, the codes and canons, by which the individual reads the text. The model consists of a hierarchy of feedbacks governed by a theme-and-variations identity (itself a construct through this very process of perception). A personal identity sets the standards for canons ("otherwise" cultural feedback loops) which in turn set the standards for codes ("not otherwise" cultural feedback loops) which in turn set the standards for "not otherwise" physical and physiological feedback loops. A personal identity governs these three levels, consciously and unconsciously using them to serve that I's idea of pleasure and to defeat that I's idea of pain. The I itself, however, is decentered, some necessarily other I's way of phrasing the viewer's individuality through just this kind of identity-governs-feedback process.

I cannot tell whether this is too complicated a model of an audience's response for a humanistic readership. Really, though, compared to the hermetic complexities of modern film and literary theory, I cannot believe that it is. I propose it because I do not know a better way to relate a real individual response to the film that evoked it and to the tests we all use for seeing movies. I believe it is the strongest model we critics presently have for what goes on when you and I "I" a film, a poem, a story, any text, anything. That is, we can explain with it. It gains further strength from "harder" disciplines than literary theory: psychoanalysis, experimental psychology, and neuroscience. For me, it is especially satisfying. Professor Holland's identity theory forms the ultimate intellectualization of Norm the moviegoer's need for pattern and unity. Nevertheless, I have to confess that this model is not one that most critics of film or literature use. Perhaps, then, this is a cue to eye, to I, some critics in action.

two

I-ing Critics

Criticism As Public(ation)

Agnes', Ted's, and Norm's responses illustrate the kind of thing audiences do. They saw a movie both in shared and in wholly individual ways. We can understand how they did these two seemingly contradictory things if we apply a model of a unique, theme-and variations identity governing a hierarchy of hypothesizing loops. Some of these hypotheses are shared by all humans, some by all humans within a culture, and some by all humans within an interpretive community within a culture.

That is what audiences do. What do critics do? In a sense a critic is no more than an audience member who speaks to and for the rest of us in a more public and formal way than Agnes, Ted, and Norm did. Literary criticism in this sense simply means making public statements about literature or making public statements, prompted by literature, about society, history, psychology, or, in general, the human condition.

Despite its public nature, however, I suspect the average citizen finds literary criticism as we academics know it a mystery wrapped in an enigma. There is some popular criticism for a wide audience: people review books and movies in print or on television, and that is certainly a kind of criticism. But reviewing is far removed from the arcane goings-on of professors of literature. In Europe there is a tradition of a learned laity. There are even learned journals directed at amateurs. Not so in the United States. Here what is "learned" in that word's two-syllable sense is largely confined to professors.

The American public, when it looks at a professor, sees someone who is supposed to be instructing the public's college-age children. But professors know that teaching is only the tip of the iceberg, at least in the United States. As a professorial adage has it, we are paid for teaching but promoted for publishing. From the professor's point of view teaching may be very rewarding—it usually is—but it does not provide the kind of rewards one's dean provides: raises, travel, research time, rank, tenure, and chairs.

Thirty years ago, colleges and universities in the United States were informally divided into "publishing institutions" and "teaching institutions." No longer. Academic administrators at every kind of institution have taken as a gauge of the liveliness and merit of both individuals and departments how much and where they are publishing. From the research institute to the community college the pressure is on. Publish or perish.

For the American professor of literature (as opposed to creative writing) that demand usually leads to writing essays and books for other professors of literature (like this book). As a result the critic no longer aims simply to be a more adept and public audience than Agnes, Ted, and Norm. The aim is also to turn out more and more "criticism," that is, more and more essays in learned journals, more and more books with university presses. Since the 1960s academic "criticism" has become a growth industry. At any given moment the sheer bulk is astonishing, and the rate of growth is something even the greediest Wall Streeter could envy.

Again, then, if we were to look at a group of academic literary critics as we have looked at Agnes, Ted, and Norm, what would they be doing? And why? There are the traditional aims of criticism. The critic was often said to be a handmaiden of the muse, that is, someone who enhances the artistic transaction. The critic made sure that audiences achieved the ethical and psychological enrichment the arts offer. The critic might do this by, for example, interpretation. The critic might bring to public attention texts that had been ignored or misunderstood. The critic might add to the knowledge or wisdom an audience brings to a text. The critic might discover truths. All these traditional aims are served by the critic serving as an exemplary member of the audience.

To these traditional aims, we have to add today another, less noble: academic publication. Any critical theory must admit the generation of a series of academic publications. The series must be, in theory at least, unlimited and, alas, in practice it often seems so. Any theoretical stance must provide a basis for ever more and more critical performances. We need to keep this practical fact in mind as we I critics.

These are generalizations, however. Really to I critics, we need an example. That is, we need a text, and we need some critics.

A Text and
a Critic

In the first few years I was teaching, I used to use one particular poem as an important test case:

> Thirty days hath September,
> April, June, and November,
> And all the rest have thirty-one
> Save February . . .

And at that point I mumble to myself something like, "which has twenty-eight until leap year when it has twenty-nine."

Is that even literature? If it looks like a duck, if it walks like a duck . . . If the text runs halfway across the page like a poem, if it scans like a poem, if it rhymes like a poem—surely it *is* a poem, and poems are a subset of literature.

Further, this poem has, in the test of value honored by no less magisterial a critic than Samuel Johnson, outlived its century. Indeed, it has outlived it many times over:

> Thirty dayes hath Nouember,
> Aprill, Iune, and September,

> February hath xxviij alone,
> And all the rest have xxxi.

That one is "a rule to know how many dayes euery moneth in the yere hath" from Richard Grafton's 1562 *Abridgement of the Chronicles of England*. Here is another from the sixteenth century:

> Thirty days hath September,
> April, June, and November,
> And all the rest have thirty-one,
> Excepting February alone,
> And that has twenty-eight days clear
> And twenty-nine in each leap-year.

You can find a half dozen versions in English and Latin of "Thirty days" both in England and the United States from the sixteenth, seventeenth, and eighteenth centuries. It would be fun to quote them but you have probably gotten the idea already. This is a poem of questionable merit but so popular it is probably the only sixteenth-century poem most ordinary citizens know by heart.

For that reason, "Thirty days" has always seemed to me an ultimate challenge to critical methods. If a critical method can't say something about this poem, so widely known and quoted, maybe there is something wrong with the method. Conversely, if a critical method *can* say something interesting about this odd little poem, seemingly so devoid of significance, the method must be able to say something interesting about *any* poem.

What, then, might a critic write about "Thirty days"? What depends on when. That is, what a critic does depends a great deal on when he or she is doing it in the half century since World War II. I think I can best explore the possibilities by a glance at the recent history of the "lit-crit" enterprise.

"English," as we know it in the United States, came into being after the Civil War as one thread in the hurried weaving of American universities. Industrialists, businessmen, and legislators felt an urgent need for the knowledge that would, ultimately, permit the industrial growth of the latter half of the century. Based on the traditional model of the classics, "English" was to provide "culture" for those who would by brains and violent competition build this modern industrial nation-state. They would be the undergraduates, and professionals in "English" would teach them. Because "English" began with the model of classics, professors of English emulated the philological and historical researches of their colleagues in Greek and Latin.

At its core, "English" in the new American universities meant the reading of the great texts of our literature. Although the canonical list of "greats" is currently under strenuous debate, this project largely continues to hold true for undergraduates. The business of an English department is to teach the great texts, whatever we judge them to be. At first, professors taught poems and fictions as "expressive realism." A story or a play described a world. A lyric described a world in a mind. The reader's task was to understand those worlds and assess their moral import. The student was to think about literary characters as if they were real people and literary episodes as if they were real events. Having done so, one could report, assess, and moralize one's experience. Often the voice of professorial authority excluded other possible experiences. There were "right" readings, even so far as feelings were concerned.

For the professors teaching these right readings, though, "English" meant activities quite different from the teaching of undergraduates. "English" as a profession meant "philology": learning Anglo-Saxon, Middle English, and the other roots of the language of the canonical masterpieces. It meant "literary history": mastering a great many facts and dates about those texts and their sources. And it meant "bibliography": learning techniques for establishing the accuracy and provenance of those texts. These three were what the Ph.D. candidate was to study, because the sole purpose of the degree was as a credential for a future professor.

The professor was thus obliged to teach in two quite different ways. First, he (and it was usually "he") was to teach undergraduates in the traditional way. Second, if he was in a research-oriented university, he was to teach graduate students, that is, future editions of himself. And what was he to teach them? Philology, literary history, and bibliography. The system thus reproduced itself, and it has proved extremely stable. Even today, in avant-garde departments, hiring and firing and curriculum tend to be organized around the traditional categories of literary history: Medieval, Renaissance, Restoration and Eighteenth Century, and so on. When American literature entered the curriculum, it acquired its periods, and so with comparative literature. One advertises for "somebody in eighteenth-century poetry" or "somebody who could do Renaissance and modern drama."

So far as I know, in the United States, the first strong challenge to this definition of "English" came in the 1940s and 1950s in the form of the "New Criticism." A "New" critic or teacher was to put aside biography, historical background, evaluation, everything else really, until the critic had closely examined the words-on-the-page themselves. The bibliographical and philological components of English still had their usefulness in establishing those texts and the meanings of their words, but literary history became much less useful. The older ideal of expressive realism faded. Instead of reading through texts to the people or events they represented, a proper professor-critic was to concentrate on the text itself, as language. Moreover, the teaching of this kind of reading served both undergraduate and graduate students.

In those buttoned-down Eisenhoverian days, an all-powerful text divided the literary transaction into author, text, and reader. The author created the text, to be sure, and the text caused the reader's experience, but firm boundaries between them made them three separable parts in the literary transaction. Considering the author led at best to biography, which was (however and ahem) "not criticism." At worst, considering an author led to the "intentional fallacy," a misguided displacement of effort. The critic would be trying to determine what the words said, not from the words themselves, but from some extrinsic source like letters or biography or other contemporary texts: political, social, historical. Conversely, considering the reader led to the "affective fallacy," studying the effect of a text instead of what one should properly attend to, the text itself.

The "New Criticism" issued a great deal of theoretical lucubration, most of it now happily forgotten. What evolved was a method for reading texts that was universally applicable. No doubt others would summarize it differently, but as I practiced it, the method was to perceive the text as an overall unity. I considered each detail of the text. I looked at particular wordings, sequence, style, tone, voice, rhythm—anything and everything. I grouped these details around themes and meanings until I could demonstrate the "organic unity" of the text. That is, I could show that each detail, no matter how tiny or accidental, related to every other detail through various themes.

The business of the student, both undergraduate and graduate, was to learn "how to read" this way, that is, how to interpret. The business of the professor of English thus became *interpretation,* and so it remains to this day. New Critical publication typically took the form of a twenty- to thirty-page essay "explicating" a text, literally "unfolding" it, showing how some or all the details fit together.

Unlike literary history, the method does not depend upon a rich store of cultural upbringing. Anyone with brains and sensibility could analyze a text. As a result the "New Criticism" opened the great tradition of English literature to people of any or no cultural inheritance. In an upwardly mobile society, students whose parents had never graduated from high school could become *littérateurs.* The New Criticism democratized "English," and it arrived in American universities at the same time as the huge influx of World War II veterans whose education was paid for by the G. I. Bill. Many of these students could never otherwise have dreamed of going to college, let alone acquiring a Ph.D. in English.

New Criticism evolved somewhat differently in England. There F. R. Leavis assumed a commanding position and made the enterprise of "English" into the passing of forceful judgments on the quality or morality of various texts. The Leavisite mode has always seemed to me the extension of the British class system to literature so as to establish a not-to-be-questioned elite. Nevertheless, these judgments required close attention to the text, since they depended on careful analysis or "close reading." Hence one could fairly speak of "the Anglo-American New Criticism." The New Criticism, as such, did not exist on the continent where the student of non-classical literature followed the traditional model of philology, bibliography, and literary history.

What would an American New Critic say about "Thirty days hath September"? New Critics favored poetry that took a lot of explaining, like Donne or Herbert or Milton. "Thirty days" hardly qualifies. As it happens, though, there is a New Critical reading of this poem, and by one of the best.

Theodore Spencer, whose brief, brilliant career as a literary historian and critic spanned the 1930s and '40s, set out in 1943 to burlesque what he took to be the pretentiousness of much New Criticism. He announced he would "explain what we may describe as [the] fundamental *dynamic*" of

> Thirty days hath September
> April, June and November:
> All the rest have thirty-one,
> Excepting February alone,
> Which has only eight and a score
> Till leap-year gives it one day more.

Spencer proceeded, in the New Critical manner, by singling out details. He mentioned the listing of the months in a non-calendrical order. He pointed to the choice of "excepting":

> The tragic note is struck the moment "February" is mentioned. For the initial sound of the word "excepting" is "X," and as that sound strikes the sensibility of the reader's ear a number of associations subconsciously accumulate. We think of the spot, the murderous and lonely spot, which "X" has so frequently marked; we remember the examinations of our childhood where the wrong answers were implacably signaled with "X"; we think of ex-kings and exile, of lonely crossroads and executions, of the inexorable anonymity of those who cannot sign their names . . .
>
> The lonely "February" (notice how the "alone" in line four is echoed by the "only" in line five), the solitary and maladjusted individual who is obviously the hero and crucial figure of the poem, is not condemned to the routine which his fellows, in their different ways, must forever obey. Like Hamlet, he has a capacity for change.
>
> But . . . in spite of all his variety . . . "February" cannot quite accomplish (and in this his tragedy consists) the *quantitative* value of the society in which circumstances have put him. No matter how often he may alternate from twenty-eight to twenty-nine . . . he can never achieve the bourgeois, if anonymous, security of "thirty-one," nor equal the more modest and aristocratic assurance of "thirty." Decade after decade, century after century, millennium after millennium, he is eternally frustrated. The only symbol of change in a changeless society, he is continually beaten down. Once every four

years he tries to rise, to achieve the high, if delusive, level of his dreams. But he fails. He is always one day short, and the three years before the recurrence of his next effort are a sad interval in which the remembrance of previous disappointment melts into the futility of hope, only to sink back once more into the frustration of despair.

Spencer's parody seems to me deadly accurate, and I do not want to make myself the over-serious and ponderous butt of Spencer's ridicule. Nevertheless, I think this is exactly the kind of thing an orthodox New Critic might have written. Spencer leans on a detail like the "ex-" in "excepting" to bring out all kinds of meanings. Spencer then brings all the details together around themes of more and less, difference and sameness, aristocratic security and bourgeois wealth. Spencer reads the poem into a coherent "dynamic": February's tragic inability to achieve thirty or thirty-one days.

12

A Derridian Critic

Spenser wrote his spoof in 1943. What might a professor of English write today about the poem? How would a postmodern or a poststructuralist critic approach "Thirty days"? I don't know any such readings, and I myself do postmodern criticism too haltingly to provide one. Instead, I wrote to a half dozen poststructuralist friends and colleagues, enclosing the version of "Thirty days" from *Bartlett's Familiar Quotations.* "Could you sketch out," I asked, "some idea of how you think a poststructuralist reading might go?" (Or Lacanian or Derridian—I varied my phrasing according to my estimate of my correspondent's critical posture.) "Please, nothing elaborate or time-consuming (unless the problem intrigues you). But what kind of method or evidence would you, as a wise and skilled postmodernist [or Lacanian or Derridian or poststructuralist] use?" My fellow-critics very generously responded, indeed, so generously that I can quote only small fractions of their total responses.

Even so, they allow us to compare Theodore Spencer's New Critical reading of "Thirty days" with a deconstructive approach to the poem. I will call this critic

Professor Adrian Ade, my pseudonym for a distinguished follower of the theories of philosopher Jacques Derrida. Notice how, instead of just starting to interpret, he situates his response in terms of my request:

> A demand for time—under whatever calendar—daunts one. And can be answered only with a calendar trick, a *coup du calendrier* (e.g., flying east to west to gain a day, west to east to lose a day; or the discussion between two persons talking about a calendar trick and then using the phrase in later publications as a personal clue/joke/reference . . .
>
> But all we have here is a child's rhyme, in your designation "the following poem." In it five "months" are named: September, April, June, and November, and finally February. Already a calendar trick—at least in the Gregorian calendar. The seventh month of the Roman calendar, here the ninth month. And the ninth month of the Roman calendar, the eleventh month . . .
>
> A question too of the feminine: Juno and Aphrodite are named [June, April], and the festival of purification, *februa*. Numbers and women, all within a question of money, *kalends* as the day the interest is due.
>
> A question of knowledge: "And all the rest": seven (or eight, until the fourth line) months must be remembered. The named within its *un*named and unable to be saturated contexts (the Gregorian calendar, the other months, the reference of day to night, year and calendar as the "rhythm" of time). The "moons" [months] are defined by the days (not the nights). All this knowing slips behind the *clarity* of the exceptions—February and leap year as acts of purification.
>
> All in a child's rhyme to the reader's mind.

What on earth has happened? Adrian's *praxis*, to use current jargon, differs wildly from what Spencer wrote. He makes no push toward a unity, no attempt to interrelate the themes he develops (women, months, money), no real effort to bring out a human significance for the poem (although surely there is an important relation for humans between women and months). Something quite drastic has happened since the New Criticism of Theodore Spencer's day.

Nevertheless, like Spencer, Ade sees the critic's task as interpretation or explanation (not, as critics before Spencer might, reporting one's experience, getting out whatever lifelikeness one could from this lyric, or finding its sources in folklore). Like Spencer, Ade homes in on details. Like Spencer with "Ex-," Ade relies on the etymology of both the important and the seemingly unimportant words, as does most Derridian criticism I have read. Ade brings in a variety of other texts, dealing with them on a par with the poem in question. By contrast, when Spencer mentions another text, he does so only to analogize to and so explain "Thirty days."

Unlike Spencer, Ade lets one word in the text, "days," evoke its opposite, nights, and then he treats the evoked word as if it were as much a part of the poem as "days." He writes using certain stylistic traits, avoiding, for example, subject-object sentences. (They would "privilege" subjects and objects in a philosophical sense.) Instead he writes without verbs ("A question of") or in passive verbs without subjects ("must be remembered," "are defined by"). All this deconstructs (undoes the usual hierarchies in) the text.

What happened? It is probably too soon to write the history of the transition from modern to postmodern or, in literary criticism, from the New Criticism to the variety of methods that have succeeded it. All I can offer is a thumbnail sketch, personal and all too brief.

For me, this transition began in 1966, although others date it earlier. The core of the New Critics' position, as I see it, was its reaction against earlier practice. No longer should one treat a text only as part of a larger literary history external to the text. Nor was a text an occasion for a rhapsodic or polemical account of one's experience. Nor did a text refer mimetically to people and things outside itself. All these critical tactics directed attention away from the text to something else: the history of its production, its reception, or the "story" it told. The New Critic's reaction was to focus on the text to the exclusion of everything "extrinsic."

The approach acknowledged that a poem or a fiction had a history, but it was to be looked at as if it were itself wholly self-contained, answerable only to its own inner logic. The New Criticism posited an autonomous and objective text, usually a single text, this particular poem or this particular novel. It did not talk about readers. It simply assumed an autonomous subjective reader reading that text. But that reader read it in a lawful way often expressed in those days by the critical (not unlike the royal) "we." "We sense the irony in . . ." "We are amused to find . . ." "We feel . . ." New Critics wrote as though the ordinary reader were constrained to some one response announced by the all-seeing critic. More properly, the reader was constrained by the text, which the critic could perceive more skillfully than those swept up in his "we." Listen to Spencer: "We think of the spot . . ." "we remember the examinations of our childhood . . ." "we think of ex-kings and exile, of lonely crossroads . . ." Do we? Did you? That doesn't seem to matter.

Nevertheless the New Criticism had an immense success. In department after department it became the dominant mode. Usually it accommodated elements of literary history. That way a critic-professor would practice critical reading but within a certain period and thereby find a niche in the job market.

Along with the triumph of the New Criticism came the increased pressure for publication, so that the journals of the profession became filled with "explications" of this or that text, each new publication implying that it had finally arrived at "the" reading of this particular text. Sometimes it seemed as though English literature would be exhausted. Critics would establish "the" reading for every poem, story, play, and movie. Then, with nothing more to publish about, there would be a great deal of perishing. Surely this was one of the reasons some critics began to challenge New Critical orthodoxy.

13

The Challenges

The early 1950s brought the first challenge to this cozy synthesis of textual criticism and literary history: the so-called Chicago critics. Often these critics took Aristotle's *Poetics* as their point of departure, and some therefore called them the Neo-Aristotelians. R. S. Crane and others wanted criticism to develop a coherent theoretical and philosophical basis.

Then, in 1957, Northrop Frye made one of the most interesting challenges to and extensions of the New Critical picture. Although Frye read individual texts like a New Critic (and a most gifted one), he embedded individual literary works in a system of classification and interrelation that embraced all of literature and finally all our verbal structures. Frye rooted his system in such universal human *nonliterary* experiences as higher and lower, time, and the seasons.

Another kind of challenge came from phenomenological critics who insisted on treating, not the single text but a writer's whole *oeuvre*. A writer's poems or novels thus were thought of not as a mass of details to be ordered but as a world to be entered and immediately experienced.

For me, however, it was a landmark conference in the autumn of 1966 at Johns Hopkins University that marked the beginning of the real challenges to New Critical orthodoxy, the postmodern challenges. A group of prominent American critics were invited to listen to what a group of prominent Continental, mostly French, critics were saying. The conference was a deliberate effort on the part of some American critics to "Europeanize" their colleagues—for two reasons. First, Anglo-American New Criticism was quite strictly Anglo-American—parochial, if you will. Second, it was also Anglo-American in its distrust of theory. Very much in the American grain, it was a practical criticism, devoted to working on particular texts (and therefore threatening to draw the well dry). Save for Frye, it was devoid of overarching theory. Save for the Chicago critics and the phenomenologists, it was isolated from philosophical trends and unaware of its own preconceptions.

By contrast, the conference presented to its American "colloquists" an array of European thinkers of whom Jacques Lacan and Jacques Derrida have since become the most famous. The papers embraced philosophy and "theory." Much of the theory discussed was "structuralist," which seemed to me then (and now) very like the American New Criticism in its theoretical assumptions. The structuralist sees a unitary text with an internal logic to be discovered by the critic. The structuralists, however, tried to build these structures on cultural anthropology, linguistics, political science, or philosophy—in the European tradition of *Wissenschaft* or *les sciences de l'homme*. The structuralists, moreover, did not assert kinship with the unphilosophical Anglo-American tradition, but with earlier European versions of "formalist" criticism, the Moscow Linguistic Circle (1915) and its successor in Prague (1926). Continental structuralists could also draw on Marxist thought, something hard to do in Cold War America.

Some of the theory, however, foreshadowed various schools of poststructuralist thought, the kind of thing which Adrian Ade is emulating. These positions subvert the modernist or structuralist or New Critical assumption of the autonomous text with its own inner logic facing a skilled but obedient reader.

Other challenges were mounting as well. In Germany, from

Wolfgang Iser and Hans Robert Jauss came German *Rezeption-sästhetik*, the understanding of texts through the reception they have historically received. The text is structured in the New Critical or structuralist manner but only as a series of schemata that a succession of readers must actualize before the book as a whole comes into existence. Or American reader-response criticism: the insistence that it is the reader who makes meaning, not the text. The critic is to write within that understanding. The critic should not claim to be simply explaining or structuring a text (or *oeuvre*) "out there." Rather, the critic should acknowledge that he or she is sharing the critic's own "in here" experience of the text. The aim is for the critic's reader to have a new "in here" experience. Or semiotics: the study of "anything you can tell a lie with," in Umberto Eco's happy phrase. A semiotic critic pays heed to the codes and systems by which we read texts, hence divides a text into codes and messages. Or deconstruction: the sense that this particular text is only one inscription of an "intertextuality," a sea of language in which we live and in which meanings are always undercut by other, conflicting meanings.

Yet another challenge besides critical schools were the social and political convictions that critics bring into their postmodern readings: Marxist, feminist, or anticolonial. All of this a critic writing in Spencer's mode would carefully omit. The New Criticism was mostly apolitical.

These postmodern challengers are alike in rejecting (or in thinking they have rejected) the New Critic's systematic reader and carefully isolated text. They substitute an indeterminate text and an indeterminate subject and a great deal of philosophizing and jargon—as we shall see when we continue our sampling.

14

Three Postmoderns

Consider another postmodern critic, pseudonymous Ben Bee, as a sample of the challenges to the New Criticism. Ben has written several versatile and witty Derridian critical essays and thus offers a second example of a deconstructive approach. Like Ade, he emphasized the poem's being a "mnemonic device." "It reminds me," Ben says, of other poems he knows "by heart." "Writing is a mnemonic technology," and hence this poem "could represent the essence of this memory function, opening out onto the whole issue of the history of writing, and the interdependence of thought, language and technology."

Drawing on Derrida's readings of a line in Nietzsche, then of Heidegger's reading of Nietzsche, both leading into various other associations, Ben cites Derrida: "how any bit of language is open to detachment from one context, and reassignment to another context, that it may be demotivated and remotivated in terms of significance, to infinity." Thus freed, Ben proposes:

Both of the foregoing perspectives, combined with an Eco-esque semiotics, suggest that the poem could be read in terms of the history of time (if that is not a redundancy), and the different dating systems (a term which further leads to the practice of computer dating and the semantic fields of love relations [here, Ben pointed to his earlier "by heart"]), Stonehenge, Mayan calendars, Roman synthesis of pagan and Christian calendars, Chinese and Jewish calendars, French revolution. The importance of time in the psychoanalytic cure might be noted, the time of understanding, and the way in which patients and analysts play with time in the transference; Lacan's experiments with the short session; the interminability of the cure . . .

I guess what I am suggesting is . . . to construct an inventory of the paradigms or semantic fields relevant to this text, leading, if pushed to an extreme, to a certain perspective on and arrangement of the "encyclopedia" or codes of our culture. Rather than constituting an interpretation, this inventory would provide a "commonplace book" from which a reader-scriptor might generate a further text of his/her own.

In Bee's technique, the original text becomes the basis for the free creation of an aftertext that he calls a "further text of [the reader's] own." Notice how he lets his commentary run from time to "dating" to matters of the heart. That is what interpretation or criticism is in the deconstructive mode. Bee's method is altogether different from Spencer's focus on the words-on-the-page (that "ex-," for example) as having a unified human significance.

My third postmodern declined the gambit entirely, writing that he would not approach the poem at all. Cecil Cee, a highly intelligent critic of films, fiction, and literary criticism, wrote:

I don't think that anyone *can* propose a "postmodernist reading" of this or any other poem. I would argue that postmodernism as an event issues from the advent of the mechanically reproducible image whose volatility/mobility (what Derrida . . . calls "iterability," the fundamental property of all signs) diffuses and scatters fixed meanings. Postmodernism's basic tactic of appropriation (. . . "grafting") demonstrates repeatedly that *any* text or single sign can be lifted from *any* context and pressed into service in another context which could not have been anticipated by the text's "author". . . .

What does iterability imply for the mnemonic poem that interests you? You have chosen a limit case, one that threatens poststructuralist ideas of textuality, since such a poem, with its rigidly fixed signified(s), would seem to have little possibility for engendering what Barthes called "the pleasure of the text," . . . those signifiers

without signifieds, or those signifiers which *he* could . . . detach
from their signifieds. Well, yes. But nevertheless, one can imagine
other uses of these lines, other contexts into which they might be
inserted (contexts in which they might become sinister, as the "Ten
Little Indians" poem becomes in the Agatha Christie story): what if
they were to be recited by a madman? After all, we thought we
knew what a Campbell Soup can meant until Warhol "moved" that
sign into a different context.

Ade and Bee let their minds roam. Cecil Cee turned to theory, but
like Bee he called attention to the way the words or "signifiers"
in the poem can be freely moved about from context to context,
meaning first one thing then another. In Cee's sketch, the Campbell Soup can means, and iterability implies that signs diffuse and
scatter meanings. Like Spencer, Cee treated the poem as the subject of "meaning"—it is the text that makes meaning—but, he
says, in a way wholly dependent upon the context, that is, the use
to which it is put.

My fourth respondent, Daniel Dee, is an energetic man who
resists categorization. "Thirty days" reminded him of a cocky,
Cockney, lockerroom ballad from his rugby playing days:

CHORUS: We're off to see the Wild West Show . . .
VOICE: And in this cage, Lad-ies and Gentlemen, we 'ave the
multi-spotted Leo-pard.
FEMALE VOICE: The multi-spotted Leopard?
VOICE: Yes, the multi-spotted Leo-pard. This strange and won-
drous hanimal 'as one spot for every day of the year, making three
'undred and sixty-five spots in hall.
FEMALE VOICE: (Oxford accent):
But what about a leap-year?
VOICE: 'Enry, lift hup the hanimal's tail and show the lady the
twenty-ninth of February.

After a paragraph on Derrida's deconstruction of the hierarchy of phonic voice over written sign (with references to Brecht,
Barthes, Flaubert, Socrates, and the classicist Eric Havelock), Dan
notes that an "oral formula" can be oppressive political speech:

Remember, remember
The fifth of November
GUNPOWDER, TREASON AND PLOT.

But, he says, he sees no ideology in "Thirty days." No? He reverses himself, noting that it is a gift in a system of professional
exchange (between me and five of my fellow-critics). He refuses
to look at the text. "I shan't look at the work but at the outwork,
not at the poem but at its frame . . . Moving, then, from center to
margin, let me investigate the request surrounding the object of
analysis." He segues into a dialogue analyzing my motives, and
its being a dialogue is, I presume, part of his approach. "[Norm]
is intellectually curious." "He has consciously identified a group
of theorists whose solidarity is disturbing." (True.) He says his
own associations (the bawdy ballad, a Guy Fawkes Day rhyme)
are "filled with apprehensions about women, religious bigotry,
and physicality" and even "aggression, envy, and cynicism."

> Look, all I was trying to do was to point to the situatedness of any
> utterance, its implication in questions of personal and political
> power. Any explication of "Thirty days" which ignores these mar-
> ginal implications is suspect. The text has a context, the context is
> not innocent. Beyond this, the context [with citations of Derrida,
> Kant, anthropologist Victor Turner, and critic Ronald Paulson] may
> contain the more important parts, may be the (im)proper site (cite)
> of interpretation.

He concludes that "Norm is getting exactly what he wants . . .
Material for his article," while his own motive is "To impress
Norm. Touché."

Although Dan's sketch differs markedly in style, content, and
theory from Ade's or Bee's, it also shares certain tactics. He moves
"away from" the poem (here, from text to pre-text, margin, outwork, or *parergon*). He lets his mind roam away from the poem,
but these are not exactly "free" associations, for he privileges ety-
mologically, philosophically, or literarily erudite comments. He
resists commitment to a single point of view (the dialogue form).

What is different about Dan's response is the frank, even
harsh, acknowledgment of his own motives and his exploration
of mine in a quasi-political comment on the typos and format of
the letter in which I quoted a "Thirty days" and asked him to
respond. Dee's response, by its very difference from the others,
highlights the issue I find crucial to them all: What is the position
of the reader-writer?

15

A Psychoanalytic Critic

When I ask about literary critics this way, I am also asking, of course, about myself. I too am a critic. What do I do? And why? Where do I fit into all these developments? Answer: I don't. I am outside the fray. (There's an identity theme for me there if you can catch it.) No, that's not exactly right. I am much concerned about all these theoretical developments and something of a participant in them. But I am and always have been something of an odd duck in the critical game as well. Someone outside the fray. What then would *I* say about "Thirty days"? What do *I* do? And why?

As a schoolboy I listened to the wonderful Sunday night radio shows of the 1930s and '40s. Then Monday mornings I would puzzle over the differences between my pals' preferences and my own. Why did Charlie prefer Fred Allen to Jack Benny? Why did Burky remember that particular line from *I Love a Mystery*? Why does Hutch think Fibber McGee's joke so funny? I was asking, I believe, How do I fit in?

Decades later, as a teacher of literature, even in my most formalist moments, I wondered about responses.

I might hold theoretically that a certain story had a "right" reading that I was to encourage as a teacher. Nevertheless, I was intrigued by the different ways people judged or enjoyed what they were reading right. In particular, I wondered about laughter. I had set up and was teaching a course in comedy, because I was still wondering about Fred Allen and Jack Benny. My interest in laughter drew me to psychological criticism.

Eventually, because Freud's book on jokes was the best theory I found, I decided to try psychoanalytic criticism. That is, I would use psychoanalytic psychology to make critical statements about literature. Thirty years ago, though, psychoanalysis moped on the margins of respectable academic scholarship and criticism. Psychoanalytic critics were few, and many of those languished at unexciting institutions. Leonard and Eleanor Manheim edited the group's mimeographed newsletter and mini-journal, *Literature and Psychology,* out of their living room. Other journal editors were averse to psychoanalysis, hence publication could be difficult. Psychoanalytic criticism lent itself all too well to parodies.

In 1960, orthodox literary critics and scholars laughed at interpretations in a strange jargon, bizarre symbolisms, and unbelievable complexes. Some psychoanalytic writers about literature, notably Kenneth Burke, Leon Edel, Erik Erikson, and Lionel Trilling, did translate the heavy-handed language into a more graceful prose and did make a human sense of the symbolism or the complexes. Yet I remember, when Erikson taught at Harvard, advisers from the English Department energetically *dis*couraging students from taking his seminars.

I can guess at an explanation. In 1960 the "New Criticism" headed the table of literary studies. Regular literary critics were saying, Concentrate on the way the words come together to form an aesthetic unity and complexity. Psychoanalysis, however, does not talk about words, but about persons. The psychoanalytic critics of those days wanted to read *through* texts toward the "real" persons they represented. "Real" meant the authors or the characters and mostly their oedipal themes and conflicts. The psychoanalytic critic would diagnose an author or character as obsessional or paranoid or homosexual, and this diagnosis became a paraphrase, something to be substituted (heresy!) for the actual wording of the text. The imagery and figures of speech so important to the New Criticism did not count as much as verisimilitude. Nevertheless, a great deal of interesting work was done in this vein and still is, for example, the revealing character studies of Bernard Paris. The orthodox literary critic, however, was and is likely to demur: But what is literature if not words and the special choice of words? What about literary form?

That question brings us back to "Thirty days." In the first few years I was teaching psychoanalytic literary criticism, in the early 1960s, I used to use this poem as a test case. I would ask my students, Can we say anything psychoanalytic about it? If we were analyzing "Mary had a little lamb," we could talk about dependency, self-object differentiation, the separating mother, Bowlby's attachment, challenging authority, or breaking obsessional routine. "Mary had a little lamb" has persons in it. But "Thirty days"? It seems a poem of pure form. My yellowed teaching notes from those years just say, "No symbolism—let's go on." Can we do more now? Can we say something about form?

Now, thirty years later, I face quite a different hierarchy. Psychoanalytic literary criticism, far from being the poor relation at the refectory table, finds itself seated above the salt. These days, if you are a literary theorist, you brand yourself passé if you cannot talk easily of Freud and Lacan, perhaps Winnicott, or conceivably Kohut or Kernberg (but not Kris or Hartmann or Erikson or Laing—they are as grandly "over" as the Beatles).

What happened? I think of psychoanalytic literary criticism, indeed psychoanalysis itself, as passing through three stages, each building on, enlarging, and including the one before it. The first of these historical stages dates from Freud's discovery of latent and manifest content in symptoms, dreams, jokes, and "Freudian slips." As he found latencies in many other mental activities, he posited a general explanation, the conflict between "manifest" and "latent," ultimately, "conscious" and "unconscious," thought of as systems, even locations in the brain. By the polarity between unconscious and conscious, the analyst could explain a great deal.

"First-phase" psychoanalysis uncovered (and the psychoanalytic critic's metaphors will often be those of digging out something secret) the latent or unconscious "content" of the text. Usually, that is some oedipal theme in the author or in a character, interpreted as real persons. Classical analysis elicits from a literary work features of the oedipus complex and the phallic and anal stages. Typically, the psychoanalytic critic will rely heavily on "Freudian symbols."

We usually date psychoanalysis' second phase from Freud's positing a superego, an ego, and an id in 1923. Its basic explanation poises ego against nonego. That is, one interprets the mind's synthesizing, unifying functions against what they have to synthesize: the demands of external reality or the id or the superego or the compulsion to repeat.

In the literary theory of this second phase of psychoanalysis, the text imitates Freud's post–1923 id-ego-superego mind. By regression in the service of the ego, an author puts satisfying fantasies ("unconscious content") in a text. The text has literary forms, like metonymy, metaphor, rhyme, or parallelism, which act for both author and reader like defenses or adaptations. They temper and transform fantasy content into ethical themes that meet the claims of ego and superego. "The" reader introjects—takes into his or her own mind—the psychological process embodied in the text. "The" reader is thus able to satisfy the multiple functioning of his or her own ego, superego, and id by transforming the various elements in any given literary work from fantasy through defense toward meaning.

Response in those days was still something one could safely assume. Readers were thought to be fairly uniform, and critics easily wrote of "the" reader. A text does something to or, more exactly, for "the" reader. It is a dream dreamed for us. The reader incorporates the id-ego-superego process embodied in the poem, varying it according to his (usually "his") own psychological patterns. In the tradition of the New Criticism, however, the variations in response were not important. What counted was the text and the psychological transformation it seemed to embody.

The picture of the literary transaction psychoanalysis had developed by 1965 was neat and powerful, but something was missing. We weren't able to say anything about "Thirty days." In my classes in the 1960s, we used to conclude that one could talk about any poem as a model of a psyche, in which its form was the literary analogy of a psychological defense. To read the form as a defense, though, one had to know what the poem was, so to speak, defending against. One had to consider the "fantasy content" of the poem, usually evidenced by symbolism. What if the poem has no fantasy content? What could the psychoanalytic critic say about a sonata? About a Jackson Pollock? That is why I thought "Thirty days" so important a test case. I can see in it no "unconscious content," no fantasy, nothing for its form to defend against.

A third phase of psychoanalytic criticism brought an answer. Poems and stories don't have defenses. People do. Poems and stories don't have fantasies. People do. It is a mistake to posit a "fantasy content" for "Thirty days" or any other literary work. One has to explore personal responses to the poem to find out what fantasies and defenses people actually make from it. That is why we have looked at Agnes, Ted, and Norm looking at *The Story of O*.

In the 1970s, literary critics began considering something new, the *relation* between reader and text. Psychoanalysis too was moving into a new phase and becoming similarly interpersonal. Researchers and clinicians, for example, focused on "self-object differentiation," the child's creation of an identity by separating from the symbiotic unity of mother and child. "Object-relations theory," the analysis of the child's early relations with mother, father, and "significant others," was replacing Freud's biological "instincts," wholly inside the child's body. Freud's *intra*psychic picture of the mind had evolved into an *inter*psychic model, in which the human being is always in relation to objects, hence decentered, never alone. We exist in a "potential space." The boundaries between self and "reality" were no longer solid as they had been in first- and second-phase theory. Psychoanalysis had become "postmodern."

In this third phase of psychoanalysis, Murray Schwartz asked in a well-known article, "Where is literature?" A text is no longer a thing in and of itself with a "fantasy content" that the author's drives "put there." The New Critics' crisp trisection of the literary transaction into author, text, and reader melts. Instead, the reality we are describing is the *relations* between authors and their creations (sublimation, compensation, reparation) and the *relations* between readers and what they read. Where is literature? Between text and author. Between text and reader.

When other critics and I began to explore readers' free associations to texts, we found that readers did respond in the transformational way described by the second phase. They did convert
fantasies through formal defenses toward themes, *but each individual did so differently from the rest.* This we have seen with
Agnes, Ted, and Norm re-creating *The Story of O.* Their responses look somewhat alike, because they share the physical film
and certain techniques for understanding it. At the same time,
their responses vary far too much to assume a single "fantasy
content" or even a shared "formal defense." We can account for
the wide differences in their readings only by saying they were
governed by widely different personal needs and defenses. The
day of "the" reader is over—at least for those of us who have
looked at actual readers.

Hence, today's psychoanalytic critic cannot declare one "fantasy content" for a movie or a story. Rather, readers project their
own fantasies onto the materials of the text. Similarly, readers
impose their own defenses—all by a complex interaction between
an I and the physical text and cultural codes for interpretation
and understanding. Analyses showed responses like Agnes' finding the pain purposeful in *The Story of O* or Ted's concern with
managing domination by finding consent. As a result, reader-
response critics concluded we could no longer sustain the traditional literary idea of a stable text with a determinate "meaning."
Rather, readers make meaning.

This conclusion about readers led to an even more disturbing
realization. We critics also had needs and defenses. We were not
explorers discovering features of a text "out there" with "real"
boundaries and meaning. What we were describing as facts
stemmed from our own critical activity. In getting at meaning, we
would share some professional maneuvers, but each of us interpreted differently—and was bound to. We had different back-
grounds, different genders, different bodies, different wishes,
fears, defenses, and identities. And they matter.

That is why I, as a psychoanalytic critic of today, turn away
from the mere text of "Thirty days" to Mrs. Guiney.

> Mrs. Guiney said, I want you to memorize how many days each
> month has, so when you need to know you won't have to stop and
> recite that silly rhyme. Yes, ma'am. Now, though, I can admit—

indeed, exult—that I never did. I never learned the days in the months, never had occasion to, really, until many years later when I got involved with investments, financial reports, and interest payments. So even now, every once in a while, I have to recite it to myself. January? "Thirty days hath September, April, June, and November." Thirty-one, then. Dear Mrs. Guiney, I got round you. Dear Mrs. Guiney, I failed you.

She was a blue-eyed, white-haired termagant who kept twenty or so of us seventh- and eighth-grade boys very much in line. She taught us arithmetic and penmanship, and she taught us with a vengeance. Woe the witless lad whose homework was late. The preteen who snickered or talked in class was likely to end up standing in the corner. And she could be wonderfully funny. Up goes a hand. "Mrs. Guiney, what shall I do with this homework you just handed back?" "FRAME IT AND MAIL IT TO THE KAISER!!" she shouted, as we all guffawed at her hapless questioner.

She played favorites unblushingly. I was lucky enough to be one of her pets, but poor Bruce Gelb could never seem to win a good word from her, even though his penmanship and arithmetic were surely no worse than mine. Underneath all her severity and shouting, though, there was real warmth. I think she shed some of that warmth on me, although my penmanship has never come up to her standards.

I remember her with real affection like another tough, blue-eyed, white-haired lady, my wife's aunt, who encouraged me, financially and otherwise, to get psychoanalytic training. She was a fierce one, too, and I was always a little afraid of her, but she was also warm and kindly, and I was one of her favorites. She would say she was glad Jane had married me, and not somebody else, and she was always trying to help me along. Even as she was dying, she was working to get me appointed to various lectureships.

Finally I begin to think of my grandmother, a putterer around her house in faded print dresses and steel-rimmed glasses that matched her dark grey hair. She suffered from diabetes, and her insulin shots and foot baths repelled an eight-year-old me. I was crazy about my grandfather, but I never felt affection for her, only a sort of distasteful respect, tinged with fear, but she must have felt only affection for me . . .

Enough. Let me stop and, in the manner of psychoanalytic work (as I do it anyway), try to hear (with, as psychoanalysts say, the third ear) what these associations are saying. Elderly women of whom I was a little afraid, because they were aggressive, strong, even fearsome, but who favored me. What might those themes have to do with "Thirty days"? The way I find out is to thread them back through the poem and see what kind of return I get.

Being singled out, distinguished, favored—surely I read much in this poem about making distinctions. Thirty days or thirty-one. Leap year or ordinary year. Named months and unnamed. The special complexity of February. Scanned lines and unscanned. The first, firm rhymes as opposed to the unremembered ending.

There are no women in this poem, though, unless one can think of months or perhaps time as Woman. More specifically, however, my associations ran to women who were initially threatening, but who favored me, even loved me. Distinctions, then, ultimately led to my being favored specifically as a promising boy or young man by an older woman of whom I was a little afraid.

The women in my associations were all old and are now dead, while I, in my associations, was a boy or young man. I am not now. If so—and now association is merging into interpretation—I can hear in that crucial rhyme on "-ember" a double assertion: one, the importance of having or being a bright, glowing "ember" or a "member," the other the "embers" I associate with the dying of a fire or the dying of a year in September and November and December.

I make then, from this not very emotional poem, some very emotional themes indeed. Needless to say, were I writing a critical essay on "Thirty days," I would (probably) not burden my reader with tales of Mrs. Guiney or my grandmother. My memories are only steps (usually) on the way to a more sharable reading of the poem. Were I writing a critical note on "Thirty days," as Ade and Bee and Cee and Dan did, I would evoke the primal human distinctions. I would talk of infant separating from (fearsome) mother, the young and growing from the old and dying, and male boy from female mother. I would wish for the parceling out of goodies to that favored boy: love, psychoanalytic training, fame, long life.

The poem, as I read it, promises that making distinctions and divisions will favor me specifically as an ambitious and threatened male. Notice that I have been doing that in this very chapter, looking for your assent and approval with my divisions of psychoanalysis, psychoanalytic criticism, and the critical process. Thus, I can draw only the faintest boundaries between my associations, the text, and the context in which I am writing them.

Notice too that that preceding sentence is precisely *not* making distinctions. My conclusion adopts just the opposite action from the one the poem promises to reward. I have met once more the deep ambivalence, the navel of early conflict, that, psychoanalysis teaches us, finally underlies every interpretation. Here, I find it in my act of making meaning. I trace this "subversion" of my conscious reading to the profound ambivalence in our earliest relation with a caregiving other. Deconstructionists and other postmodern critics attribute such contradictions to the text—but more of that in part three.

"Thirty days" promises that primal human distinctions will favor me. It promises that favor *for me,* not necessarily for you or for any other reader. Nevertheless, when I transact the poem that way—and that is the verb I customarily use for this kind of "poem opening," *transact*—I make myself more intensely aware of some features that no one would deny are "in" the poem: thirty vs. thirty-one, named vs. unnamed, -ember and non-ember months, or leap and non-leap years. *In "transacting," the poem and I are parts of one process.* I—my identity—tests the poem by various hypotheses, and I get feedback from it.

Transacting is the process we saw Agnes, Ted, and Norm engaged in in part one. In this chapter my transaction of "Thirty days" makes *having* something important, having the favor of those older women, having an ember or a member, having investments. Although at first I thought them insignificant, I now think "have" or "hath" are important words in the poem. Curiously those two words persist in all the versions I found, even when the poem varied in larger ways, like rhyming on November instead of September. Thus, given my third-phase reading I can talk in, now, a second-phase way, about a theme of possession or holding on as if it were "in" the poem.

Better, though, is a mode from third-phase psychoanalytic criticism. I can point to aspects of the poem you are likely to perceive as I do, like "have" or "hath," and ask if you too find them important. I can ask if you get the same feeling of being or not being favored that I do. That is what reader-response criticism does. It opens up possibilities of response.

My associations, threaded back through the poem, make new readings possible. I can even use my concern with distinctions to read the poem in the earliest psychoanalytic way, as picturing the psychology of real persons in familiar symbolisms. Eleven of the months *have* something: they are named or they have thirty-one instead of thirty days. Somewhat along Spencer's line, poor February is a victim, smaller than all the rest. He is unable definitely to have or not have, yet he is *the* most special of all, a phallic victim-hero—someone rather like Rudolph the Red-Nosed Reindeer.

Yet it is not clear that I could have arrived at these first- and second-phase readings from looking only at the poem, without my associations. Neither is it clear that I could support these readings solely by evidence from the text. Rather, we have to recognize that first- and second-phase psychoanalytic readings, traditionally thought of as "objective," are really third-phase readings: personal transactions of the poem. This transactive process of interpretation rests on my associations, even if, as is the custom, I were to speak of impersonally discovering things "in" the poem.

My "third-phase" psychoanalytic criticism of "Thirty days" thus resembles the postmodern readings by Ade, Bee, Cee, and Dee. Is that true of all psychoanalytic critics? We have two more in the sample.

Psychoanalytic Critics

For another example of today's psychoanalytic criticism, consider this response by Eli Ede. When he learned of my asking for responses to "Thirty days," he volunteered his own. Ede was a graduate student specializing in literature-and-psychology and well-versed in both postmodern and third-phase psychoanalytic criticism. Eli was in much the same position I was in when I chose to study psychoanalysis thirty years ago, but he faced an altogether different intellectual (and economic!) environment. Postmodern, psychoanalytic, and reader-response methods are as natural to him as formalist or New Critical thought was to me in 1960.

He divided his response in two. In the first—

> I remember very clearly the rainy day in Southern California when I realized, at the age of twelve and in the sixth grade, that there was something I *should* know but didn't, and it had something to do with months and their number of days, with being able to correctly identify the number of days in each month, and with, therefore, *being correct.*

After his embarrassment at not knowing, "Someone recited the 'thirty days' mnemonic, and I knew that I had learned a lesson. Or, rather, I sensed that something had happened between the teacher, Mr. Kern, and myself that wouldn't have happened if I had known the right answer and that had made me feel uncomfortable and self-conscious."

> "Thirty days hath September / April, June, and November"—except that the days are not all alike. And I started to become aware of myself in relation to a frowning teacher on one day, apparently like any other day, but for me very, very different. I can still remember being aware that something had changed, that something was different.

Eli divided his answer between that kind of reminiscence and a complex intellectual analysis of "cognitive reduction," "referential meaning," and "grammatical mood," which ended:

> Herein lies the peremptory aspect of the poem when read in light of the imperative: the months have their number of days because they have been declared to have their number of days. And when the imperative is framed in the declarative, what is a human act of defining reality acquires the appearance of natural fact. In learning the poem a child learns much more than the apparent lesson that the months have 30 or 31 days with the exception of February.
>
> This short poem, then, reflects much about the structure of a kind of learning which entails the establishment of a way of experiencing the way things are. I see the poem as embodying the issues of authority and obedience which are present in much learning, in the interpersonal context of much learning. In this regard, I learned about the poem in the context of an emotionally significant personal experience in which I became aware that my teacher thought that I had overstepped a boundary, his boundary.

In this way, through free association (in its classical psychoanalytic sense), Eli arrived at a reading in terms of teacher's power that might suit Daniel Dee or deconstructionists in general. He also associated freely from personal reminiscence to intellectual analysis to the general themes of authority and obedience that passionately concerned him in his thinking in general: "I see the poem as embodying . . ." Unlike the "regular" postmodernists, this psychoanalytic reader makes his own role in the reading overt and decisive.

My final sample of psychoanalytic reading is Lacanian. Compare the two psychoanalytic readings we have already seen, the four postmodern readings, and Theodore Spencer's New Critical reading of "Thirty days" with the reading by a fellow-critic whom I will call Professor Fred Fay.

Fred was as dismayed by "Thirty days" as a classical psychoanalytic critic would be: "At first glance, the jingle seems unpromising: there is a lack of subjective and/or personal material to psychoanalyze." He suggested, however, one Lacanian possibility: reading through the grid of the three psychic registers: the Imaginary, the Symbolic, and the Real.

"The Real of the poem refers to the periodicity of the Earth's annual revolution around the sun," he wrote, and he mentioned other measurements and complexities of numbering days within a solar year. The great problem of the calendar, he remarked, is to reconcile the lunar reckoning of religious festivals and the solar year. This "projection of the sacred onto the Real for religious purposes is actually an Imaginary process, and the construction of calendars to meet this imperative is a Symbolic-order interpretation of the Imaginary and the Real."

The Imaginary (pre-verbal) register could lead to the missing subjective element:

> The two universal structures of the psyche (Desire and Law) and Lacan's four key signifiers (birth; love/relationship; procreation; death) would seem to have little place in the poem. And yet why, if the poem is only a mnemonic, do virtually all persons in the English-speaking world know this poem by heart? Or . . . what is the extra effect of more-than-language in poetic utterance which makes it memorable?
>
> The role of February in the poem is interesting . . . . February is separated from the other eleven months and stands alone. Now separation, not language *per se* (as is sometimes erroneously stated), is really the bottom line in Lacanian teaching. It is the infant's separation from the illusory symbiotic bond of union with the (m)Other at around 18 months (due to the castrating effect of the intervening law of the Name-of-the-Father) that both gives rise to absence or lack in the first place, and creates the need for the substitutive ref-

erential system of language to compensate for that lack thereafter. . . . February 29th is both *fort* and *da*. This ambiguity around the separation and presence/absence experiences is undoubtedly very powerful and evocative. It strongly reinforces the emotion of "excepting" and "alone," where February could be felt as an animistic displacement (or metonymy) for the castrated child.

Fay's analysis proceeded by a mapping of Lacanian theory onto the text, just as classical first- and second-phase psychoanalytic criticism mapped the psychoanalytic theory of those days and just as an American analyst of today might map onto the poem theory from Kohut or Kernberg. Fay found elements in the poem that corresponded to familiar psychoanalytic themes: castration, the *fort-da* game, and mother-child or self-object differentiation (which corresponds to my own reading of the poem as about "distinctions").

At the same time, however, Fay felt free (or compelled), through Lacanian theory, to follow out "arbitrary" conventions:

If we separate the 'twenty-eight days clear' (l. 5) into two 'clear' halves, we get 14 times 2. February 14, interestingly enough, is St. Valentine's Day . . . the only date in the calendar that celebrates love relationships in this way, since (m)Other's or Mothers' Day cannot be said strictly to fall in this category. While the association of February as evocative of separation trauma and St. Valentine as evocative of the substitution of the other for the Other may be over-ingenious on my part, the idea does impose itself irresistibly once we have opened up this line of inquiry.

Fay reported that his wife, also a professor and Lacanian, added

the very interesting and true observation that it is in leap years (i.e., when February has its peculiar 29th day) that women are, exceptionally, permitted to propose marriage to a man. In Lacanian terms, one could say that February's love-cum-relationship specialness succeeds in subverting or at least inverting the Symbolic Order.

And Fred concluded, "This whole line of speculation, far-fetched as [it] may have seemed at the beginning, makes more and more sense the more one pursues it."

In the Fays' response, I see again the freedom characteristic of postmodern criticism. Both the Fays show, as I did, an easy

willingness to "go away from" the poem. In this, today's psychoanalytic critics are very different from their first- and second-
phase forebears. In this they are more like the other postmoderns
than like Spencer. Yet there are important differences between the
psychoanalytic critics and all the others.

Differences

In I-ing critics, we have acquired a sampling: a New Critic, three psychoanalytic critics, and four postmodern critics. What can we conclude about what critics do, particularly as compared to what Agnes, Ted, and Norm did? What do they do that is alike, what different? Our seven critics of today look somewhat similar, particularly when we look at them against the background of Spencer's New Critical reading, and they look somewhat different.

Reading Holland and Spencer and Ade, Bee, Cee, Dee, Ede, and Fay, we are seeing the changes in criticism over the decades of this century. There are differences between the critic of a half-century ago, Spencer, and these critics of today, and there are differences between the critics of today. There are differences between the psychoanalytic and the non-psychoanalytic critics, and there are differences between the psychoanalytic critics. I see these differences around four issues:

What are the boundaries, if any, of the text?
What is the role of the responder in the responding?

97

What is an appropriate response?

When you have an appropriate response, what do you do with it?

Let me take them one by one.

What are the boundaries of the text? One axis we can draw between old and new, psychoanalytic and non-psychoanalytic criticism is, To what extent does the critic treat the text as a defined, bounded structure? A critic of Theodore Spencer's stamp thought the boundaries of the text were obvious: the edge of the poem, the words on the page, the pages in the book. Today, however, these seven critics—*without exception!*—freely move away from the poem as a self-contained entity.

This is part of a larger critical shift. The earliest reactions to the New Criticism turned away from the individual poem or novel to consider a writer's whole *oeuvre* or a whole genre. Nowadays, particularly among deconstructionists, a text really has no boundaries. It is simply one wave in a vast sea of textuality or intertextuality. Today, psychoanalytic and non-psychoanalytic critics alike open the poem outward. There is the text, but it has a pre-text and an aftertext to which it is bound by a process of intertextuality.

This loss of boundaries became particularly clear in Cee's reading (or refusal to read) "Thirty days."

> One can imagine other uses of these lines, other contexts into which they might be inserted (contexts in which they might become sinister, as the "Ten Little Indians" poem becomes in the Agatha Christie story): what if they were to be recited by a madman? After all, we thought we knew what a Campbell Soup can meant until Warhol 'moved' that sign into a different context.

In Cee's sketch, the Campbell Soup can means, and iterability implies that signs diffuse and scatter meanings. Like Spencer, Cee treats the poem as the subject of "meaning"—it is the text that makes meaning—but, he says, in a way wholly dependent upon the context, that is, the use to which it is put.

"Is put." My passive verb, like Cee's, masks a question, our second, *What is the role of the responder in the responding?* Who does what in the reading transaction? This poem can be "pressed into service," "might be inserted"—Cee's passives leave open the question of who does the pressing and inserting. Once the lines are inserted, who finds them sinister? Or is it, as in Cee's phrasing, that they simply "become" sinister. I hear in such wordings that something of much interest to me, namely, Who does what in the reading transaction?, is not a live issue to Cee. Do readers make meaning or do poems mean? Neither Ade nor Bee nor Cee asks the question. For both the critics of today and Spencer from 1943, what the I does remains profoundly ambiguous.

For most of our eight critics some action by language (like "intertextuality") leads to an answer to our second question. The role of the responder? Not much. The New Critics of Spencer's era also left the responder, the I, out. They assumed the poem produced its own response or, as I did when I was a New Critic, they simply bracketed the process by which the reader arrived at a reading. We don't know anything about that. We have no way of talking about what goes on in the reading process. Let's talk about the text.

Poststructural critics like Ade, Bee, Cee, and Dee do much the same. They write at least some of the time as though "Thirty days" emitted its own aftertext. The poem gives off meanings the way a lamp radiates light, and readers have little to do with it. As Ade and Cee put the matter, the text "diffuses and scatters fixed meanings." Dee's text contains and implies. Bee's has "significance." Today's critics talk without hesitation about the free play of language or the linkage of signifier and signified imposing itself willy-nilly on "the" reader (like Valentine's Day on Fay). All this leaves little for the responder to do.

At the same time, however, both Bee and Dee acknowledge their own participation in the poem's act of meaning. Bee, in particular, mentions several ways the poem "could be read." He even makes a suggestion parallel to my own reader-response view that, once we grant the reader's creativity in reading, the text becomes a commonplace-book or "promptuary" (a collection of sayings, quotations, or phrasings from which its owner can build letters, sermons, poems, or conversation—the responder's own text).

Dee goes both ways. He acknowledges the role in his response of his relation to me, his political views, and his professional values. He also removes the meaning from the text and relocates it in the context—in that, he is different from the others.

He does not deal with the possibility that he, the reader, makes the meanings he attributes to that context—in that he is like the others.

Fay, the Lacanian, also goes both ways in speaking of his own role as a creative reader. "While the association [Valentine's Day] may be over-ingenious on my part, the idea does impose itself irresistibly once we have opened up this line of inquiry." Fay himself provides the aftertext but then the aftertext imposes itself. In the question of the responder, I think Fay's reading resembles the New Critic, Theodore Spencer's.

Spencer saw an objective poem "out there" and "in here" a subjective (fallible) reader of that poem. Critics like Ade or Bee also see a poem out there and a reader in here. They concede that dichotomy (ultimately, they are conceding a dichotomy between "subjectivity" and "objectivity"), but they refuse (as believing postmodernists) to situate the reading "in" either one. Lacanians and deconstructivists and New Critics are equally, to use the proper term, *formalist.* That is, they assume that a text creates meanings, and either the I has little to do with that process or they have little to say about what the I does.

By contrast, Holland and Ede have a clearer idea of how the I relates to "Thirty days." We are free associating. I think Spencer, and Ade, Bee, Cee, Dee, and Fay are also free associating, but they don't admit it. They leave the role of the I in reading ambiguous or unacknowledged. There is then, a division between Holland and Ede, on the one hand, and the rest of the eight critics on the other as to the reader's activity.

Given an indeterminate text, then, and an indeterminate responder, *What is an appropriate response?* Again, Spencer's approach provided an unequivocal answer. Because he was parodying the New Critics, Spencer did exactly the kind of thing they would do. The critic's business was to explicate—unfold—the unity of the text, to show how all the parts fitted together. Accordingly, Spencer showed how the order in which the months were listed or the "ex-" in "except" developed February's Tantalus-like tragedy. An appropriate response for Spencer's era was to point to the organic interrelation of all the details in the text.

What is an appropriate response today? Are there any limits

to what a postmodern critic can say in relation to a text? Not unless you think there are limits to free association. Is there, then, any such thing as a misreading? Only in the sense of a "wrong" free association (and, of course, there is no such thing). You could say, as some modern critics do, following Harold Bloom, that *all* readings are misreadings. That is, all readings mis-take the original one way or another. I see no reason, however, to call that a *mis*reading, any more than I would call free associations misassociations. That prefix "mis-" marks the assumption that there is a not-misreading, a reading that is not a mis-, and we have seen that is not so. There are only readings and different rules by which the reading game is played. Bloom is simply saying all readings (or all "strong" readings) answer some reader's needs, not the writer's.

Then, are there any limits to what a postmodern critic can say in relation to a text? Spencer thought common sense excluded certain moves by the critic. His parody proceeds from that assumption, and it is worth remembering that it was published in the staunchly middlebrow *New Republic*. By contrast, for the modern critics, anything goes. Ede and I talked about our teachers, Dee about a bawdy ballad, Ade about Roman calendars, Bee about computer dating, and so on and on. These new, associative modes of criticism include and never exclude. Contemporary criticism admits Ade's or Bee's most far-fetched associations as well as all the familiar moves of traditional New Criticism or the vagaries of old and new psychoanalytic critics. In that sense, any response is an appropriate response.

Hence, this theoretical position allows for an unlimited series of professorial publications. This, I believe, has to be taken into account as one of the functions of a literary theory, at least in America in the 1990s. By contrast, Spencer's method and theory held out the promise of a "correct" reading. New Critical method threatened that enough "correct" readings would finally say all that could be said about even *Hamlet,* to say nothing of "Thirty days." New Criticism would eventually have shut off the professorial flow. Possibly this is one reason for the popularity of the postmodern technique of what amounts to free association. There is no theoretical limit.

There is, however, a difference between the psychoanalytic

and the non-psychoanalytic postmoderns. Both use something akin to free association, but the non-psychoanalytic interpreters limit themselves to an impersonal or extrapersonal "free play of signifiers": highly intellectual references to etymology, Nietzsche, Heidegger, or language about language. By contrast, Ede and I, two of the three psychoanalytic critics, arrive at memories of personally important persons or events or themes. Our associations could arouse strong feelings: sexuality, aging, the family, teachers, coercive authority, having and not having. Our postmodern psychoanalytic criticism looks like Freud's analyses of Ibsen, Dostoevsky, or Shakespeare, and even more, like his analyses of his own dreams. Freud's analyses led to wishes about work and family and sexuality, not Nietzsche or lunar calendars. In that sense, our postmodern psychoanalytic criticsm makes a return to Freud.

At least some postmodern psychoanalytic criticism does. In the Fays' associations to "Thirty days," as in all Lacanian criticism I have read, the associations tend to be abstract, intellectual, cultural, or etymological rather than personal. If they are "free associations," they do not lead to the Fays' work or family. There is, then, a distinction to be drawn between Lacanian psychoanalytic criticism and other kinds as to what is an "appropriate response."

This difference in style of association leads naturally to my fourth criterion of difference among these critics: *When you have an appropriate response, what do you do with it?* The psychoanalytic critics, Fay and Ede and I, treated our associations differently than the other postmoderns did. Having associated, we returned to the poem. We threaded our associations and interpretations back through the text and thereby evoked further associations and themes from the poem. Fay contrasted love relationships to the distinctions among months drawn in the poem. Ede related the poem to his own awareness of boundaries and the coercive element in education. I tried to learn something about myself, how I hoped distinctions between humans would favor me. Perhaps because we are psychological critics, we gave the poem a human significance. But then the non-psychological Spencer did the same.

By contrast, Ade, Bee, Cee, and Dee moved away from the poem and stayed away. For these poststructuralist critics, the aftertext became an end in itself, a quasi-poem to stand alongside the original. Bee says of his procedure, "A reader-scriptor might generate a further text of his/her own," and Ade, Bee, Cee, and Dee did just that.

The psychoanalytic and non-psychoanalytic critics, then, did read in systematically different ways. For the psychoanalytic critics—this psychoanalytic critic, anyway—that aftertext of associations served to open up and articulate the relationship between the critic and the first text. I could pass my associations about older women through "Thirty days," using the aftertext to complicate and deepen my relationship with the original mnemonic.

In short, there are four kinds of differences in this sampling of critics. First, the modern critic, Spencer, has a clear idea of the boundaries of the text. None of today's critics did. Second, the psychoanalytic critics—two of them, anyway—clearly acknowledged the role of the self in responding to the poem. Neither the modern nor the postmodern nor the Lacanian critics did.

Third, the modern critic (Spencer) could define an appropriate response. The postmoderns could not. In effect, any association would serve. Within the postmodern group, however, there were two kinds of associations. The psychological critics—two of them, anyway—favored personal and familial memories. The poststructuralists, Ade, Bee, Cee, and Dee, and the Lacanian critic Fay favored philosophical and intellectual associations. For them, a text led to other *texts*, not to persons or experiences.

Fourth, Fay and Ede and I, the psychoanalytic critics, threaded our associations back through the poem. The other postmoderns moved away from it and stayed away. The psychoanalytic critics, I think, saw themselves engaged in a process that involved both self and poem. The postmoderns, I think, saw themselves awash in a sea of language.

What underlies these four differences in critical practice is the way they think of the relation between the I and the text. If you think language is active regardless of any I directing it, then you write one kind of criticism. If you think the I is the active party, if you attribute critical activity to the critic, then you write another. Since common sense would suggest that it is critics who do criticism, we need to consider the theory that leads to the opposite idea (that it is the text that analyzes itself). That is part three of this book. In the meantime, can we sum up this I-ing of critics at work?

Doing literary criticism in this postmodern era, we critics feel, regardless of our school, that the text no longer has limits. Anything goes as a response. What we differ about, and we differ profoundly about it, is why. Was this opening up of the text language's doing? Or was it a human decision? The question brings us to what is called in these latter days of the twentieth century "theory"—not the theory *of* anything, just plain theory. We need to I some theorists. What do they say about the I?

three

I-ing Theorists

The I
in Trouble

Not so long ago, I attended a conference with a typical 1980s title: Self and Other. There I heard about the disappearing self, the vanishing self, the deconstructed self, the self on the edge, the self within the self (presumably some kind of indigestion), the marginal self, the self degree zero, and so on. I got worried, having just published a book called *The I*, having therefore a certain vested interest in the self above and beyond one's usual concern for oneself. My worries, alas, proved correct. The I is in big trouble. The best literary theorists of today seem to have declared war on the I or the self, and *you*'s and *I*'s are vanishing wherever you (if you will still allow me that pronoun) look.

J. Hillis Miller, for example, writes from the point of view of deconstructionism: "The self is a linguistic construction rather than being the given, the rock, a solid *point de départ*." "There is no literal language of consciousness, the self being itself a figure or an effect of language." "The self is a figurative construction—a metalepsis." (In case you are not up on the cacozelic terms of modern rhetoricians, rather like Hamlet's parody of Osric, "metalepsis" is the figure of speech that attributes a present effect to a remote cause. Your Chrysler breaks down at midnight on a deserted country road, and you swear at Lee Iacocca.) Miller is saying the self, the I, is at best distantly connected to any behavior you can see. Ultimately, Miller is saying the I has disappeared, and most practitioners of deconstructionism would say the same. Vincent Leitch in his excellent "advanced introduction" to deconstructive criticism states flatly: "In general, deconstruction turns its criticism upon the concept 'self.'"

Almost as baffling as the deconstructive vanishing of the self is the glee associated with its disappearance. Leitch dedicates his introduction to "all lost brothers and sisters." I get the feeling that he thinks anyone who enlists under his flickering banner is as beautiful and damned as Scott or Zelda. Michel Foucault, although no deconstructionist, evidently shared this enthusiasm for his own disappearance: "It is comforting, however, and a source of profound relief to think that man is only a recent invention, a figure not yet two centuries old, a new wrinkle in our knowledge, and that he will disappear again as soon as that knowledge has discovered a new form." Oh, my. Here I was just getting used to being around on this planet. Foucault may have found the disappearance of man comforting, but I don't, particularly when I think about the blunderers in the white house with the red telephone.

The self disappears most readily when it is engaged in reading, because in the metaphysics of deconstructionism, texts do their own reading. Barbara Johnson, for example, in a precise capsule statement of deconstruction American-style, asserts:

> A deconstructive reading is an attempt to show how the conspicuously foregrounded statements in a text are systematically related to discordant signifying elements that the text has thrown into its shadows or margins . . . In this sense it involves a reversal of values, a revaluation of the signifying function of everything that, in a signified-based theory of meaning, would constitute "noise." Jacques Derrida has chosen to speak of the values involved in this reversal in terms of "speech" and "writing," in which "speech" stands for the privilege accorded to meaning as immediacy, unity, identity, truth, and presence, while "writing" stands for the devalued functions of distance, difference, dissimulation, and deferment.

What I notice in Johnson's remarks is the playful busyness of the text. It has "signifying elements" which the text, all by itself, "has thrown into its shadows or margins." It has a "signifying function," which is different from the conventional "signified-based theory of meaning." Somewhere in the paragraph is "an attempt to show," which presumably entails an attempter, but he or she is scarcely there. In the same way, Johnson says there are "warring forces of signification within the text." She can write, "The reasons a reading might consider itself *right* are motivated and undercut by its own interests, blindnesses, desires, and fatigue." In her prose, texts and interpretations (nouns) do the kinds of things that people used to do (verbs).

Thus J. Hillis Miller can describe reading as "an attempt, no doubt an impossible attempt, to confront what language itself has always already erased or forgotten, namely, the performative or positional power of language . . ." The role of the critic follows from the text's activity: "The text performs on itself the act of deconstruction without any help from the critic." "The critic still has his uses, though this use may be no more than to identify an act of deconstruction which has always already, in each case differently, been performed by the text on itself." And, like the critic, the teacher still has his uses. Miller in his role as president of the Modern Language Association counseled his fellow professors:

> The teacher's authority, when she or he has it, comes from an impersonal response to the work being read, a response that transcends the "I." It is not the subjectivity of the teacher that is obligated to the work but an impersonal power of reading that he or she shares, to some extent, with all other readers of the same work. . . . Teaching is an interlinguistic transaction, not an intersubjective one. It is a reaction necessitated by an implacable demand made by the language of the work on its reader and manifested in its turn by the teacher to his or her students.

Paul de Man carries on the same procedure when—No, I shouldn't say it that way. The same procedure is carried out when Paul de Man's reading of Proust says it is not Paul de Man's:

> The reading is not "our" reading, since it uses only the linguistic elements provided by the text itself . . . The deconstruction is not something we have added to the text but it constituted the text in

the first place. A literary text simultaneously asserts and denies the authority of its own rhetorical mode . . .

As Barbara Johnson hints, one forerunner of all this is Nietzsche's *The Will to Power,* for example, his attack on Descartes:

> "There is thinking: therefore there is something that thinks": this is the upshot of all Descartes' argumentation. But that means positing as "true *a priori*" our belief in the concept of substance—that when there is thought there has to be something "that thinks" is simply a formulation of our grammatical custom that adds a doer to every deed. In short, this is . . . a logical-metaphysical postulate—

The next step is obvious. "The 'subject' is only a fiction." The I is not something self-evident, something that simply is. Rather, we posit, invent, "fict" that I. "When one has grasped that the 'subject' is not something that creates effects, but only a fiction, much follows." For example, "It is only after the model of the subject that we have invented the reality of things and projected them into the medley of sensations."

Everything then follows upon an act of interpretation, and especially self and object. Further, "One may not ask: 'who then interprets?' for the interpretation itself is a form of the will to power, exists (but not as a 'being' but as a process, a becoming) as an affect." That is to say, once we recognize that everything is interpreted, the subject, along with reality, causality, and morality, becomes a construct of that interpretive process. Nietzsche calls it the will to power, the will to mastery and coherence, an emotion that is independent of any one of us. In this sense, the subject, reality, causality, morality, all become fictions. Hence, for Nietzsche, the I disappears or, more exactly, it becomes a construct having the same kind of being as physical objects or moral judgments. Its construction depends on an "affect," that is, an emotion.

The idea that everything—morality, science, and the I—follows from an act of interpretation is quite in accord with modern constructivist psychology (as described in chapter nine). Nietzsche's positings quite resemble the setting of a cruise control or other interpreting feedback in that both depend on feelings (if one can speak of an electronic circuit as feeling discomfort, and I suppose you can). In general, Nietzsche's ideas quite accord with the model of chapter nine, although his prose sounds very different.

Oddly enough, then, from my special perspective as a reader-response critic, the deconstructors of the I look less as though they found their spiritual father in Nietzsche and more as though they descend from the true-blue New Critics exemplified for us by Theodore Spencer. As we have seen, the New Critics held that the first business of the critic was to interpret the words-on-the-page. They thus assumed from the outset an "objective" text independent of its audience, and this text had a determinate meaning. One reads, for example, in the famous Brooks and Warren textbook, "Poems . . . 'mean' something . . . But poems characteristically express their meanings not through abstractions but through concrete particulars." Or, "All really good poetry attains its unity by establishing meaningful relationships among its apparently discordant elements." Back in 1935, I. A. Richards was writing, "Every poem is a fabric of meaning." Northrop Frye, summarizing such interpretive techniques in a 1963 handbook for graduate students, asserted: "Poetry is . . . a structure of words that contains meaning." One could multiply indefinitely statements like these describing the basic premise of what once was called "New" and now is called "traditional" or "formalist" criticism. The idea is that the text determines meaning or that meaning is "in" the text, the text provides its own structure and unity, and so on.

As someone who studies readers' responses, I see no fundamental difference between these claims and many statements by representative critics of today. Jonathan Culler, for example, writes in a 1982 handbook, the successor to the one for which Frye was writing in 1963, that a text is a "signifying practice." True, for the older critics the text creates its own unity, while for the newer ones the text creates its own disunity. For both, however, it is the text that does the work. We are dealing with the old New Critics and the new Old Critics. Or the New Cryptics, to judge from the style which many of them aspire to—and achieve.

The New Critics were proceeding from a commonplace subject-object metaphysics. An author writes (or causes) a text, and a text causes a response in a reader, but the three are separate and independent. The New Critical model separated objective text with its determinate meaning from subjective author or subjective reader. The author communicates to the reader, but only through the objective text.

For the New Critics, a text "had" its particular meaning, which it delivered to the right-reading reader. Readers were *supposed* to arrive at themes, structures, or (sometimes) values within a certain range of correctness. Although there might be differences among readers, any skilled or tasteful reader would render a reading within that range. If some particular reader did not, the critic had to question the reader's state of mind. (Richards was most particular on this.) Hence it was the business of literary education to teach the skills (and state of mind) that would enable readers to arrive at acceptable readings. I take it this training is exactly what Jonathan Culler, surely a representative critic of today, has in mind when he cries up "literary competence."

Consider E. D. Hirsch, Jr., whom many people would call the most conservative theorist of today. His principles recapture a historicism prior even to the New Critics. "I argued that, in academic criticism, the significance and use of a text ought to be rooted in its fixed meaning, since otherwise criticism would lack a stable object of inquiry and would merely float on tides of preference. . . . I intended to provide a firm justification for those who wished to pursue historical scholarship." Hirsch believes the text carries with it a fixed meaning, just as de Man believes the text "simultaneously asserts and denies the authority of its own rhetorical mode." For both theorists, the text does all the work.

Geoffrey Hartman shows how both traditional and deconstructive interpretations share similar notions of an impersonal meaning. Deconstruction, he says,

> refuses to identify the force of literature with any concept of embodied meaning and shows how deeply such logocentric or incarnationist perspectives have influenced the way we think about art. We assume that, by the miracle of art, the "presence of the word" is equivalent to the presence of meaning. But the opposite can also be urged, that the word carries with it a certain absence or indeterminacy of meaning.

Either way, though, it is the text that makes meaning or absence of meaning.

In short, whether we look at the newest of the new or the oldest of the old, we find literary theorists dismissing the I as a maker of meanings. Texts make meanings, people don't. The reason is the theorists' conception of language. We can see it in Hartman's "the word carries with it." This is a classic example of the "conduit metaphor" and the idea, which we need now to explore, that the text is active.

19

The Active Text

Both the postmodern Hartman and the conservative Hirsch build their ideas on the "conduit metaphor" for language—so identified and named by the linguist Michael Reddy. The basic assumption is an ancient one: words carry or contain meanings. It follows, then, that a word has an inside and an outside. The meaning is inside the word, whose outside (at least at first glance) consists of its physical sound or shape. As one of Shakespeare's competitors, Thomas Nashe, quaintly put it, literature is "sower pils of reprehension wrapt up in sweete words." More formally, ideas (or meanings) are objects. Linguistic expressions are containers. Communication is sending. "The speaker puts ideas (objects) into words (containers) and sends them (along a conduit) to a hearer who takes the ideas/objects out of the word/containers"—that is how Lakoff and Johnson sum up this cluster of metaphors.

Words, so understood, surround meanings as books enclose pages. For example, think of the student question that an enthusiastically analytic professor is most likely to hear—

Do you really think Shakespeare put all this stuff in there?

Or what I, as a reader-response critic, hear all the time from my more conservative colleagues:

The meaning is right there, *in* the words on the page!

A word has a physical outside and a psychological inside. That is, a writer puts something from his psyche inside this outer container. A reader, given that outer physical text, takes the psychological inside from it. A poem becomes a tube. You put intention in at one end and take meaning out at the other. Then, once you have got the "meaning," you can go on (in Hirsch's vocabulary) to "significance." That is, you can derive some personal association or use or special variation you add to the meaning proper.

In this model, shared by New Critics and New Cryptics alike, a text is a "communication channel" that delivers its contents the way pipelines do. The reader becomes relatively passive. Whatever the reader does doesn't really matter. He or she will be filled up like an oil tank or a martini glass or, for the deconstructionist, emptied as by a vacuum cleaner hose. There is a pre-packaged meaning (or absence of meaning) that the text simply delivers like the post office or, if a really good text, like Federal Express. It is in this sense, I take it, that Barbara Johnson can talk about a reading that "considers itself right" or J. Hillis Miller can talk about a text having deconstructed itself. It is in exactly the same sense that I. A. Richards could talk about a "fabric of meaning" or Northrop Frye about "a structure of words that contains meaning." They were assuming like Jonathan Culler today that literature is "a signifying practice." These new New Critics hold exactly the same position, at least so far as the process of meaning is concerned, as the old New Critics. The text determines meaning or its absence. The text is active.

The real problem, as I see it, is that neither group has faced the questions raised by the only radical change in critical theory and practice that the 1960s and 1970s yielded. That is, in the 1960s and 1970s, some critics, notably Stanley Fish, Wolfgang Iser, and I—Homer Brown called us the Holy Family (as opposed to the "Gang of Four" then at Yale)—began calling attention to the reader's response. By and large, until then, the dominant New

Critical mode assumed "the" reader's reaction to be automatic, predictable, common to all, and therefore not much worth discussing. By contrast, we claimed (in quite different ways, to be sure) that the reader was central. I, for one, argued it was the reader who decides such things as interpretations, evaluation, the boundaries of the text, or the technique for looking at the text. Literents (my word for combining readers and hearers of literature) experience any given book in quite individual ways. They also experience literature in shared ways, depending on the kind of expectations they have or the interpretive community they belong to (like Agnes, Ted, and Norm).

Today, we have a great burgeoning of literary theory. Unfortunately, few of these theorists have met the challenge of the reader-response critics, namely, to explain the similarities and differences in a group of responses to a literary text.

Traditional critics would say some are right and some are wrong, and they would dismiss the wrong ones without much concerning themselves how they happened. A modern deconstructionist, J. Hillis Miller, uses the "law of misreading" to deal with the same problem. That is, for the postmodernist, it hardly needs saying that all readings are misreadings. All readings fail to exhaust the possibilities of the text. (Notice that "exhaust" there is a conduit metaphor.) What would it mean, asks Miller, to get Heidegger and Derrida right, to read them correctly? "Even if the law of misreading applies here also, there are obviously strong and weak critical misreadings, more or less vital ones," and he goes on to belabor the author he is reviewing for exhibiting contradictions in his own text instead of the contradictions in William Carlos Williams'. Frankly, except for a change in vocabulary, Miller's idea of vital or less vital misreadings sounds to me very like one of the cornerstones of the New Criticism. I. A. Richards opposed "misunderstanding" to "good understanding" in, for example, *Practical Criticism* (1929). Richards would prescribe education, training, or even therapy to replace misunderstanding with correct understanding. Miller prescribes for his unfortunate reviewee the reading of Derrida and Heidegger and the pre-Socratics in their original languages.

Is there much difference? Both the old New Critics and the new New Critics assume that there is some rightness of reading, true meaning, deconstruction, or signifying practice that has already been established, somehow, by the text. Critics, teachers, or readers come along after that has already taken place, and "get" it. In Richards' terms, they "understand" it. In Miller's, they "identify" it, like someone pointing to a package at the post office. Today's theorists simply postulate automatically that texts generate their own readings or misreadings, and the human reader of literature doesn't much matter. They assume the text generates its own meaning, even when they want it to be an uncertainty of meaning.

Here, for example, is Roland Barthes talking about the indeterminacy of language. Notice how he assumes the language imposes *some* meaning in any case, although,

> It is very rare that [language] imposes at the outset a full meaning which it is impossible to distort. This comes from the abstractness of its concept; the concept of *tree* is vague, it lends itself to multiple contingencies. True, a language always has at its disposal a whole appropriating organization (*this* tree, *the* tree *which*, etc.). But there always remains, around the final meaning, a halo of virtualities where other possible meanings are floating; the meaning can almost always be *interpreted*.

The text does all the work, floating meanings hither and yon. To be sure, Barthes gives us that peculiar passive "interpreted" at the end, where we glimpse a person doing some interpreting. Except for that, though, for Barthes, it is language (or, in the rest of *Mythologies,* myth) that does all the meaning-work.

How about the I in this view of language? Where does the self come into the reading process? Barthes writes in *S/Z:*

> *I read the text.* This statement, consonant with the "genius" of the language (subject, verb, complement), is not always true. . . . I do not make [the text] undergo a predicative operation called *reading,* consequent upon its being, and *I* is not an innocent subject, anterior to the text, which will deal subsequently with the text as it would an object to dismantle or a site to occupy. This "I" which approaches the text is already itself a plurality of other texts, of infinite codes or, more precisely, codes whose origin is lost.

As I interpret this passage, Barthes is saying that, because a reader has read other books, because there are codes for reading, these books and codes replace the self who is reading. I think Barthes has simply said that 'the I *uses* codes' is the same as 'the I *is* codes.' I believe many of the New Cryptics make the same move, although, obviously, 'the I *uses* codes' is not the same thing as 'the I *is* codes.' Neither does 'the I *is* codes,' follow logically from 'the I *uses* codes.' Nor does 'I *have read* books' entail 'I *am* the books I have read,' although I suppose a sufficiently romantic (or pedantic) reader might make that claim. The confusion arises from the idea that language is active, and the I is not. What the I does to understand language doesn't much matter.

Derrida

We can see this premise, language is active, in the writings of the theorist who represents something of a new orthodoxy in America today, the philosopher Jacques Derrida. We have heard from three of his American disciples, Miller, Johnson, and de Man. Unlike them, however, Derrida rarely analyzes an individual poem or novel. As a philosopher, he writes more about language as a whole. When he does so, he creates the image of a vast, tumbling sea of language. We have already seen it in part two: the endless play of language that Ade and Bee and Cee refer to in their responses. Words yield meanings, but the meanings only exist in other words, so that you can never arrive at some final meaning which is free of language.

Hence Derrida can write,

> But is it by chance . . . that the meaning of meaning (in the general sense of meaning . . .) is infinite implication? the unchecked referral of signifier to signifier? If its force is a certain pure and infinite equivocalness, which gives signified meaning no respite, no rest, but engages it within its own economy to go on signifying and to differ/defer? . . . That which is written is never identical to itself.

In Derrida's phrasing, what is active is language or something like language, signifying.

The signifier, the process of meaning, signifying, implication, referral, differing, deferring—these are all so active that, in Derrida's thinking, they become a kind of force or violence, something irresistible. This is the reason Derrida's language bristles with all those *musts*. Meaning or the understanding of meaning ceases to be a psychological process involving a human being. Instead, meaning becomes something language does by itself, for itself, to itself. This process creates a vast tumbling net of intertextuality, driven by mysterious "forces" that cause every text to circulate through other texts. Ultimately, I suppose, these "forces" are the necessities of logical entailment or, perhaps, semantic implication. They may be what Derrida means by "writing."

At any rate, there is no end (and no beginning) to the process. Here are Derrida's words. They come from the first time I heard him speak, in the landmark 1966 conference at Johns Hopkins University I mentioned in chapter thirteen, and this essay is a favorite of those who anthologize such things. Derrida said then (and in the "presence" metaphor we use when we write of books, he "says" still) that language deconstructs itself. At the root of Western philosophy is

> a process of giving it [any structure] a center or of referring it to a point of presence, a fixed origin. The function of this center was not only to orient, balance, and organize the structure—one cannot in fact conceive of an unorganized structure—but above all to make sure that the organizing principle of the structure would limit what we might call the *freeplay* of the structure. No doubt that by orienting and organizing the coherence of the system, the center of a structure permits the freeplay of its elements inside the total form. And even today the notion of a structure lacking any center represents the unthinkable itself.

Having established this limiting function of the center, Derrida goes on to deconstruct it:

> Thus it has always been thought that the center, which is by definition unique, constituted that very thing within a structure which governs the structure, while escaping structurality. This is why classical thought concerning structure could say that the center is, paradoxically, *within* the structure and *outside it*. The center is at the

center of the totality, and yet, since the center does not belong to the totality (is not part of the totality), the totality *has its center else-where*. The center is not the center . . . .

He deconstructs the idea of a transcendental center by showing that, once we become explicit about such a center, it necessarily rests on language.

Everything became discourse . . . everything became a system where the central signified, the original or transcendental signified, is never absolutely present outside a system of differences. The absence of the transcendental signified extends the domain and the interplay of signification *ad infinitum*.

There can never be, then, some center, some absolute point, some "presence" that provides either an origin or an end of the chain of signifyings. Derrida reads the history of metaphysics as a history of the various names given these transcendent centers: essence, existence, substance, subject, transcendentality, con-sciousness, God, man, and so forth. None provides stability. In-stead of some center that limits a structure, every structure "must be thought of as a series of substitutions of center for center, as a linked chain of determinations of the center." Note, again, that he says it is the center that determines the (next) center.

Further, as Derrida makes clear, this applies to experience it-self. You can never arrive at some "referent" which is not in-volved with the language you use to think about that referent, hence also involved with signifiers, signifieds, and a system of dif-ferences.

Derrida's terms here, "signified," "signifier," "system of dif-ferences," are terms of art. To understand both the strength and the flaw in Derrida's thought, we need to look to the theory of language these terms invoke. Which brings us, I nervously write, to linguistics. We need to consider the figure on whom Derrida, his disciples Miller and Johnson, Barthes, Foucault, and virtually all New Cryptics (including my friends Ade, Bee, and Cee in part two), rely for their account of language. We need to look at the turn-of-the-century linguist Ferdinand de Saussure. I know of Derrida's intricate critique and "reinscription" of Saussure, and I will return to it. At this point, though, I want to examine these hundred-year-old ideas about meaning.

Saussure

Saussure defined communication as taking place along two channels, speaking and hearing. A speaker draws on a communal storehouse or system of language (*langue*) for his individual speaking (*parole*). The hearer then associates the sounds he hears (*parole*) with the concepts prescribed by *langue*.

In Saussure's account of the way we understand language, the receiver is passive and communication is automatic. The "speaking-circuit" has "an active and a passive part: everything that goes from the associative center of the speaker to the ear of the listener is active, and everything that goes from the ear of the listener to his associative center is passive." In understanding, "Through the functioning of the receptive and co-ordinating faculties, impressions (*des empreintes*) that are perceptibly the same for all are made (*se forment*) on the minds of speakers."

According to Saussure, the verbal stimulus, the sound [hors] or [tri] simply "imprints" itself on the brain. He draws pictures of trees and horses to illustrate what is signified, namely ideas in our minds about trees and horses. His metaphors are telling: language stamps itself like printing on the blank mind. Impressions form themselves by themselves on that mind like photographic images coming up in the developer. The salient fact for Saussure is that these impressions are the same for all. Hence, Saussure concluded that language is only a social fact. The hearer is passive, and differences are unimportant or secondary.

How does language accomplish this on its passive hearer? A sign—an individual signifying element—combines a concept and a sound. There is the sign "tree." The sign associates the sound [tri] to the idea of a tree. There is the sign "horse" and it associates the sound [hors] to the idea of a horse. The idea of a horse has none of the properties of the sound [hors], yet sound (signifier) and concept (signified) are arbitrarily bound together in the sign "horse." Such a sign is, in Saussure's metaphor, like "a chemical compound, like water, a combination of hydrogen and oxygen; taken separately, neither element has any of the properties of water."

Saussure's metaphor does not illustrate or explain what for me is the crucial question. How can a physical thing, the sound [hors] (*matière phonique,* he calls it) be bound like the atoms in a molecule to an idea of that thing? The sound is a physical thing, the idea a mental state. Saussure just says the two are bound together. Something physical simply generates something psychological. The verbal stimulus, he says, "imprints" itself on the brain (whether we think of that stimulus and its response as simple signs or as differences between signs).

Saussure's whole idea of the way we understand language rests on this doubtful premise. We understand language because language simply signifies. In his picture of a person's speaking language, *parole,* Saussure allows for the individual's psychology in choosing and arranging words from the system of *langue.* He allows no such freedom, however, in understanding language. We understand language by some sort of automatic reflex-arc in which a word emits a meaning, as it were, which readers take unthinkingly into their minds.

Now I think his account has a certain commonsense simplicity. That is, if you say to me [hors], I get an idea of a horse (in my case, a rather city-bred idea). My understanding seems completely automatic. I am not sure if even by a great effort of will I could hear or read that italicized word and not experience some idea of a horse. Saussure, however, has offered no explanation whatever of this psychological phenomenon.

Fans of Saussure, however, will quickly point out that I have omitted Saussure's sophistication of this first picture. Indeed he later characterizes this first picture as "grossly misleading." Saussure substitutes a more complex idea for the simple picture of the signifier as sound and the signified as concept. The sound, he says, is *already* psychological. "The word-image stands apart from the sound itself and . . . it [the word-image] is just as psychological as the concept which is associated with it." "The linguistic sign," he claims,

> unites, not a thing and a name, but a concept and a sound-image [*image acoustique*]. The sound-image is sensory, and if I happen to call it "material," it is only in that sense, and by way of opposing it to the other term of the association, the concept, which is generally more abstract.

I would say it this way. When we hear someone say [árd•vark], we are hearing not the specifc pitch or accent of the speaker, but the invariant [árd•vark]. We hear whatever of the distinctive features of [árd•vark] everybody would identify as [árd•vark]. As a result of our hearing the [árd•vark] distinctive features, Saussure claimed, the aardvark-concept imprints itself in our minds. These distinctive features of the sound of the word Saussure calls the sound-image. Thus both sides of Saussure's "sign," both the signifier (= sound-image) and the signified (= concept), are psychological. But, again, how did we get from physical *matière phonique* to psychological sound-image?

This more psychological version of the signifier rests on Saussure's idea of *difference*. Both the signifier and the signified function—they are such—only because they are different from other signifiers and other signifieds. Saussure begins with the example of all the different ways one might write the letter *t*. We recognize a *t* in many different handwritings, because all that matters is that the *t* have a vertical stroke and cross-bar partway down. Then it is different from an *a* or a *w* and all the other letters of the alphabet. "In language there are only differences"—Saussure's most famous statement.

Saussure treats, first, phonemes, and then, by extension,

words as these pairings of difference. A [b] is different from a [p] in that, although both are plosives, only one is voiced. A [t] is different from a [d] in that, although both are dentals, only one is voiced. Thus one can arrange all the phonemes by this system of binary, on-off, digital differences: plosive or not, dental or not, voiced or not, and so on. (After Saussure, Roman Jakobson defined and identified these distinctive features very exactly.)

So with letters or words. In Saussure's system, just as a *p* is a *p* because it is not a *b* (and not *a, c, d, e* . . .), so [árd•vark] is an *aardvark* because it is not [ar] or [á•land] or [al•borg] or [ál•wulf], that is, not *Aar* or *Aaland* or *Aalborg* or *aalwolf*. And the same differencing applies to all the hundreds of thousands of other words (signs) an English speaker uses. A signifier signifies because it is different from all other signifiers. Its sound-image embodies a system of binary differences from all other sound-images.

The same, says Saussure, holds true for the signified. An aardvark (the signified, now, or the referent or the concept) is such because it is not the concept of a dog, a cat, a rat, a mouse, a house, etc. "Whether we take the signified or the signifier, language has . . . only conceptual and phonic differences that have issued from the system. The idea or phonic substance [*matière phonique*] that a sign contains [*dans un signe*] is of less importance than the other signs that surround it." Saussure is saying it is the *difference* between this sound-image and all other sound-images that signifies the *difference* between this concept and all other concepts.

He says it again this way:

> A linguistic system is a series of differences of sound combined with a series of differences of ideas; but the pairing of a certain number of acoustical signs with as many cuts made from the mass of thought engenders a system of values; and this system serves as the effective link between the phonic and psychological elements within each sign. Although both the signified and the signifier are purely differential and negative when considered separately, their combination is a positive fact; it is even the sole type of facts that language has, for maintaining the parallelism between the two classes of differences is the distinctive function of the linguistic institution.

Earlier in his course of lectures, Saussure had compared the sign to a chemical compound like water. Water consists of a pair of elements, hydrogen and oxygen, without resembling either. So a sign combines the signifier-signified pair without resembling either. Now he images the pairing of these differenced signifiers with their differenced signifieds as a vast plane:

> Language can also be compared with a sheet of paper: thought is the front and the sound the back; one cannot cut the front [i.e., into these patterns of differences] without cutting the back at the same time; likewise in language, one can neither divide sound from thought nor thought from sound.

I would summarize him this way. Language consists of two negatives and a positive. The two negatives are the differences, phonological or psychological. They mark off this signifier from that and this signified from that. The positive is the process of signifying, which remains unchanged from his earlier, simpler account. What language does, literally *does* in this positive sense, is maintain the relations between two classes of differences, one acoustic, one mental. It links a phonic difference to a psychological difference, as a sheet of paper links its two sides or a chemical compound links two elements.

Now, from my psychological, reader-response point of view, something curious has happened in Saussure's model. He started with the sound [hors] that I can feel in my throat or vibrating on my ear. He ended up with a concept in my mind, the concept of a horse as different from twenty billion other things. How did he do that? He seems to have solved the mind-body problem while nobody was looking. Saussure makes the jump from physical world to psychological concept in two stages. First, from sound to sound-image. Second, from sound-image to concept. I'll take them one at a time.

How did Saussure get from the sound [hors] in someone's voice to the sound-image "horse" in my mind? Apparently he jumped the chasm between body and mind by some process he labels psychological imprinting, that metaphor he has used twice, or "the representation of it [the sound] that the testimony of our senses gives us" (my translation of "*la répresentation que nous en donne le témoignage de nos sens*"). Saussure seems to assume that we hear the physical sound of a word, and our senses automatically give us the "sound-image" of the word. Click. Just like that. Saussure imagines the process as all outside-in. Something impinges on our senses and causes a state of mind.

But that is not the case. A word-sound does not become a Saussurean "sound-image" without some activity on the part of its hearer. The process is both outside-in and inside-out.

By automatically associating the physical sound and the heard word, the sound-image, Saussure has dropped out the whole process of interpreting phonemes. If you look at the wave-forms of words on an oscilloscope, you can see that the sound of a given phoneme looks—is—very different depending on the context in which it occurs. You see, too, that different phonemes have no clear boundary. Adjacent phonemes run into one another. Further, the presence of an [l] or an [m] next to a [d] may completely change the waveform of the [d]. You can try it yourself. Pronounce the letter [t] by itself or in [tip]. Then prounounce the word [toud], *toad*. In [tip] the [t] is unvoiced. In [toud] it feels almost as heavily voiced as the [d]. You can feel in your throat how you partially voice the [t] as part of the diphthong [ou].

"One of the most characteristic aspects of language is its relative 'fuzziness,'" notes Eric Lenneberg. There are no vocabulary items in which meaning is sharply defined, and no phoneme has absolute acoustic boundaries. Syntax is also fuzzy, "and it is this fuzziness that makes it impossible to separate syntax from semantics, thus wedding the realm of language irrevocably to the realm of knowledge in general."

Yet despite the fuzziness of the boundaries, we do somehow process phonemes. Apparently we understand the word first, and then we use the word to understand the phonemes. Yet we also used the phonemes to get at the word in the first place. That complex, circular, bootstrapped processing—that feedback process, if you will—is why it is so difficult to get computers to understand spoken language. The computer's binary, step-by-step methods work poorly in such complex interactions, while humans can do them easily.

We go through complex inferences to hear a word. Psychologists have demonstrated these processes over and over again, and we lay people become aware of these inferences when we try to understand someone talking on a staticky radio or speaking accented English. There is a large body of evidence that hearing a word is not a matter of the distinctive features of a word-sound "imprinting" themselves on a passive hearer. The hearer has to know things and do things in order to hear a word. Saussure,

however, simply lumps this whole complex psychological processing into the single phrase "sound-image." What he has done
is translate a human process, a verb, if you will, into a thing-out-
there, a noun, and transferred the human activity to the thing-
out-there. What he has done is drop out the psychology of the
hearer, although it is essential to converting mere sound into what
Saussure calls an *image acoustique*. In short, Saussure's system of
differences does not work *even* at the level of phonemes.

Saussure makes the same mistake, even more crucially, in his
central idea: signifying. Here again are some key passages. Now
I want you to look at them more critically. "In language there are
only differences." "Whether we take the signified or the signifier,
language has ... only conceptual and phonic differences that
have issued from the system. The idea or phonic substance [*matière phonique*] that a sign contains [*dans un signe*] is of less importance than the other signs that surround it." (Notice, in passing, the conduit metaphor in "*dans un signe*." Notice, too, how
he treats idea and *matière phonique*, psychological concept and
physical substance, as interchangeable.) Finally, "A linguistic system is a series of differences of sound combined with a series of
differences of ideas; but the pairing of a certain number of acoust-
ical signs with as many cuts made from the mass of thought en-
genders a system of values; and this system serves as the effective
link between the phonic and psychological elements within each
sign."

As with Saussure's noun "sound-image," his noun "sign" and
its verb "signifies" cover up a lot of activity on the part of the
hearer. Any elementary textbook in the psychology of reading
will show that word-sounds do not simply imprint word-images
on our psyches. Understanding involves complex interpretive acts
that Saussure loses by compressing them into the noun "difference." To anyone who has seen the difficulty psychologists and
psycholinguists have in making the connection from sound to
sense, his claims are sheer flimflam—intellectual sleight-of-hand.

Incidentally, the people who today work with children learning to speak, with beginning readers, or with illiterates don't even
hold with the fundamental difference that Saussure posited. That
is, one cannot draw his sharp line between actively speaking and
writing language and passively hearing or reading language. The

same skills and inferences are involved in both. I am thinking of Margaret Meek in London or Frank Smith in Canada and the United States, the centers that study reading at the universities of London and Illinois, Rand Spiro, Arthur Applebee, and many another. They have written extensive accounts of beginning readers and the kinds of active feedback processes they have to learn in order to understand language.

One does not go from words to concepts by a simple imprinting. The easy idea that one word or one concept is different from the rest does not cover the inferences we make when we distinguish a word or a concept. Nor does the word "signifies" account for the many inferences we make when we go from word to concept. To trace comprehensions from the physical to the psychological, you have to do more than just say the physical is already psychological.

In short, Saussure's either-or differences do not account for our understanding of language at the level either of phonemes or of signs. Saussure's differences among signifiers, among different signifieds, and different signs, among different phonemes, and between language and the world—none of them explain what they are supposed to explain, compared to contemporary cognitive psychology. Saussure did not solve—indeed he did not address the problem of how a physical sound becomes a psychological concept. He simply proclaimed that it does.

By this equation of physical differences with mental differences, he papered over the psychological puzzles of response, *and he did so deliberately and explicitly.* Saussure was writing long before there was a psychology that could deal with our speaking or understanding speech or writing. He may have understood that. At any rate, he wisely chose to dismiss psychology from his account of the way we understand language.

As he tells us at the beginning and end of his lectures, his aim was to model language in purely linguistic terms, free of psychology, sociology, or anthropology. "The true and unique object of linguistics is language studied in and for itself." "From the very outset we must put both feet on the ground of language [*le terrain de la langue*] and use language as the norm of all other manifestations of speech." Saussure sought a purely linguistic account of language, and in this he succeeded. He gave a formal account of language, untangled from ethnography, social or individual psychology, physiology, philology, and everything else that is not linguistics. By so doing, he founded one branch of modern linguistics. Fine.

He erred, however, by psychologizing the idea of signifying. He promoted his purely formal account of language into a psychological account of what we do when we understand language. It is as if you formalized the laws of arithmetic and then claimed that you had also shown how our minds work when we do sums. In Saussure's model, a signifier's difference from other signifiers simply imprints a difference from other ideas in the hearer's mind, and this is where Saussure thinks he eludes psychology. He has only swept it under the rug, though, hiding the psychological process in "imprints." Saussure's "signifying," far from being something the theorist of literature or film can take for granted, rests on a highly questionable but unexamined set of *psychological* premises.

Interestingly, Saussure did not make this error when he described the way we speak—perhaps because simple introspection tells us our minds busily frame phrases and sentences when we speak. When he described how we understand language, however, he continued to drop psychology out, even in his more sophisticated account based on differences. Perhaps he did so because simple introspection will not reveal the activity of the mind when we hear and interpret the simpler forms of language.

By dropping out psychology or, more precisely, psycholinguistics, he shortcircuited any possible analysis of hearing or understanding language. In Saussure's theory, a physical sound automatically becomes a sound-image, a pattern of differences. That pattern of differences automatically becomes a concept. This is "black boxing" or "bracketing" with a vengeance. What looks like a simple, even banal assumption about how words mean is really a global assumption about human psychology.

Saussure formalized language as a sheet of signifying differences mapped onto a sheet of signified differences. Whatever its *linguistic* credibility (and that is very limited at present), this idea of signifying entails a radically behaviorist, stimulus-response psychology of perception. Saussure's assumption runs counter to most modern thinking about the mind and brain. In 1964, Chomsky identified (as I do) the structural linguistics that derives from Saussure as "radical behaviorist reductionism." It is an extreme stimulus-response, behaviorist picture of the mind that among psychologists, even the most devout of Skinnerians might not endorse.

The idea that texts signify puts the text in the active role, like a stimulus in the stimulus-response model. A feedback model like that of chapter nine is, I admit, an over-simplification. Even so it does allow us to account for the variability of response to a given filmic image and for the complicated way in which audiences edit and rewrite the stimulus in front of them, as in the Kuleshov effect. Stimulus-response cannot account for the fluidity of your or my response either to a film or to a novel, and Saussurean linguistics suffers from the same rigidity.

So far, I have set out what's wrong with "signifying" from a psychological point of view. A second trouble with Saussure is linguistic. Psycholinguistics aside, Saussure's is surely an early and imperfect conception of language, compared to ideas now available to us.

What's wrong with it? It rests, as I have said, on a conduit metaphor for language, the old belief that words have an inside and an outside, surely no better than a figure of speech. It is a dictionary view of language—as though I could understand French by memorizing Larousse or, in Saussure's more sophisticated version, by memorizing all the binary polarities for all the words in the Larousse dictionary. Indeed, Saussure says as much: "Language exists in the form of a sum of impressions deposited in the brain of each member of a community, almost like a dictionary of which identical copies have been distributed to each individual." I think that is a very primitive conception of language, just about what you would expect in 1890 or so. It is a conception of language that really works only for proper or common nouns. "Tree" and "horse" are the examples of signs Saussure favored. What "signified" comes to your mind when I say "hope"? Do you think it could be expressed as a system of differences the way one might use a system of differences to define the sound "hope"? Saussure's "signifying" does not handle abstract words well. Nor common words like *over* or *set*. The word "over" has been found to have ninety-eight different senses. In the *Oxford English Dictionary* the verb "set" has a hundred fifty-four divisions, one of them with forty-four subdivisions. Its examples and definitions cover more than twenty-two elephant folio pages. Hugh Kenner calls the "set" entry in the *OED* a lexicographer's epic, because it is fully four-fifths the length of *Paradise Lost*. How on earth would Saussure's simple "sign" deal with such polysemy? True, as a mathematical exercise, ten or twenty binary choices might cover the signifieds (although the signifier would be just one). But these meanings grow from one another; they evolve, overlap, and intertwine.

How can such a model as Saussure's account for the constant change in language? When *contra* entered our political vocabulary, did it readjust all the billions of patterns of difference from *aal* to *zyxt*? How can Saussure's linguistics explain ambiguity? "John hit the ball, then Herbert." How can it model the way we combine words into sentences? How does it explain your ability to understand a sentence you have never heard before? You may well recognize those last questions. I am simply raising the same issues Noam Chomsky raised about phrase-structure grammars. It was he who in 1957 decisively refuted Saussure.

22

Chomsky

In a lecture of 1988, Chomsky traced the changes in the field of linguistics since he had been a graduate student in the early 1950s.

> For example, when I was a graduate student, a "real result"—I define that operationally, I mean something you could hand in and they would give you a Ph.D. for it—a "real result" was, you take some language, Cherokee, say, and figure out what the basic elements of it are, the sounds, maybe the words, and so on. You make some statements about the patterns into which those things fall, you hand it in, and you get a Ph.D., and so on. That's a "real result."

Chomsky went on to describe two stages *after* that first stage, a Bloomfieldian linguistics that was already advanced compared to Saussure's, followed by Chomsky's own beginning work. The first, Bloomfieldian, approach, he noted, becomes in these later phases merely an organization of data with which to begin to tackle the real and much harder problems.

By the way, there is a profound irony here, as John Ellis notes. "Even though Saussure is now quoted everywhere in France, there appears to be no understanding there of the fact that Saussure's work radi-

133

cally altered linguistics in the English-speaking world many decades ago while he was being ignored elsewhere."

In Chomsky's work, however, the post-Saussurean Bloomfield is only a way-station on the path to the real questions. They are—

> *What constitutes knowledge of language?*
> *How is knowledge of language acquired?*
> *How is knowledge of language put to use?*

Notice how Chomsky has focused on language as a *psychological* phenomenon. By contrast, Saussure treats language as existing in some sort of Platonic space, apart from the humans who use it.

Language in that sense, Chomsky notes, does not exist except as different individuals and communities speak it. It is no more than a *façon de parler*.

> In ordinary usage . . . when we speak of a language, we have in mind some kind of *social* phenomenon, a shared property of a community. What kind of community? There is no clear answer to this question. . . . The term "language" as used in ordinary discourse involves obscure sociopolitical and normative facts. It is doubtful that we can give a coherent account of how the term is actually used. . . . But in pursuing a serious inquiry into language, we require some conceptual precision and therefore must refine, modify, or simply replace the concepts of ordinary usage . . . It may be possible and worthwhile to undertake the study of language in its sociopolitical dimensions, but this further inquiry can proceed only to the extent that we have some grasp of the properties and principles of language in a narrower sense, in the sense of individual psychology. It will be a study of how the systems represented in the mind/brains of various interacting speakers differ and are related within a commmunity characterized in part at least in nonlinguistic terms.

To paraphrase, people set the boundaries of English by rather arbitrary "sociopolitical" or "normative-teleological" factors. People say things like, "Black English isn't English." Or, "Anyone who uses *ain't* isn't speaking English." Saussure's idea of "language," it seems to me, is open to this objection. He assumes all hearers understand the system of signifiers the same way. *Langue* is behavior. It is what is "out there," what is said.

For Chomsky, however, language in a precise sense is something individuals have in their heads.

I am using the term "language" to refer to an *individual* phenomenon, a system represented in the mind/brain of a particular individual. If we could investigate in sufficient detail, we would find that no two individuals share exactly the same language in this sense, even identical twins who grow up in the same social environment. Two individuals can communicate to the extent that their languages are sufficiently similar.

In other words, Chomsky's notion of language allows us to explore such notions as Black English or "women's language." It accords with reader-response thinking and feminist criticism, but it is opposed to structuralism or post-structuralism.

To distinguish these two senses of "language," Chomsky's recent writings use the terms "E-language," externalized language, and "I-language," internalized language. E-language is an artifact. "Languages in this sense are not real-world objects but are artificial, somewhat arbitrary, and perhaps not very interesting constructs." That is, no one could set the boundaries of E-English except by arbitrary "normative-teleological" factors. Paradoxically, I-language, because it is psychological, is a more realistic concept:

> When we speak of a person as knowing a language, we do not mean that he or she knows an infinite set of sentences, or sound-meaning pairs taken in extension, or a set of acts or behaviors; rather, what we mean is that the person knows what makes sound and meaning relate to one another in a specific way, what makes them "hang together," a particular characterization of a function, perhaps. The person has "a notion of structure" and knows an I-language ["internalized language"] as characterized by the linguists' grammar. When we say that it is a rule of English that objects follow verbs . . . we are not saying that it is a rule of some set of sentences or behaviors, but rather that it is a rule of a system of rules, English, an I-language. The rules of the language are not rules of some infinite set of formal objects [like Saussure's signs] or potential actions [like Skinner's behaviors] but are rules that form or constitute the language, like . . . rules of chess (not a set of moves, but a game, a particular rule system).

That is why, from a Chomskyan point of view, "The E-language ['externalized language'] that was the object of study in most of traditional or structuralist grammar or behavioral psychology is now regarded as an epiphenomenon at best." "Theories of I-languages, universal and particular grammars, are on a par with scientific theories in other domains; theories of E-languages, if sensible at all, have some different and more obscure status because there is no corresponding real-world object."

As we have seen with Agnes, Ted, Norm, the critics from Ade to Fay, and even Spencer, the way we use, even the way we know, language expresses our individuality. Chomsky's notion of language, in other words, fits the model of chapter nine as well as our everyday experience. I see an analogy, moreover. In a realistic or scientific approach to reader-response, the real responses of Agnes, Ted, and Norm are to I-language as the "assumed" responses of an abstract audience are to E-language. The idea of "the" reader or "the" interpretation is an obscurely defined social phenomenon with no clear real-world status.

In contrast to Chomsky, Saussure has no way of accounting for individual styles, because he is locked into a view of language as external, E-language. His only concession to psychology and an I-language is his idea that language exists as though identical dictionaries had been placed in each of our minds. That is one basic trouble with Saussure. Language in Saussure's sense is not a real thing—at least according to Chomsky.

Another difficulty is that Saussure built his linguistics on the unit of the word. One part of Chomsky's 1957 revolution in linguistics was to change that unit of analysis to the sentence. He made his well-known demand, that a grammar should be able to generate all and only the well-formed sentences of a language. Saussure does not even come close to this target.

Long before Chomsky, however, linguists had realized that it would take something more than Saussure's word-bound linguistics to interrelate words in phrases and sentences. Indeed some nineteenth century linguists, Hermann Paul, Karl Brugmann, and William Dwight Whitney, experimented with the idea of deep structures. Saussure knew of their work, and there is at least one passage in students' notes on Saussure's lectures where he seems himself (under the influence of Whitney) to adopt the idea. In his *Cours*, however, he insists, as we have seen, on confining himself to the linguistic surface. Hence he was able to offer only a very primitive way of explaining how we put words together to form sentences. Indeed, I find Saussure's idea of a sentence difficult to grasp at all.

Saussure seems to conclude that one builds sentences along "two natural co-ordinates": association and syntagms. Association groups words (or inflections or any morpheme, really) according to meanings. Associations determine what is possible at any given slot in the sentence. He defined the "syntagm" as consecutive signifier-signified units. Syntagmatics arranges elements in linear order, thereby creating slots, but one cannot (according to Saussure) study word order apart from its concrete manifestations. That is, one cannot consider the slots apart from the words that actually fill them. "To think that there is an incorporeal syntax outside material units distributed in space would be a mistake." Thus he rules deep structure out.

Furthermore, the only syntagms in *langue,* he proclaimed, were pat phrases dictated by tradition, things like "Good morning" or "il y a." Once a language fact depends on individual freedom, we are in the realm of *parole.* Hence, he concluded, "The sentence . . . . belongs to speaking [*parole*], not to language [*langue*]." Chomsky sums up Saussure's position this way: "In Saussurean structuralism, a language [*langue*] was taken to be a system of sounds and an associated system of concepts; the notion of sentence was left in a kind of limbo, perhaps to be accommodated within the study of language use." "Saussurean structuralism had placed . . . 'free expressions' outside of the scope of the study of language structure, of Saussure's *langue.*" As a result, "The fundamental question of the use and understanding of new sentences is left without any explanation." Chomsky notes the links of this position to behaviorist psychology in that both avoid the notion of the autonomous individual, and I shall return to that connection.

Enlarging on Saussure's brief and inconclusive remarks about association and syntagm, Roman Jakobson helped out with two principles to account for sentences. It is obvious that we make sentences by putting one word after another. First, "The man." Then "hit." Then "the." Then "ball." It is equally obvious that at any given point in that process we can substitute other words. Instead of "The man," we could say "The woman," or "Herbert." Instead of "ball," we could substitute other nouns or phrases to produce, "The man hit the child," or "The man hit the nail on the head," or "The man hit the road." Jakobson thus formalized

Saussure's two-axis model of sentence formation. Following Saussure, he named these two principles the paradigmatic (the vertical axis of selection) and the syntagmatic (the horizontal axis of sequential combination).

The trouble with Jakobson's system is that it doesn't account for the way we build sentences any better than Saussure's. If I understand Jakobson and Saussure correctly, they are describing what Chomsky calls a "finite-state grammar." In such a grammar, "Sentences are generated by means of a series of choices made 'from left to right'; that is to say, after the first, or leftmost element has been selected, [the probability of] every subsequent choice is determined by the immediately preceding elements."

In 1957, Chomsky's *Syntactic Structures* proved that such a grammar is inadequate for many English sentences. Consider a sentence like,

Anyone who denies that is lying.

is lying does not depend on *that*. Rather, there is a dependency between *Anyone* at the beginning of the sentence and *is lying* at the end. One cannot simply generate the sentence from left to right.

Similarly, if-then or either-or constructions create dependencies beyond simple left to right.

If he went home or he left the office

is not an English sentence. Think of pronouns. "John hit the ball and then he ran to first base." Or relative clauses. "This is the dog that worried the cat that killed the rat that ate the malt that lay in the house that Jack built." Or passives. "The ball was hit by Jack." Or pragmatics—our ordinary fuzzy ways of connecting sentences to one another. "Joe Bob's pit bull bit me yesterday. They are a dangerous breed."

Consider the pair of sentences in Chomsky's well-known example:

John is eager to please.
John is easy to please.

At first glance, they look as though they were built along Jakobsonian lines. Just substitute "eager" for "easy." But the underlying meanings are quite different. In the first sentence, John is active, in the second, passive. In the first John is doing things, in the second John is being done for.

There are still more complex examples (studied in the later phases of Chomsky's work on "binding theory"). Identical sequences of "signifiers" can have quite different meanings:

> John is too angry to talk to Bill.
>
> John is too angry to talk to.

In one case, John is doing the talking, in the other, someone other than John, but the seven-word sequence of signifiers is the same. Evidently, not only a single signifier, but a whole sequence of signifiers can signify different signifieds. Similarly,

> I wonder who the hunters expected to see them.
>
> I wonder who the hunters expected to see.

In the first sentence, the hunters are seen. In the second, they do the seeing.

> The horse raced round the barn.
>
> The horse raced round the barn fell.

In the first sentence, the horse did the racing. In the second, someone else did.

There is no need to belabor the point. When we compose or understand sentences we use structures other than the surface produced. Furthermore, these structures can be exceedingly complex. I would find it quite impossible to say why, in the "hunters" sentences, I know that the first "them" refers to the hunters themselves.

It was weaknesses such as these that led Chomsky in 1957 to prove the inadequacy of "finite-state grammars." Such a grammar cannot cope with any rule in which the choice of words in one part of a sentence is dictated by the choice of words in an earlier or later part. And a great many of the rules by which we make sentences are of that type.

In the first half of the twentieth century, to deal with the building of sentences, linguists had developed phrase-structure grammars (or "immediate constituent" grammars). These grammars built phrases and sentences by rewrite rules. A sentence S has a subject and a predicate. That is, S can be rewritten into subject and predicate. The subject may in turn be rewritten into a noun phrase (NP). A noun phrase can be rewritten into a proper noun (PN) or an article, an optional adjective, and a noun (Art [+ Adj] + N). A verb phrase can be rewritten into a verb plus a noun-phrase object (V + NP). These are the "immediate constituents" of first the sentence, then the noun phrase, then the verb phrase.

This kind of analysis, Chomsky showed in his 1957 book, is open to ambiguity. For example,

the old men and women

might mean old men and old women or old men and women in general. You would have to know how the phrase was derived to disambiguate it. Similarly,

The shooting of the hunters was terrible.

You need to know the sentence's origin, that is, the deep structure it was derived from, to know whether the hunters are dead or just bad shots.

Thus, a phrase-structure grammar has considerable power, more than Saussure's associations and syntagms or Jakobson's metaphor and metonymy, for example. You can use a phrase-structure grammar to assign phrase markers (like NP). Chomsky himself incorporated phrase-structure rules into transformational grammar. Even so, a phrase-structure grammar is weak. A phrase-structure grammar cannot show how *The man hit the ball* and *The ball was hit by the man* in some sense belong together. Phrase structure grammars are context-free, while a transformational grammar is context-sensitive and, in general, therefore, more powerful. Chomsky, however, did not claim to have disproved phrase-structure grammars in 1957, and many linguists still use them.

In his earlier thinking, Chomsky distinguished "competence," the language speaker's ability to frame and understand sentences (now I-language), from "performance," the exercise of that ability with particular sentences (now E-language). Since the 1970s, Chomsky has begun what amounts to a major deepening and strengthening of this inquiry into what speakers and hearers do.

He has focused on what he calls "Plato's problem." How do we know as much as we do with as little evidence as we have? How are we able to disambiguate such sentences as those in the preceding paragraphs when we have never heard them before and even a grammar teacher would be hard put to explain why they work as they do? How do children learn a full "English" from the few and imperfect samples they hear?

This is not the place, however, nor am I the person to attempt an explanation of X-bar theory, theta marking, PG parameters, the move-α rule, or other features of Chomsky's newer, stronger, and, despite such terms, simpler grammar. Much of Chomsky's work is not accepted by other linguists, notably his idea of an innate language faculty. I am not asking you to accept Chomsky's own linguistics, however. My point is simply that Chomsky's work rendered Saussure's linguistics, indeed much of post-Saussurean linguistics, obsolete. I am not claiming that Chomsky is right, only that Chomsky has proven that Saussure is wrong. Linguists who reject Chomsky claim to be going beyond Chomsky, or they cling to phrase-structure grammars. They are not turning back to Saussure.

Saussure's views are not held, so far as I know, by modern linguists, only by literary critics and the occasional philosopher. A theory (like Saussure's) that language understanding is purely semantic, reports Mitchell Marcus, is "fundamentally inadequate to process the full range of natural language" and "held by no current researchers, to my knowledge." In writing this section of this book, for example, I had trouble finding linguistic texts that even refer to Saussure. His is an "impoverished and thoroughly inadequate conception of language," according to Chomsky. "Wrong on a grand scale," cognitive linguist Mark Turner calls it, when extended from phonemes to words. And it has elicited wrong film and literary theory on a grand scale. One can find dozens of books of literary theory bogged down in signifiers and signifieds, but only a handful that refer to Chomsky.

Saussure's account of language deals only with surface features and makes no provision for deep structures or transformations between deep and surface structures. There is no way in Saussure's system to build a sentence taking into account what has gone before and what is planned to come after. There is no way, really, in Jakobson's either. Chomsky's adjectives, "impoverished" and "thoroughly inadequate," are not unduly harsh, just painfully accurate. Saussure and Jakobson were both distinguished, even great, linguists. But it is the fate of scientists, even of great scientists, to have their ideas superseded.

Saussure and Jakobson developed their ideas of signifier and signified and metaphor and metonymy before Chomsky's 1957 revolution in linguistics. In 1964, Chomsky summed up Saussure's thinking this way:

> Saussure . . . regards *langue* as basically a store of signs with their grammatical properties, that is, a store of word-like elements, fixed phrases and, perhaps, certain limited phrase types . . . . He was thus quite unable to come to grips with the recursive processes underlying sentence formation, and he appears to regard sentence formation as a matter of *parole* rather than *langue,* of free and voluntary creation rather than systematic rule (or perhaps, in some obscure way, as on the border between *langue* and *parole*). There is no place in his scheme for "rule-governed creativity" of the kind involved in the ordinary everyday use of language.
>
> Modern linguistics [Chomsky was speaking in 1962] is much under the influence of Saussure's conception of *langue* as an inventory of elements . . . and his preoccupation with systems of elements rather than the systems of rules which were the focus of attention in traditional grammar . . . . In general, modern descriptive statements pay little attention to the "creative" aspect of language . . . . This narrowing of the range of interest, as compared with traditional grammar, apparently has the effect of making it impossible to select an inventory of elements correctly, since it seems [according to Chomsky's proofs in *Syntactic Structures*] that no inventory (not even that of phonemes) can be determined without reference to the principles by which sentences are constructed in the language . . . . To the extent that this is true, "structural linguistics" will have suffered from a failure to appreciate the extent and depth of interconnections among various parts of a language system.

Thus, when Saussure defines his linguistic unit as "a slice of sound which to the exclusion of everything that precedes and follows it in the spoken chain is the signifier of a certain concept," he has created a false model, not only of a sentence, but even of a word.

In short, simply as a matter of linguistics, Saussure's idea, that a language consists of systems of differenced signifier-signified pairings, fails. These terms, "signifier," "signified," "signifying," "system of differences," which bulk so large in contemporary literary theory, refer to things that are no longer valid linguistic concepts. They come from "this preoccupation with inventory and with taxonomic procedures" for which Saussure is responsible: "It has failed totally [writes Chomsky] to come to grips with the 'creative' aspect of language use, that is, the ability to form and understand previously unheard sentences." "Signifying" just doesn't work as a concept. "Signifier," "signified," "system of differences"—these are meaningless so far as language is concerned.

What is needed to account for the human use of language, for speaking and understanding, is a *combination* of personal creativity and of rules. In other words, what is needed is some such model of the human as that of chapter nine. And that takes us from linguistics to psychology.

We have seen that Saussure's system breaks down linguistically. It also breaks down psychologically. As a psychological critic, I am more concerned with the psychological failure, but it is related to the linguistic. Chomsky continued his 1957 rebuttal of Saussure's grammar and the phrase-structure grammars that succeeded Saussure's with a devastating review of B. F. Skinner's *Verbal Behavior*. Skinner had attempted to explain human language skills in stimulus-response, behaviorist terms. In both the linguistic and the psychological spheres, Chomsky showed that it is logically and empirically impossible to account for language proficiency in terms of stimulus-response chains.

So far as psychology was concerned, Chomsky's linguistic achievements gave an important push away from behaviorism. More generally, Chomsky's work brought into question the customary but narrow definitions of psychology. "Psychology is the scientific study of behavior." Or, "Psychology is the discovery of lawful relationships between observable stimuli and observable responses." Psychologists became increasingly interested in looking inside the mind that had been bracketed and put off limits under the influence of behaviorism.

Chomsky's work was only one among a number of such challenges, however. Others were: the general failure of academic psychology to deal with higher-level processes; new work in perception, cognition, and memory; and especially the interest in getting computers to model high-level human behavior. These and other developments created something of a revolution in psychology. A new generation of psychologists refused to consider internal, inferred mental processes as chimeras (the behaviorists' dogma). Instead, they chose, like Chomsky, to investigate what the mind knows and how it knows it. As a result, Chomsky's linguistics became, he wrote, "one of the strands that led to the development of the cognitive sciences in the contemporary sense." Chomsky's shares with other approaches the belief that certain aspects of the mind/brain can be usefully construed on the model of computational systems of rules. These rule systems form and modify mental representations, and we put them to use in interpretation and action.

By contrast, traditional psychology avoids the idea of mental structures. The focus is on stimuli that "evoke" or even "control" responses. Higher-order structures, processes, and patterns of behavior can at best be understood as concatenations of simple units of stimulus and response. Today's cognitive psychology or "cognitive science" we have sampled in chapter nine, and it is quite different. It finds one pattern recurring in domain after domain of human experience. Perception, comprehension, and interpretation all involve the use of existing knowledge, in complex as well as simple units, to obtain and understand sensory input. The individual actively directs and processes inputs. In the most common model, the individual imposes from above, as it were, schemata on what the senses say, and the senses in turn provide input "from below" that the schemata must cope with. All of human experience involves this type of interaction of "top-down" and "inside out" activity on the part of the human with "bottom-up" and "outside in" input from the world.

In other words, both to compose sentences and to understand them, we depend upon the whole body of knowledge we bring to bear.

> To rephrase the point [writes Chomsky] in the terms of contemporary discussion: the cognitive system involved in use of language is "cognitively penetrable" in the sense of Pylyshyn (1984) and other

current work; that is, our goals, beliefs, expectations, and so forth clearly enter into our decision to use the rules in one way or another, and principles of rational inference and the like may also play a role in these decisions. This is true not only of what we decide to say but how we decide to say it, and similar factors enter at some level into determining how we understand what we hear.

In other words, both Chomsky's idea and the model of chapter nine reflect the modern notion of linguistic rules, as opposed to signifier-signifieds, and, in Chomsky's phrasing, "the classical view that the use of these rules in speech is free and indeterminate."

Chomsky refers here to Zenon Pylyshyn. Just as Chomsky proved in 1959 that a behaviorist account of language fails, so Fodor and Pylyshyn proved in 1981 that even J. J. Gibson's sophisticated quasi-behaviorist, stimulus-response account of "direct" perception fails, at least for words. Fodor and Pylyshyn were disproving something like Saussure's easy link from *matière phonique* to "sound-image." Interestingly, they refer to an experiment in which hearers used cough-sounds to stand for various phonemes in just the way Kuleshov's audience used the image of Mosjukhin's face to stand for various emotions. Signifying as an activity of the text fails on *both* psychological *and* linguistic grounds.

In thinking about "rule-governed creativity," it is important to distinguish two kinds of rules. We have the relatively hard-wired codes for language and for the perception of our surroundings. We have more fluid codes for the perception of word meanings or literary interpretations. Chomsky acknowledges that

> the process of sentence perception is cognitively penetrable, influenced by factors that might involve expectations, reasoning, and so on.
>
> But while the system of language use is cognitively penetrable in this sense, the system of principles of S_0 [the initial or infant state of the language acquisition system] presumably is not; it merely functions as a kind of automatism. In normal cases, the same is true of the system of speech perception and much of speech production."

In other words, the system through which we learn is, in Chomsky's view, part of our biological endowment. Our expectations, reasoning, goals, or beliefs cannot change it. They can change, however, the way we learn and use that system. Therefore no two individuals learn and use language in exactly the same way. Chomsky's model allows for individual styles of understanding language, even if we accept his idea that the language faculty is inborn.

In my terms, our writing, speech, reading, and understanding are all functions of our identities. Chomsky's principle of "rule-governed creativity," which is, he points out, a very traditional notion of language as well as a radically modern one, fits the picture of chapter nine. The identity-governing-feedback model is consistent with Chomsky's ideas. In his terms, canons are cognitively penetrable, and codes are not.

By contrast, Saussure's concept of signifying or his notion that we have identical dictionaries in our heads belong to an older mode. They are very much out of kilter with modern psycholinguistics. His two transitions, from *matière phonique* to sound-image and from sound-image to concept, are all outside-in (as, indeed, his diagrams show). He does not allow for the considerable activity of the reader or hearer as described by psychology and psycholinguistics since the 1950s.

Unfortunately, this radical change in the psychology of language understanding and interpretation seems not to have made its way into literature professors' current preoccupation with "theory." There, otherwise innovative people play the conservative. They trot out Saussure against psychology or reader-response the way fundamentalist preachers quote the Bible to cry down evolution or family planning. Most literary theorists I know would subscribe to Saussure's claim, "The word is a unit that strikes the mind [*s'impose à l'esprit*], something central in the mechanism of language." Texts are still active and controlling in the literary world, although linguistic texts have evidently not been active enough to penetrate the theoretical fog.

Literary theorists, by following Saussure, tacitly adopt his radically behaviorist view of our understanding of language. Psychologically, however, Saussure overextended himself. As we have seen in the preceding chapter, he let his purely linguistic, formal account of language pretend to a psychological validity. It is easy to see what has gone wrong if we consider arithmetic instead of language. In a formal sense, adding one to the first number "generates" all the rest of the integers. Yes, in a purely formal way,

$$n + 1, (n + 1) + 1, ((n + 1) + 1) + 1, \ldots$$

"signifies" all the whole, positive numbers. But that "generates" or "signifies" does not describe what goes on in your mind or mine when we think of 365 or 186,000. Presenting $((n + 1) + 1) + 1$ to us simply does not imprint the set of positive, integral numbers on our minds. Although $y = x^2$ "generates" a parabola, it does not stimulate our plotting or perceiving that parabola. Neither does "tree" (even if it were a differential value) stimulate a concept of a tree.

A psychologized signifier-signified is all outside-in and bottom-up. It is not a strong enough model to explain your or my understanding a sentence, to say nothing of our response to a film or a novel. This is the psychological error inherent in the literary use of "signifying." It allows *neither* for the hard-wired parts of our psychology *nor* our fluctuating beliefs and goals. No purely formal description of language can serve for a psycholinguistic description of the human being actually using language.

Chomsky, by contrast, anticipated the error of extending a formal model to a psychological one, and he avoided it. Indeed he turned the whole subject-matter of linguistics around, from the epiphenomenal *langue* or E-language to the competence of speakers and hearers, I-language. Nevertheless, "A generative grammar as it stands is no more a model of the speaker than it is a model of the hearer. Rather, as has been repeatedly emphasized, it can be regarded only as *a characterization of* the intrinsic tacit knowledge or competence that underlies actual performance." This is true of his later work as well as his earlier. In other words, a modern grammar can offer at most a characterization of the fixed codes ("rules" in Chomsky's language) or the optional canons readers like Agnes, Ted, and Norm use in their feedback processing or use (in the language of cognitive science) as schemata. By contrast, Saussure admits nothing of codes or feedback or schemata or actual readers. Instead he offers a stimulus-response model, and even that radically simplified as compared, say, to

Skinner's. With Saussure, a word simply imposes a meaning on the mind. Skinner, at least, asked for reinforcement.

My topic, however, is not psychology or linguistics or even psycholinguistics. I am trying to look at literary theorists in the light of contemporary ideas of human psychology. I am trying to I literary theory. What we have seen so far is that contemporary literary theory relies heavily on Saussure. Saussure's account of language, however, fails in three important respects.

First, it fails linguistically. For one thing Saussure's idea of language is E-language, an externalized language, which really rests on non-linguistic criteria. For another, his conception of language includes, for all practical purposes, only a dictionary. He did not recognize that any formal account of language that will deal with sentences and discourse (to say nothing of a psychological account of language) has to include more and deeper systems than just a lexicon. It also and most importantly has to include the interactions among these different systems, between deep and surface structures. Saussure fails to meet Chomsky's 1957 critique of the finite-state or phrase-structure grammars introduced to shore up Saussure's.

Second, Saussure fails psycholinguistically. He drops out the active psychological processes by which we understand language. Somehow, physical sounds or differences in physical sounds convert automatically into psychological concepts or differences in psychological concepts. He simply assumes that signifiers evoke signifieds automatically. He simply assumes "signifying." He simply assumes that a formal description of language equals an account of the psychology of language-users as well. He attributes to language the processes that, both common sense and psycholinguistics show, must take place in hearers and readers. This is how Saussure arrives at a purely text-active model: he posits it.

Third, then, Saussure fails empirically. He assumes that speaking or writing language involves the personal performance of a human being but understanding language does not. The experimental evidence from today's cognitive science is all the other way.

Saussure's psychological errors rest on one basic assumption, namely, that language *does* things. Words mean. Differences signify. Texts control, limit, restrain, or "imprint" their readers. What Saussure has done is psychologize a way of describing an externalized language (already a suspect concept). He has taken a way of speaking formally (or "metalinguistically") about language (as when we define a word, "Healthy means not being sick"), and called it a psychological process. For Saussure, a physical signifier can simply evoke a psychological signified, and that text-active model shuffles lamely on from Saussure's nineteenth-century theories into the most postmodern literary thought.

In the language I have quoted from Barthes, Miller, and Derrida, language and texts *do things,* sometimes to readers but always to themselves. Barthes, Derrida, Miller, Johnson, De Man, Leitch, and Foucault are admittedly a disparate group of theorists, but they constitute a sample of the much larger group whom I lump together as The New Cryptics. I lump them together—and I find them cryptic—because they all talk about signifiers and signifieds as though the Chomskyan revolution in linguistics had never happened. They claim to be avant-garde, but they rest their thinking on Saussure and Jakobson and old-fashioned behaviorism.

Is this ignorance? Or laziness, since Saussure is easier to understand than Chomsky? I do not know, but I notice, for example, that in 1982, my professional society, the Modern Language Association, published a guide for "nonspecialists, particularly students" to the interdisciplinary study of literature. It included, naturally, a chapter on "Literature and Linguistics" (by Jonathan Culler, a well-known literary theorist). I find it astonishing, not to say scandalous, that *the chapter does not even mention Chomsky or the linguistic revolution.* Transformational grammar is mentioned only as useful in describing literary styles.

By contrast, the student need go to no more recondite a source than the *Encyclopedia Britannica* to get a more informed view:

> The effect of Chomsky's ideas has been phenomenal. It is hardly an exaggeration to say that there is no major theoretical issue in linguistics today that is debated in terms other than those in which he has chosen to define it, and every school of linguistics tends to define its position in relation to his.

Except, evidently, the literary theory establishment.

In writing this chapter, just as I could not find linguistics books that mention Saussure, so I had trouble finding "theory" books that mention Chomsky. (I found one or two but they misrepresented his ideas.) At the same time, film and literary theorists by the dozens quote Saussure or rely on his terminology and claims. It is as though the linguistic revolution of 1957 hadn't happened yet. It is as though most of the literary professoriate had stuck its collective head in the sand.

Derrida Again

One salient member of the literary professoriate would be, on anybody's list, Jacques Derrida. He is also typical of the group in that, for all his careful, intelligent, and even brilliant rethinking of Saussure, he never really gives up the idea of signifying and the active text. Derrida starts from Saussure's account of signifying, and his later modifications, however much they may invert or transform signifiers and signifieds, never change the process of signification. That remains unquestioned—as in *Of Grammatology*: "From the moment that there is meaning there are nothing but signs. We think only in signs." He could hardly be more explicit than that.

At the same time, the concept is not wholly satisfactory, and he will do remarkable things with it.

> From the moment anyone wishes this to show, as I suggested a moment ago, that there is no transcendental or privileged signified and that the domain or the interplay of signification has, henceforth, no limit, he ought to extend his refusal to the concept and to the word sign itself—which is precisely what cannot be done. For the signification 'sign' has always been comprehended and

determined, in its sense, as sign-of, signifier referring to a signified, signifier different from its signified.

As I understand Derrida here, he is admitting that his whole argument rests on signifier-signified. Nevertheless, he challenges the difference between them by proposing to erase that difference.

> If one erases the radical difference between signifier and signified, it is the word signifier itself which ought to be abandoned as a metaphysical concept. . . . But we cannot do without the concept of the sign, we cannot give up this metaphysical complicity without also giving up the critique we are directing against this complicity, without the risk of erasing difference [altogether] in the self-identity of a signified reducing into itself its signifier, or, what amounts to the same thing, simply expelling it outside itself.

Notice that these alternatives at the end of the passage, which he treats as false, unthinkable, or impossible, he nevertheless creates from Saussure's idea of language. He therefore concludes that he cannot carry on his critique of signifier-signified, he cannot maintain his concept of difference, except in the very language of signifier-signified.

Derrida proceeds from the assumption that the only true model of language is signifier-signified, and it leads him to his critique of the idea of presence. "The first consequence to be drawn from this [signifier-signified—NNH] is that the signified concept is never present in itself, in an adequate presence that would refer only to itself. Every concept is necessarily and essentially inscribed in a chain or system, within which it refers to another and to other concepts, by the systematic play of differences." That is why, if I understand him correctly, he introduced the concept of the "trace," to make this implicit chain explicit.

His translator, Gayatri Spivak, defines "trace" as "the radically other within the structure of difference that is the sign." That is, in the system of differences which is Saussure's notion of language, the trace marks the fact that the sign is always half not there. Signifying always involves the other, the non-signified— what is different, differed, or deferred. Hence the trace "is the mark of the absence of a presence, an always already absent present, of the lack at the origin that is the condition of thought and experience." Thought, in other words, depends on Saussure's differences. Therefore, "The trace is in fact the absolute origin of sense in general. Which amounts to saying once again that there is no absolute origin of sense in general. The trace is the *différance* which opens appearance and signification." The trace may not be a signifier as such, but it is what makes signification—and thought itself—possible.

Thus, when Derrida speaks of the limitlessness of language, he has in mind something like Saussure's giant sheet of paper in which differenced signifiers and signifieds—now "traces"— stretch out to infinity. Because the "signified" results from the difference between two signifiers, and they in turn result from their difference from other signifiers, there is no limit to this "system of differences." It has neither end nor beginning ("origin"). The meaning of a sign depends on what the sign *is not*. Hence its meaning is always deferred from the sign itself. Moreover, within a sentence, each word draws some of its meaning from the words that have gone before and the words that come after. And one can detect in any given word or sign, traces of the other signs that it was, so to speak, differenced from. Indeed, it is not just a matter of "one can detect"—this deferral and differencing is a kind of force that drives what Derrida calls the "freeplay" of language.

Derrida's freeplay, however, as Rajnath and John M. Ellis point out, makes a radical extension of Saussure. Derrida follows Saussure in saying that meaning comes from the differences between signifiers. "No element can function as a sign without referring to another element which itself is not simply present." Derrida's "referring," however, goes beyond Saussure's notion of difference, making it more active. Then Derrida goes still further: "This interweaving results in each 'element' . . . being constituted on the basis of the trace within it of the other elements of the chain or system." Again, "trace" goes beyond Saussure's "difference." It is more active, more tangible. It remains present in what is being differenced from. Then Derrida goes from "trace" to "erasure." What is said by the signifier is cancelled out, erased, by the traces. "The sign present is marked by the traces of the signs absent [and that] precludes the possibility of saying anything with finality," is the way Rajnath sums up the position. "The nature of language makes any kind of presence impossible, as the absences, i.e., the traces of the absent signs, keep disrupting it." The traces have become very active indeed, making it impossible to say anything with finality.

In the same way, Derrida posits the supplement. "The movement of signification adds something, which results in the fact that there is always more, but this addition is a floating one because it comes to perform a vicarious function, to supplement a lack on the part of the signified." The very lack, the difference that makes a signifier a signifier, leads to a superabundance. The combination, then, of absence and presence, of erasure and supplement, of subtracting and adding, if I understand them correctly, leads to "freeplay," very loosely put, the idea that anything can mean anything, and nothing can mean anything final.

Now clearly this goes far beyond Saussure. As Ellis points out, it is by substituting the term *play* for Saussure's precise term *differences,* that Derrida "proves" that there are no longer the kind of differences that really define a given sign or word.

> Saussure had said that meaning is created by the opposition of terms, that is, by *specific* differences. Derrida imports into this scheme the word *play,* which immediately says a great deal more, but that word is introduced into his text without any argument for what it suggests; it is introduced casually, as if only a more colorful term were involved. But *play* has already suggested that the mechanism of differentiation is much less controlled and specific than it was before the word was introduced. Having done this, Derrida then completes the movement of his argument with the introduction of "limitless," "indeterminate," and "infinite," now making the implications of *play* quite explicit and taking them to an extreme. This is a very radical new turn in Saussure's argument—and yet Derrida allows his prose to introduce these new terms as if they were simply linguistic flourishes and the expression of an energetic, forceful style—there is no pause to explain why he or we should accept the substance of what is being said."

Actually, I think (*pace* Ellis) that there *is* a kind of justification. Derrida has been assuming all along that the linguistic processes described by Saussure, signification and the differencing of signs, act like forces. If so, then there is no reason for them to stop, and each sign evoked by difference will introduce a new set of differences. But there is no justification for making Saussure's signifiers and differences into forces, and indeed, there is no longer any justification for Saussure's signifiers and differences.

Justification or no, language for Derrida lacks the stability that Saussure found. Saussure's neat pairings of signifier and signified came from a finite system of distinctive features. By contrast, Derrida's signifier and signified go on and on in endless differencing or differing or deferring (all terms involved in Derrida's own word, *différance*). And since our minds only work in signs, and nothing is ever fully present in signs, *everything* becomes flickering and unstable, both present and absent, present and future. It follows therefore that human beings are not the master of language, since the forces of language cannot be mastered. I try to mean, but my meaning is dispersed, divided, at odds with itself. Indeed, *I* myself am one of my meanings, as much a fiction, as little a stable entity as they. In Terry Eagleton's phrasing, "Because language is the very air I breathe, I can never have a pure, unblemished meaning or experience at all."

Wow! With one masterful stroke, Derrida seems to have gotten rid of meaning, structures, categories, and mankind itself. Yet the whole argument rests on the idea of signification. As Eagleton sums the position up, "If the theory of signification . . . is at all valid, then there is something in *writing itself* which finally evades all systems and logics."

But that's the trouble. It is *not* valid. Saussure's is finally a flat earth theory. If we consider only how the hearing and the understanding of a word feel to us, if we only introspect, his account has a certain commonsensical appeal. It *seems* right, just as the horizon *seems* to define a flat earth. A better linguistics, though, and a great deal of psychological evidence show that Saussure's theory leaves out a world of complexities. The text-active model leaves out all of human activity in interpreting language or the world.

So does Derrida. In what follows, he is responding to an interviewer who asked him the pleasantly naive question so often posed to reader-response critics like me. "Do you believe [that any interpretation is as good as any other] and how do you select some interpretations as being better than others?" He replied:

> JD - I am not a pluralist and I would never say that every interpretation is equal but *I* do not select. The interpretations select themselves. . . . I would not say that some interpretations are truer than others. I would say that some are more powerful than others. The

hierarchy is between forces and not between true and false. There are interpretations which account for more meaning and this is the criterion.

[Interviewer:] You would reject then the view that meaning is any response whatever to a sign? that meaning is determined by the person who reads the sign?

JD - Yes, of course. Meaning is determined by a system of forces which is not personal. It does not depend on the subjective identity but on the field of different forces, the conflict of forces, which produce interpretations.

He is making a classic statement of a text-active position. Words are a force. Meaning—what is signified—results from that force. Looked at psychologically, Derrida's new trace is as active as Saussure's old signifier was. Psychologically, they are both committed to a stimulus-response model for our understanding of language.

Nevertheless, Derrida does makes some allowance for the activity of writers and, more surprisingly, readers. Both the writer's writing and our reading involve the *production* of language and meaning.

The writer writes *in* a language and *in* a logic whose proper system, laws, and life his discourse by definition cannot dominate absolutely. He uses them only by letting himself . . . be governed by the system. And the reader must always aim at a certain relationship, unperceived by the writer, between what he [the writer, but also the reader?] commands and what he does not command of the patterns of the language that he uses. This relationship . . . is a signifying structure that critical reading should *produce*.

I take it, Derrida is here drawing on a model of production rather like Saussure's *langue* and *parole*. "The system" of *langue* produces meanings, dominating its writer or reader. But there is a part, *parole,* in which the writer or reader commands.

In this passage Derrida describes what I call a bi-active model, part text-active and part reader-active. Some people call this "interactive," but this "interactive" is not the same as the feedbacks of chapter nine. In Derrida's picture, the text controls part and the reader controls part, but Derrida treats the two parts as independent. Reading produces meaning, but within an already existing process of signifying that is entirely linguistic and has no personal element. That is why this bi-active picture does not meet Chomsky's demand that we think in terms of "rule-governed creativity," because the creativity and the rules have been separated. The writer commands in one part and is commanded in the other. Part of reading (or writing) comes from rules without creativity, part from creativity without rules.

Contrast this version of interaction, this half-action, half-acted-upon, with the feedback interaction of chapters five and nine. There the reader initiates and controls the whole transaction, getting reactions from the text. The text is at all times dependent on the reader's questioning it. At the same time, however, the hearer's understanding, the reader's reading, the writer's writing, or the speaker's speaking can take place *only* by and through the rules described by Chomskyan or post-Chomskyan linguistics. This is what Chomsky means by "rule-governed creativity." It is what I mean when I say that language and the other rules by which we perceive and experience "both enable and limit" us. We *use* codes and canons. Derrida's writer has a much simpler, either-or relation to language. Either the writer commands or does not command (and is therefore commanded by) language.

Nevertheless Derrida's reader, like the New Critics' reader, is expected to do "critical reading" that "should produce" a "signifying structure." I hear the same sort of ethical injunction as I. A. Richards' or Cleanth Brooks' or, for that matter, E. D. Hirsch's demands of the literary critic. Indeed, one of Derrida's acolytes, J. Hillis Miller, makes this requirement explicit. "Texts have a 'plain sense' and . . . the main business of criticism is to identify this. We 'deconstructionists' have said that over and over, both in assertion and practice. . . . Yes, the plain sense is what we are after, believe it or not, though that pursuit, of course, includes identifying and deciphering rhetorical complexities (ironies, for example) in the text in question." To someone trained as a New Critic, as I was, or, for that matter, Miller was, all this seems quite familiar, even old-hat. We are still seeing the structuralist and New Critical assumption of a fixed meaning "in" the text. We are even being told to seek out ironies (which are, of course, "in" the text, not in the eye of the beholder). It is Cleanth Brooks all over again, just as if the last thirty years of linguistics and psycholinguistics had never happened.

Derrida himself, however, goes on to qualify. His kind of reading (as opposed to the American deconstructionists') does not get at any "truth" in or about the text, since there are no such things as "plain sense." Neither does his kind of reading duplicate the text by eliciting the author's intention, since that intention does not determine the text. Nor does the critical reading "transgress the text toward something other than it," toward a reality outside the text. (Except for the first, these are all positions parallel to those taken long ago by New Critics.)

At this point in Derrida's reasoning, it seems to me, he is very close to what the cognitive scientists find. One cannot make claims of absolute truth, communication, or verisimilitude, because the truth or message or reality appealed to is itself the result of interpretation. In other words, the cognitive scientists come to the same conclusion as Derrida, but for a different reason. I do not mean simply that they rely on experiment and evidence, he on philosophizing. In addition, the cognitive scientists would say that we can never know anything *except by our own processes of cognition.* It is in this sense that all reality is symbolic reality.

This is a widely accepted, I would even say commonplace, intellectual position in the latter half of the twentieth century. One name for it is "symbolic realism," as developed for example, by the sociologist R. H. Brown:

> We cannot know what reality is in any absolute or objectivist fashion; instead, all we can know is our symbolic constructions, the symbolic realities that are defined by our particular paradigms or frames of vision. Symbolic realism is the view that the only realities accessible to us as knowledge are symbolically constructed.

Derrida is making the same point, *but he rests our symbolic constructions, not in our psychological processes of construction, but in the differences, hence the "forces" of language.* It is the nature of writing (conceived first as Saussurean *langue* and then exaggerated), endlessly differing and deferring, that makes the truth, message, or reality uncertain.

Derrida is interestingly close here to the cognitive scientists. One could even analogize from Derrida's "trace" to the infinitesimal error signals required to keep a feedback network active. But Derrida is, finally, very different. He has substituted a rather narrow and limited idea of language for our psychological processes of perception and cognition.

It is at this point in the argument that Derrida delivers his famous dictum: "*Il n'y a pas de hors-texte.*" "There is nothing outside the text." Partly there is nothing outside the text because everything takes place in language. Partly, then, Derrida is simply stating a position like "symbolic realism." He is after bigger game, though.

That bigger game shows most clearly (for me) in his demonstration that there is no real difference between speech and writing. As I understand Derrida in the passage that follows, he says that, in speech no less than in writing, there are (or we identify) certain fixed, stable features (like Saussure's binary differences). We hear a voice saying *aardvark* as different from a voice saying *art park* or *hard part,* because we recognize those features, regardless of the pitch or accent of the speaker. We know, moreover, Derrida says, that these features are invariable; they have "self-identity." They can be "iterated" over and over again, regardless of their (non-existent) origin or any referent pointing to the external world or their putative hearers or readers. We can say *aardvark* in any context including this one (if you could hear me), and you would hear [árd•vark] and understand aardvark. These distinctive features are *differences* or *absences,* built into the difference-system of language (assumed from Saussure). This is how Derrida puts it:

> Let us consider any element of spoken language .... let us say that a certain self-identity of this element (mark, sign, etc.) is required to permit its recognition and repetition. Through empirical variations of tone, voice, etc., possibly of a certain accent, for example, we must be able to recognize the identity, roughly speaking, of a signifying form. Why is this identity paradoxically the division or dissociation of itself, which will make of this phonic sign a grapheme? Because this unity of the signifying form only constitutes itself by virtue of its iterability, by the possibility of its being repeated in the absence not only of its "referent," which is self-evident, but in the absence of a determinate signified or of the intention of actual signification, as well as of all intention of present communication. This structural possibility of being weaned from the referent or from the signified (hence from communication and from its context) seems to me to make every mark, including those which are oral, a grapheme

in general; which is to say, as we have seen, the non-present *remainder* [*restance*] of a differential mark cut off from its putative "production" or origin. And I shall even extend this law to all "experience" in general if it is conceded that there is no experience consisting of *pure* presence but only of chains of differential marks.

It seems to me that Derrida gives here the nub of his thought. Language works as language because it can be repeated. It can be repeated because within it are stable systems of difference, and they are stable regardless of variations of tone, accent, handwriting, and so on, and, more importantly, regardless of intention or reference. These differences are established by the language-system, not by speakers, hearers, readers, or writers. That is why these differences do not depend on the "meaning" or what the word refers to. Then, it is because they are independent of intention or reference, notes Raymond Tallis, that Derrida can claim that "referential discourse is an illusion in so far as language cannot reach out to an *extra-linguistic* reality."

The idea that language or "writing" consists of systems of difference is thus essential to Derrida's argument. These systems are built into every element of language and experience, and any one text takes part in the infinite differencing, interplay, and intertextuality of language in the large. How do we know that? Because language can be re-said and re-understood in any context, any accent, tone, pitch, and so on. As we have read a few paragraphs above, "Every concept is necessarily and essentially inscribed in a chain or system, within which it refers to another and to other concepts, by the systematic play of differences."

Hmmm. Isn't there a logical *non sequitur* here? Does the idea that language can be repeated in any context entail the idea that language cannot refer to or depend upon anything outside itself? That deduction seems to require, as Raymond Tallis points out, another assumption: that all structures or systems are closed. (The central nervous system? Hardly.) Or at least the language system? But isn't that assumption, that language is a closed system, precisely the point at issue? It seems to me that what is to be proved, language cannot reach out to some extra-linguistic reality, has simply and tacitly been assumed.

Then, too, is Derrida empirically correct in insisting that the stable elements of language are differences, remainders, absences, "a differential mark" *in* the language? Only if you believe Saussure with his idea that binary differences sufficiently describe language. If you believe Chomsky, cognitive psychology, or me, it is the codes we use, our rules for making and understanding sentences, that are stable. Words are stable only in that we get appropriate feedback when we apply our stable codes and rules. We learned these codes and rules as children, we took them into our minds, and you and I can communicate because we share those codes and rules. We do not communicate by the mere fact that we share the words you are reading, even if those words were "a differential mark." Merely equipping me with a Latin dictionary does not enable me to read a Latin text. I have to know the codes and rules. The physical words, in this view, become just one part of a continuing, widely shared psychological, and much more complex transaction of sentences.

Think back to some of the examples Chomsky used:

John is too angry to talk to Bill.
John is too angry to talk to.

How would you explain the change in the meaning of in the seven signifiers that begin those sentences by "a system of differences"? You can't. "Signification" is no explanation at all. You have to know other, more subtle rules.

Incidentally, there is another problem with Derrida's argument here, a logical inconsistency that Raymond Tallis points out. If it is true that "there is no experience consisting of *pure* presence but only of chains of differential marks," then how can we perceive the *matière phonique,* the raw phonemes, that in Saussure's system (or any linguistics, I suppose) must precede and underlie the perception of the differences between the phonemes? One has to perceive without differences in order to perceive that the differences are differences, I should think.

But let us, for the sake of the argument, accept Derrida's idea that the only stable features of language are systems of difference. Indeed, for Derrida, they are more than stable. They are *forces.* "Force," he writes in "Force and Signification," "is the other of language without which language would not be what it is." If I understand him correctly, he is claiming that the "other" of language, its arbitrary pairing of differenced signifiers and signifieds to coerce meanings, hence its linking of absence to presence and present to future, is a force. Hence he can write in terms of chains, breaks, ruptures, in general, "violence," when writing about language, because the link between signifier and signified is a force. This is his reason for thinking the text is active.

This force, this activity, is, I believe, what Derrida means when he uses the term "writing." He refers to "writing in general," distinguishing it from writing in ordinary usage, because it is something not reducible to language. By "writing," he means, it seems to me, this peculiar quasi-causality, this arbitrary assignment, that binds signifier to signified, absence to presence, and present to future. It is (in his quasi-Saussurean view) the thing that makes language language. "And thus we say 'writing' for all that gives rise to inscription in general, whether it is literal or not and even if what it distributes in space is alien to the order of the voice: cinematography, choreography, of course, but also pictorial, musical, sculptural 'writing.' "

"If 'writing' signifies inscription and especially the durable institution of a sign (and that is the only irreducible kernel of the concept of writing), writing in general covers the entire field of linguistic signs. . . . The very idea of institution—and hence the arbitrariness of the signs—is unthinkable before the possibility of writing and outside of its horizon." "Institution" here means the establishment of a system of differences in the Saussurean sense. Thus, "writing" (in Derrida's quasi-Saussurean view) is the thing that makes language language. It acts on human beings like a force.

Derrida makes the same mistake as Saussure. He confuses two senses of "meaning." He confuses "meaning" as one element in a formal description of language with "meaning" as a psychological event in somebody's mind.

Like Saussure, Derrida psychologizes language rules. His "force," or its generalized form, "writing," makes explicit the behaviorism that was implicit in Saussure. He makes the signifier-signified link explicitly coercive, a force. Psychologically, this move corresponds exactly to and decisively extends Saussure's stimulus-response model for our understanding of language.

What does the reader do then? As we have seen, for J. Hillis Miller, the reader is supposed to let the forces somehow lead to the "plain sense" (spiced with irony) "in" the text. Derrida's notion of reading is not much more psychological than Miller's. "Although it is not commentary, our idea of reading must be intrinsic and remain within the text." "Text," here, I understand not only as the particular text being read but the presence of both text and commentary in the vast intertextual network of forces. By contrast, the cognitive psychologists find that humans are always already interpreting. Derrida translates that universal act of interpretation into a never-ending interplay of (Saussurean) language.

Gayatri Spivak puts Derrida's idea of reading very simply, "We undo and redo a text." That means, she quotes, "to dismantle the metaphysical and rhetorical structures which are at work in [the text], not in order to reject or discard them, but to reinscribe them in another way." As I understand this definition, Derrida visualizes critical reading as the critic's taking down and rebuilding the writer's structures in the critic's own mental or written interpretation. (Notice the structuralist, Saussurean assumption of fixed, given structures independent of human processes of perception.) Derrida calls this process, "to destroy writing by the writing that is yet reading." Derrida's idea of reading is, then, the production of a text in response to a text. That sounds commonsensical enough. In both these texts, however, and in all texts, Derrida's Saussurean system of language is active over and against the intentions of writer or reader. Hence Derrida can write, " . . . it seems to us in principle impossible to separate, through interpretation or commentary, the signified from the signifier, and thus to destroy writing by the writing that is yet reading . . ." Interpretation cannot violate the fixed relations of signifiers and signifieds.

Actually, however, what Derrida wrote is: "If it seems to us in principle impossible to separate, through interpretation or commentary, the signified from the signifier, and thus to destroy writing by the writing that is yet reading, we nevertheless believe that this impossibility is historically articulated." This means, I take it, that interpretation cannot undo the fixed processes of signification. Nevertheless, people do. People make mistakes. People make mistakes even about significations. In other words, Derrida raises the possibility—even the historical actuality—of some kind of psychological activity that can undo signifier-signified linkages.

Given the idea that signification is a force, I don't see how this could happen, but I cannot find an answer to that psychological problem in Derrida's teaching.

Rather, Derrida insists again and again that he has to keep the idea of signifying as basic to his thought. It seems to me that Derrida is claiming for "writing," the pairing of signifiers with signifieds that he adapts from Saussure, the absolute presence he claims to have gotten rid of. Hence he can speak over and over again of a written sign as having "a force that breaks with its context," a "force of rupture." "Meaning is determined by a system of forces," he said in the interview I have already quoted. These forces, he says, come from language itself and they control persons.

"The person writing is inscribed in a determined textual system." That system is the freeplay of forces rather than Saussure's precise differences. The text, however, remains both active and dominant. Derrida is still thinking in terms of something like the non-entities signifier and signified. At best, Derrida has a bi-active model of reading: readers do some things but texts also do things. Like other bi-active models of reading (*Rezeptionsästhetik,* for example), his model is half text-active, whatever the claims for the reader's activity. It is half wrong therefore.

Language does things—that is (I think) Derrida's ultimate premise. Language or "writing" acts like a force. This principle is his center, his god-term, his claim to truth, however much he may claim to have gotten rid of such things as god-terms, centers, or claims to truth. For Derrida, meaning or reference—he often treats the two as synonymous—implies the signifier-signified process embodied in Saussure's sign. Moreover, by insisting that we *think* this way, he replaces human acts of interpretation with signification. He adopts Saussure's dictionary-in-the-head. He has rested his entire argument on an outmoded and discredited linguistics and a rather simple-minded behaviorist view of language and the human being.

                                           •

If I claim to have identified Derrida's god-term, I should own up to my own. I rest my thinking on on the general idea that we construct reality by trying out hypotheses against the "out there." I do not wish, though, to commit the postmodern sin of making the self a "transcendent signifier" (in the jargon of deconstructionism). I am not suggesting an autonomous self. I rely on this process as a whole—not any one of its elements or details. Even though an identity governs the feedback, it is also the result of the feedback. (That is, after all, what feedback is.)

This process (as described in chapter nine) is, the psychologists tell us, how we perceive and know the world or language. It is how we assess truth. This claim does not force us into the familiar dichotomy, that either we are "objectively" constrained by the world (or reality or texts), or it is all "subjective," or it is half-and-half. Rather, we are, in the language of Lakoff and Johnson, experiential. Or, in my own term, *transactive*. All we can be sure of is the process of knowing, not its product. We use language and other symbolic processes to perceive, to know, to interpret, to understand.

No philosopher myself, I would appeal to Hilary Putnam here. He defines a truth that could suit Derrida in that it does not require an objectivity, some "God's eye" view of things. But it would not suit Derrida in that it appeals to such humanly based ideas as coherence or fit (instead of the system of ordained and arbitrary differences Saussure posited for language):

> What makes a statement, or a whole system of statements—a theory or a conceptual scheme—rationally acceptable is, in large part, its coherence and fit; coherence of "theoretical" or less experiential beliefs with one another and with more experiential beliefs, and also coherence of experiential beliefs with theoretical beliefs. Our conceptions of coherence and acceptability are . . . deeply interwoven with our psychology. They depend upon our biology and our culture; they are by no means "value free." But they *are* our conceptions, and they are conceptions of something real. They define a kind of objectivity, *objectivity for us,* even if it is not the metaphysical objectivity of the God's Eye view.

In this, his conclusion to "Putnam's theorem," a disproof of "objective" claims, Putnam acknowledges that our idea of truth is a humanly based one. Mark Johnson sums up Putnam's position this way: "Objectivity does not require taking up God's perspective, which is impossible; rather, it requires taking up appropriately shared human perspectives that are tied to reality through our embodied imaginative understanding." We humans, after all, do have an idea of truth, something Derrida seems to deny. We act on it every time we cross the street. Similarly we believe texts can convey stable meanings. We act on that belief every time we have a prescription filled. (I suppose that is another way of saying literary theory needs a dose of common sense.)

What Putnam has done is bring to bear on a philosophical issue the new knowledge from cognitive science. (I had better admit right away, to pacify my Derridian friends, that that knowledge is, of course, based in cognitive science itself. There is no sensing or knowing things outside our own processes of cognition—a basic principle of cognitive science.) By doing so, by accepting the limitations of human thought, Putnam builds a stronger philosophy.

Derrida, by contrast, is asking philosophy to do what it cannot: "prove" truths about reality. He and many other "theorists" are trying to use philosophy to impose answers on questions that can really be answered only by a psychology. Historically, when philosophy runs up against science, philosophy loses. Think of the bishops who refused to look through Galileo's telescope. Or Hegel's proving by logic that there can be no more than seven planets. History, I think, will find Derrida's heavy reliance on behaviorist psychology and Saussure's false idea of signifying differences another example. (Yes, I can say "false," meaning that I have tested the idea against the real world, and it failed.)

These are grand and philosophical issues, however. I do not wish to lose my argument in their mazy intricacies. I am I-ing contemporary literary theorists who make the I disappear. Derrida is only the most obvious of these prestidigitorial theorists.

Vanishing the I

For most of us, "to vanish" is an intransitive verb. For magicians, however, it is transitive ("How to vanish a handkerchief"). It should be transitive for literary theorists, too, at least so far as the I is concerned. Intelligent theorists are claiming that there are no individuals at all, no I's. How was the trick accomplished? How did we get from Saussure's deliberately unpsychological account of meaning to a psychological conclusion, that the I has disappeared?

We can see the sleight-of-hand in this passage by Jonathan Culler:

> What does the pursuit of signs [sic] have to do with the disappearance of man? A whole tradition of thought treats man as essentially a thinking being, a conscious subject who endows objects around him with meaning. Indeed, we often think of the meaning of an expression as what the subject or speaker 'has in mind.' But as meaning is explained in terms of systems of signs—systems which the subject does not control—the subject is deprived of his role as source of meaning. I know a language, certainly, but since I need a linguist to tell me what it is that I know, the status and nature of the 'I' which knows is called into question . . . Although they

[the human sciences] begin by making man an object of knowledge, these disciplines find, as their work advances, that the self is dissolved as its various functions are ascribed to impersonal systems which operate through it."

I see three confusions in this passage.

First, because I cannot explain the workings of the tools that I use, does it follow that my I is called into question? If, for example, I do not understand the working of my hip, if I have to ask an orthopedist to find out what it is I am walking on, does it follow that *I* am called into question? Arithmetic. How many of us could explain the workings of arithmetic? Yet we do sums daily without disappearing. In short, Culler's claim that the incompleteness of our knowledge of linguistics calls the self into question is a simple, old-fashioned *non sequitur.*

Second, even if the self were called into question, does it then "dissolve"? Another *non sequitur.* Surely the self is a very problematic concept, "systematically elusive" in my chapter nine model. Merely questioning it, however, does not make it disappear. Otherwise, like one of these theory-magicians, I would have by this time made all kinds of theorists vanish. In short, even if signifiers signified, even if the process of signifying worked the way Culler and others seem to think, it simply does not follow that the self disappears.

More interesting, though, is Culler's third error. He renders as either-or what may be—I think is—simply both-and. *Either* I am an individual subject *or* I am the result of systems of convention. *Either* I operate through language *or* language operates through me. *Either* I control language *or* language controls me. And if language controls me, I don't exist.

Raymond Tallis sums up the argument as it appears in Derrida's writing:

If the signs I use do not originate with me and if I do not explicitly intend all the conventions and, indeed, all the utterance-conditions, that make meanings possible, then I am not present in my act. Since what I say to some degree escapes my control, exceeding or falling short of any formulated or formulable signifying intention, since it is not inwardly lit through and through by such an intention, I cannot be said to have intended the meaning of my utterance.

Granted, Tallis is a hostile critic, yet it seems to me an accurate summary of the argument as we have seen it in Derrida. Moreover, we shall see the same thesis in several more New Cryptics. Culler is only one example.

Yet we have seen in chapter nine (and my *The I* of 1985 presents in more detail) a rather simple feedback model derived from combining a psychoanalytic idea of identity with cognitive science. Such a model quite avoids Culler's or Derrida's either-or error. I *use* codes. They both enable and limit me. I cannot speak without them. I cannot speak except in their language. In that sense, they "speak through" me. Yet in no sense need we assume that they make the I disappear. Just the opposite. The codes demand an I to run them.

The assumption that codes rule out the existence of the person comes from the Saussurean notion that signifying takes place untouched by human hands (or minds). As we have seen with Derrida, his idea that there is no unmediated, unconstructed language or perception corresponds to the cognitive scientists'. But Derrida situates the act of construction in language itself. He thus drops the person out of the transaction, not as a result of reasoning, *but because it was assumed from the very first.* Culler and Derrida just took over Saussure's premise that the person did not enter into the understanding of language. What Miller, Culler, Derrida, and others assert as conclusion, then, is not a conclusion at all. It was posited from the outset, without evidence or reasoning, just on Saussure's say-so.

In another passage, Culler again spells out this either-or trap, either person or language:

> On the one hand, language seems the realm or medium in which consciousness can truly produce events, display its freedom in creative acts of origination. Language thus seems the realm of fresh starts and discontinuity. But, on the other hand, language is the realm of structures always already in place ... Creative acts of imagination, like the sudden flowering of a plant, turn out to depend on and be limited by structures already in place; and linguistic creations ... function outside the control of an originating consciousness. Note that one cannot resolve this problem by seeking a compromise, in which linguistic structures are said to make possible a limited creativity and freedom—as if it were possible to divide

language into what is free and what is determined. This is impossible, because the most common, banal, or resilient structures must have been produced, must once have been singular and creative events, while, on the other hand, the most radical creative acts turn out to be determined in various ways and to develop according to laws which are not the intentions of their "creators."

Culler asserts that because language is already in place it cannot also be something I can be creative with. Instead of taking the obvious move of saying I *use* language, he creates a bogus issue. *Either* language is free *or* language is determined. He then forces that false issue to a false conclusion: "Linguistic creations . . . function outside the control of an originating consciousness." Culler would find himself in the odd position of having to say Shakespeare was not original—he did not create anything—because his language existed as a determining code before he did.

We can watch Vincent Leitch making the same set of moves, more dramatically phrased. His active text is an invader who causes an implosion:

> Within the reader-subject resides a multiplicity of texts and codes, and this "resource" effectively rules out any conception of the reader-text transaction as a simple relation of subjectivity to objectivity. The invasions of intertextuality into the self of the reader disintegrate that enclosed self. The borders collapse, producing a disorienting complicity. The *reader* like the text, is unstable. . . . Essentially, deconstruction regards the subject as an effect of language. The "ego," a rational formulation, emerges out of a play of signifiers.

Either reading consists of some sort of a pristine, virginal *tabula rasa* subject reading an object that consists of various codes *or* there are codes in the subject as well. If there are codes in the subject, then, abracadabra, there is no subject at all!

25

Barthes

Vincent Leitch bases his vanishing of the I largely on quotations from Roland Barthes, especially his autobiography, and we have already seen how the semiotic Barthes dissolves the self in codes by the same neo-Saussurean strategy that Derrida, Culler, and Leitch use (pp. 117–118. Barthes was, however, a very various writer who went through many different phases and intellectual systems. At one point he even proposed breaking with the Saussurean model. "It is necessary to take the struggle further, to attempt to split, not signs, not signifiers on one side and signifieds on the other, but the very idea of the sign: an operation one might call a semioclasty. It is Western discourse as such, in its foundations, its elementary forms, that one must today attempt to split." But (in this very text where he proposes splitting the idea of the sign):

> The text liquidates all metalanguage . . . . The text destroys utterly, *to the point of contradiction,* its own discursive category, its sociolinguistic reference . . . . The text can, if it wants, attack the canonical structures of the language itself . . . lexicon (exuberant neologisms,

portmanteau words, transliterations), syntax (no more logical cell, no more sentence).

Barthes seems to have in mind authors like James Joyce or Lewis Carroll. He could have written that they challenge language by wrenching meanings and syntax. He gets a jazzier paragraph by resorting to the old Saussurean active text, always guaranteed to deliver a paradox. Here it is a text that seems almost to be having a tantrum, while the ebullient author has vanished.

And the reader? The reader, says Barthes, could be compared to an idle stroller walking along the side of a valley, imagining nothing, but being bombarded by lights, colors, bird calls from the other side of the valley, children's cries. These "proceed from known codes" but they are unique, "founding the stroll in difference that can be repeated only as difference," as the text re-creates itself in infinitely many different ways. "The Text is plural . . . not coexistence of meanings but passage, traversal; thus it answers not to an interpretation, liberal though it may be, but to an explosion, a dissemination." For all the excitement, though, Barthes has not come very far from Saussure's active text. In practice, Barthes never gets beyond the process of signifying, and his reader is simply a creature of stimuli.

In a late writing (from which all my subsequent quotations come), Barthes yet again approaches the relation of the interpreter to the text. Again, it is the text that does the work. "The text is a signifying practice . . . by means of which the meeting between subject and language is produced . . . . What is a signifying practice? It is first of all a differentiated signifying system, dependent on a typology of significations . . ." We are back to Saussure, and Barthes brings in the Prague School as well with several references to Jakobson. He rejects "interpretative criticism, which seeks to demonstrate that the text possesses a total and secret signified." That is, he rejects structuralist or "New" criticism, because, "The text is treated as if it were the repository of an objective signification, and this signification appears as embalmed in the work-as-product."

By contrast, the reading that Barthes advocates is livelier. At least it escapes embalming, because it proceeds, not from traditional "signification," but from "signifiance":

> When the text is read (or written) as a mobile play of signifiers, with no possible reference to one or several fixed signifieds, it becomes necessary to distinguish carefully between signification, which belongs to the level of the product, of the statement, of communication, and the signifying work, which belongs to the level of production, enunciation, symbolisation: it is this work that we call the "signifiance."

The crucial discovery that Barthes has made seems to be that texts can have multiple meanings. This idea, as I remember, was not unknown to the old New Critics, although I doubt they would have phrased their idea of the text as Barthes does: "a polysemic space where the paths of several possible meanings intersect."

Nevertheless Barthes regards his approach as a radical change. "Signification is produced not at the level of an abstraction (*langue*), as postulated by Saussure, but through an operation, a labour . . ."

Now we have seen just such a labor, when Agnes, Ted, and Norm talked about *The Story of O*. How close and yet how far is Barthes' description from what we saw.

> The notion of signifying practice restores to language its active energy; but the act which it implies is not an act of understanding . . . the subject no longer has the fine unity of the Cartesian 'cogito'; it is a plural subject, which so far only psychoanalysis has been able to approach.

Aha! We may be getting to Agnes' concern with place or Ted's with domination. But no such luck. The text is doing all the work.

> The text is a productivity . . . . the very theatre of a production where the producer and reader of the text meet: the text 'works,' at each moment and from whatever side one takes it. Even when written (fixed), it does not stop working, maintaining a process of production. The text works what? Language. it deconstructs the language of communication, representation, or expression (where the individual or collective subject may have the illusion that he is imitating something or expressing himself) and reconstructs another language, voluminous, having neither bottom nor surface, for its space is not that of the figure, the painting, the frame, but the stereographic space of the combinative play . . .

And what of the reader? Barthes here does a curious turn.

We glimpse the reader at work or, more properly, play, arriving at personal, "ludic" readings. But as soon as we get a peek, Barthes whisks the reader away. We had just entered stereographic space:

> Productivity is triggered off, the redistribution is carried out, the text comes about, as soon as, for example, the scriptor and/or the reader begin to play with the signifier, either (in the case of the author) by ceaselessly producing 'word-plays,' or (in the case of the reader) by inventing ludic meanings, even if the author of the text had not foreseen them, and even if it was historically impossible for him to foresee them: the signifier belongs to everybody; it is the text which, in fact, works tirelessly, not the artist or the consumer.

And the writer and reader disappear again, as the all-powerful text takes over.

There is, it seems to me, a failure of imagination here, astonishing in a writer as original as Barthes. Why cannot he turn his mind around to the idea of the reader's creativity rather than the abstract creativity of language? Why attribute Agnes' interest in places or Norm's in rules to the film? Why not acknowledge and enjoy their readerly creativity?

I am told, by friends more sympathetic than I to theorizing like Barthes', that there is a historical reason. The idea of the subject made thinkers of Barthes' generation uneasy. After the undistinguished performance of most French people during World War II, postwar existentialists like Sartre, Camus, or de Beauvoir laid a heavy weight of responsibility on the individual. Work like Barthes' tries to vanish that postwar guilt by vanishing the individual. Hence, Barthes can refer sarcastically to "the ego-cogito" or "the fine unity of the Cartesian 'cogito.' " Individuals are not coherent, responsible beings, but blameless creatures of circumstance: social, linguistic, or philosophical structures. Hence Barthes can convert individual readers like Agnes, Ted, and Norm or, for that matter, authors like Joyce or Carroll, into nonentities. Their readings and writings really come from an activity of the text.

Whether that decades-old guilt is what drives the New Cryptics, I do not know the French intellectual scene well enough to judge. It is clear though, that for Barthes and for many other literary theorists, as we are seeing, language is the only reality.

The subject disappears. The idea of individual acts and responsibilities has become a bourgeois, capitalistic, reactionary fiction. Instead, language does it all, wonderful, playful, irrepressible, above all, innocent language:

> 'Signifiance' invokes the idea of an infinite labour (of the signifier upon itself) . . .
>
> 'Signifiance' is 'the without-endness of the possible operations in a given field of language.'
>
> 'Signifiance,' which is the text at work . . . . the glow, the unpredictable flash of the infinities of language—is at all the levels of the work without distinction: in the sounds, which are thus no longer considered as units meant to determine the meaning (phonemes) but as drive-movements; in the monemes [words?], which are not so much semantic units as networks of associations, produced by connotation, by latent polysemy, in a generalised metonymy . . .

Jakobson again. Saussure again. The active text again. Ho-hum.

Foucault

Foucault is most widely cited in literary circles for his vigorous assertion of "the death of the author" and the author's replacement by an "author-function."

> These aspects of an individual which we designate as making him an author are only a projection, in more or less psychologizing terms, of the operations that we force texts to undergo, the connections that we make, the traits that we establish as pertinent, the continuities that we recognize, or the exclusions that we practice.

In other words, we do not know an author immediately. We construct an author. Moreover, we construct him or her in such a way as to justify our own critical practice.

This was standard ideology for the old New Critics, although quite differently expressed. One should study the literary text, not its author, they asserted. If one did speak of an author, the individual involved was an interpretation of a text, either the work of literature or the biographical texts. Such an author could neither justify nor refute any interpretation of the literary text directly. No claim was made that "the author is dead," to be sure, but the idea is much the same as Foucault's. Indeed Foucault himself acknowledges that the author's disappearance has been a constantly recurring event since the death of Mallarmé, whom Foucault regarded as the inventor of pure "literature," in 1898.

Although many modern theorists parrot striking phrases like "the death of the author" or "the disappearance of the subject," Foucault's own phrasings are quite reasonable. Indeed, they match the model of chapter nine. One constructs an author by testing hypotheses against what we know. Whether our construction feels right will depend in part on whether that construction fits with other hypotheses of ours, notably our critical practice.

"The author does not precede the works," writes Foucault, "he is a certain functional principle by which, in our culture, one limits, excludes, and chooses; in short, by which one impedes the free circulation, the free manipulation, the free composition, decomposition, and recomposition of fiction." "The author is the principle of thrift in the proliferation of meaning."

To the existing versions of this idea, Foucault adds, as one would expect, politics. "The author-function is therefore characteristic of the mode of existence, circulation and functioning of certain discourses within a society." Again, that seems perfectly reasonable and sensible.

What seems less so is Foucault's underlying justification for replacing an author by an author-function. Foucault is a theorist of a very different stripe from either Barthes or Derrida, but he, too, relies on the idea of signifying to force a dichotomy between humanity and language:

> For the entire modern *episteme* . . . that which constituted man's particular mode of being and the possibility of knowing him empirically—that entire *episteme* was bound up with the disappearance of Discourse . . . If this same language is now emerging with greater and greater insistence . . . is this not the sign that the whole of this configuration is now about to topple, and that man is in the process of perishing as the being of language continues to shine ever brighter upon our horizon? Since man was constituted at a time when language was doomed to dispersion, will he not be dispersed when language regains its unity? . . . Ought we not to admit that, since language is here once more, man will return to that serene nonexistence in which he was formerly maintained by the imperious unity of Discourse?

My aim, one of them, in this book is I-ing such statements. That is, what are they saying about the I? And what do we find out when we read such statements as this of Foucault against the model I proposed in chapter nine?

So far as the I is concerned, I hear Foucault arriving in a cloud of Wagnerian gloom at a kind of Twilight of the Human. Then, if I listen to this statement, holding the model of chapter nine in my mind in the way that one uses codes to see a film, I can see why. Foucault based his vanishing of the human on no more than a linguistic assumption that language insists or shines or, in general, does things on its own. Language has an "imperious unity" that makes the human being unnecessary. In this passage, Foucault makes, in his highly individual way, the same false move as Derrida, Culler, or Barthes.

That is, he assumes that either "language is here" or man is. He is making the Saussurean assumption in yet another form, more abstractly. Where Saussure wrote of specific phonemes and signs, Foucault deals with humanity in the large and Discourse with a capital D. Nevertheless, he creates a spurious either-or. Either language has "being" or man does. Why not both? Why are we presented with an either-or, man or discourse, instead of a both-and? That is one of the mysteries of French intellectual life.

"Some of this antagonism to the knowing subject is merely typical of Parisian discussions of the day," writes Ian Hacking, one expert on Foucault. Another, David Hoy, speaks of Foucault's "linguistic nominalism." He gave it up after *les événements,* the student riots in Paris in 1968 that nearly toppled the government. He turned instead to what he called power/knowledge as his central topic. Still others studying Foucault, like Richard Rorty, Hubert Dreyfus, and Paul Rabinow, regard his separation of discourse from man as an aberration, which he retracted in *Surveiller et punir* (1975). He learned from his mistakes, they say, as he followed his central themes: how human beings constitute themselves as subjects; how they treat one another as objects; ultimately, how the individual is supposed to constitute himself as a moral subject of his own action. Good for Foucault. He rescued the I from the death-grip of Saussure's linguistics.

Eco

Foucault rescued the I. Others have thrown the I back into the sea of intertextuality, even those far from the rarefied emptinesses of deconstructionism. Consider, for example, a leader in semiotics. Consider Umberto Eco's way of dealing with the I who hears the semioticist's signs.

> The 'ideal' reader of *Finnegans Wake* cannot be a Greek reader of the second century B.C or an illiterate man of Aran. The reader is strictly defined by the lexical and the syntactical organization of the text: the text is nothing else but the semantic-pragmatic production of its own Model Reader.

Notice, in that paragraph, how Eco slides back and forth from the ideal reader to the actual Greek or Scot. He could have phrased it this way: a Greek reader of the second century B.C. or an illiterate man of Aran would not have the codes for reading *Finnegans Wake*. Or he could have said: a reader needs to develop special codes for reading *Finnegans Wake*. Instead, Eco submits to the idea of the active, governing text. He has the text create the reader it requires. "We have seen that even the more 'open' among experimental texts direct their own free interpretation and preestablish the movement of their Model Reader."

Like the others, Eco rests on Saussure's anti-psychological premises. More specifically, Eco combines Saussure with Louis Hjelmslev. He converts Saussure's piece of paper with differences between signifiers on one side and differences between signifieds on the other into units of

> the *expression plane,* which is correlated (by a code) to units of a *content plane,* in which another system of oppositions has made pertinent certain (semantic) units, through which a given culture 'thinks' and communicates the undifferentiated continuum which is the world. The sign therefore is the correlation, the function which unites two 'functives,' expression and content.

We are back to the Saussurean process of signifying cast in slightly different language.

Eco's model is, like Derrida's, a "bi-active" model. It purports to be a compromise between "text-active" and "reader-active." That is, you could assume that the text governs its own reading. That was, more or less, what the New Critics and Saussure did, although the assumption is, in this pure form, untenable as an account of actual reading. Such a "text-active" model would determine response down even to such variations as Agnes' preoccupation with place. That really makes very little sense (although it seems to be held by Roland Barthes). Alternatively, you could assume the model I suggest in chapter nine, which makes the reader the active one. Or you could compromise as Eco and most critics of today do, saying the text acts in some respects but leaves the reader free to act in others.

Eco puts his compromise this way: "A responsible collaboration is demanded of the addressee. He must intervene to fill up semantic gaps, to reduce or to further complicate the multiple readings proposed," and so on. "Responsible" expresses the familiar ethical demands of New and other traditional critics. Then, within the control of the text, "The reader finds his freedom (i) in deciding how to activate one or another of the textual levels and (ii) in choosing which codes to apply." This seems vaguely like the model of chapter nine. Later, however, he writes, "The aesthetic text becomes a multiple source of *unpredictable* 'speech acts' whose real author remains undetermined, sometimes being the sender of the message, at others the addressee who collaborates in its development."

The model is "bi-active." It looks like a compromise, but it isn't. To be sure, to the extent Eco's model treats the reader as active, it seems to me correct. To the extent the model treats the text as active, it entails the contradictions of Saussure's linguistics. To the extent it rests on Saussure's active text it fails for the same reasons that Derrida's model fails. Half-right and half-wrong, it is not right and no compromise.

What Eco believes he gains is, precisely, an escape from psychology (like Saussure). One gives up meaning as such so as not to fall "into a mentalistic or psychologistic theory." He questions and rejects meaning as "what 'travels' within the head of an interpreter." One cannot check such an event (he claims). He questions and rejects meaning as reference to the world or as observable behavior (as I would).

Eco therefore turns to C. S. Peirce's concept of the "interpretant." An interpretant is the "testable and describable" correspondent the public assigns to a certain sign. Thus any picture of a dog, be it anatomical diagram or comic strip, would be an interpretant of "dog." Eco gives the Rosetta stone as an example: the Greek text is the interpretant for the hieroglyphic, and there are many interpretants in many modern languages for the Greek text. Notice, though, that Champollion has dropped out of the picture. Eco writes as though the Rosetta Stone did all the work without any egyptologist.

Eco melds the Saussurean idea of a signifier linked to a signified with Peirce's idea of an "expression" (or "representamen," a cultural object) linked to its "interpretants," the latter "equated with any coded intentional property of the content." All this is very like the old-fashioned signified. "A given culture displays, in any of its activities, accepted correlations between representamens (or expressions), each becoming in turn the interpretant of the other."

All this then leads to a way of interpreting signs. "In order to establish what the interpretant of a sign is, it is necessary to name it by means of another sign which in turn has another interpretant to be named by another sign and so on. At this point there begins a process of *unlimited semiosis*." As is common in this line of reasoning (very like Derrida's), passives like "to be named" elide whoever is doing the naming. "Semiosis explains itself by itself: this continual circularity is the normal condition of signification." By making "signification" purely the activity of signs or a quite unverified "public agreement" (that is, Saussurean *langue*), one drops out of the picture the real audience of Agnes, Ted, and Norm. The analysis of meaning becomes completely non-psychological.

Eco has arrived at that favorite picture for the 1980s, a signifier (or "representamen" or "interpretant") that leads to another signifier that leads to another signifier and so on and on, never coming to rest in any signified or meaning. It is very like Derrida's endless play of language. It is very like Swift's little rhyme about the fleas that have fleas "smaller still to bite 'em / And so proceed *ad infinitum*." As always in these maneuvers, the psychology of the intender or the interpreter has been replaced by what the philosopher, critic, or semioticist is good at and feels more comfortable with: texts.

In "unlimited semiosis" and "continual circularity," Eco has achieved another result that is highly gratifying for semioticists and for literary critics. They are now guaranteed employment for centuries to come. Whatever the psychology of response or meaning is, we need not concern ourselves with *that*. We can go from "cultural product" to cultural product—texts—merrily analyzing away. We need never have to trouble ourselves with the real world to which people refer those cultural objects or the psychology of those minds to which "content" finally travels.

Further—at least I believe this follows from Eco's picture—the semioticist simply points to all these interpretations as observable facts. What another school of criticism would call the critic's interpretation, semiotics promotes to a code that binds us all. The semiotician's interpretations become invulnerable, exempt from the psychological processes to which lesser beings are subject. At least this is the impression I get from some semiotic practice.

Eco set out to de-psychologize the process of meaning, and he did just that. For all the complexities and subtleties of his semiotics, however, Eco has really gone very little beyond the old Saussurean idea of the signifying text.

His whole rejection of psychology reminds me of an unfortunate passage by Tzvetan Todorov. In it Todorov justifies studying reading through the representations in a nineteenth-century novel of the characters' constructions of one another. "One of the difficulties in studying reading is . . . that reading is so hard to observe: introspection is uncertain, psycho-sociological investigation is tedious. It is therefore with a kind of relief that we find the work of construction represented in fiction itself, a much more convenient place for study." What an extraordinary piece of intellectualizing! Suppose we were talking about smoking. "Sociomedical investigation is tedious. Doing experiments over and over is a bore. It is therefore with a kind of relief that we find a fictional account of the practice." Is not reading as real a thing as smoking? And to be investigated as realistically?

In fact, of course, there are simple textbooks in the psychology of reading, dozens of them. The literature on the psychology of reading is very large but, so far as I can see, it rests in recent years wholly on the concept of feedback or even more precisely defined processes applied by an active reader. But Eco and other New Cryptics shy away from readily available psychologies of reading to assume a bi-active, really a text-active, model.

28

Iser

I have suggested that the reader-response critics avoid the errors of Eco and the others. Reader-response critics do not make the mistake of assuming the text *does* things on its own. But is that entirely true? Consider Wolfgang Iser who is the leading theorist of *Rezeptionsästhetik,* the German version of reader-response theory. Iser offers a very different theory of reading from Eco's. But it is very different from mine too, although we both consider ourselves "reader-response critics." Unlike me (and other American reader-response critics), Iser is not concerned with individuals like Agnes, Ted, and Norm. Unlike Eco he is concerned not so much with codes as with texts—and readers.

For Iser, text and reader have a "dialectic" or "dynamic" relation. That is, a given reading results partly from action by the text, partly from action by the reader. The text constitutes a series of instructions to its readers as to how to realize the text. "Texts must already contain certain conditions of actualization that will allow their meaning to be assembled in the responsive mind of the recipient." The text has "a network of response-inviting structures, which impel the reader to grasp the text." Then the reader actualizes the text by obeying those instructions.

Iser deals with the problem of an uncooperative reader by saying that he is talking about an ideal reader. The vagaries of any actual reader are no affair of his, although "The reader's own disposition will never disappear totally; it will tend instead to form the background to and a frame of reference of the act of grasping and comprehending." "The structure of the literary text consists of a sequence of schemata—built up by the repertoire and strategies—which have the function of stimulating the reader to constitute the totality of which the schemata are aspects."

Iser writes with a clarity unusual among literary theorists, and his assumptions stand out. Here, he is assuming a uniform pattern of grasping and comprehending for "the" reader, fixed by schemata in the text. Like other theorists of today, he locates in the text the schemata that a psychologist would find in individual readers.

Iser's individual reader has a wandering viewpoint, that is, "a moving viewpoint which travels along *inside* that which it has to apprehend." The text defines an outer limit, so to speak, and the reader then wanders around within that limit, taking now this point of view, now that. The reader can take advantage of the various perspectives the work offers. The reader can bring extra-textual matters to bear. But the reader always works within the instructions or limits provided by the text. Within those limits, there are indeterminacies or blanks or gaps. These the reader is free to fill up, indeed feels called upon to fill up. "The blank in the fictional text induces and guides the reader's constitutive activity." We readers are thus able "to discover an inner world of which we had hitherto not been conscious."

Iser's model is yet another of those that I call bi-active (like Derrida's or Eco's). It purports to be a compromise between text-active (the text controlling) and reader-active (the reader controlling). To the extent it treats the reader as active, it seems to me correct. But Iser's model also treats the text as active. It invites, allows, impels, induces, guides, and so on. Iser's model thus entails the contradictions of Saussure's linguistics (or, in Iser's case, Roman Ingarden's aesthetics). It is half-right and half-wrong and so not right.

It also poses with unusual clarity (compared, say, to Derrida) a problem introduced by bi-active models. Iser's model, like mine of chapter nine, attempts to explain two things. First, why readers share certain perceptions of a text. Second, why readers do not share others. Iser explains both by saying the text controls the ones we share, and we control the ones we don't share. I say we control both. In both personal identity governs, but the responses we share depend more heavily than others on codes and canons we share with others. Even so, in all responses a personal identity applies shared codes and canons.

It seems to me the identity-governing-feedbacks model has an advantage in parsimony. It explains *both* the shared perception of basic features *and* the differences in response from sex, education, class, or personality. "Interaction" (or other claims that some features of response are text-active and some reader-active) requires two different models. That duality leads to a further problem. If there are two modes by which we apprehend texts, what determines which mode is in play at any given moment? What determines the shift? One avoids this problem by looking first at the response, not the text. When you do, you find that even the most elementary responses (to "factual" questions about the text or "plain prose sense") answer to the identity-governing-feedbacks model.

Iser's model is also, like the models of Eco, Barthes, Miller, and company, thoroughly traditional. Iser, writes Stephen Mailloux, "shares with [the New Critics] a belief in interpretive validity guaranteed by constraints in a prior and independent text; and these shared assumptions make Iser's detailed account of reading extremely attractive to traditional literary theorists in America."

29

Fish

Mailloux and I are by no means the only ones to recognize the traditional quality of these bi-active models. Stanley Fish is another. In a strenuous controversy, Fish succeeded in pushing into the foreground Iser's assumption that, regardless of the dialectic between reader and text, certain elements of a text are "given." This is simply the text-active model in a slightly different version.

Iser tried to distinguish the inferences we make with fictions from the inferences we make with everyday life. Fish countered (as I would):

> Perception itself *is* an act of ideation, if by ideation we mean the inferring of a world from a set of assumptions (antecedently held) about what it must be like. To put it another way, mediated access to the world is the only access we ever have; in face to face situations or in the act of reading of a novel, the properties of objects, persons and situations emerge as a consequence of acts of construction that follow (and because they follow they are not, in any simple sense, free) from a prestructured understanding of the shapes any meaningful item could possibly have.

From Fish's point of view, or mine, it is not the text that constitutes or constructs the reader. It is the text that is "constituted" or "constructed" by the reader's ways of doing so. The same holds for everyday experience, according to the psychologists. Fish's position is that we are already embedded in professions, conventions, theories, rules, and the like. Whatever impinges on us, we perceive from the start through those professions, conventions, theories, or rules.

Fish's work in the 1980s therefore took the next and very practical step. Fish went on to consider the professional stances various belief-systems give rise to in literary criticism and in the law. Why do judges decide cases as they do? Why do literary critics interpret as they do? Allying himself with the "critical legal studies" movement, Fish has called his position "anti-foundationalism" or, sometimes, "rhetoric."

Perhaps the best place to start is with what Fish calls "foundationalism." "By foundationalism I mean any attempt to ground inquiry and communication in something more firm and stable than mere belief or unexamined practice." The foundationalist identifies some such ground, bases activities on it, and then claims they are principled or "objective." There are various requirements for such a ground. It must be "invariant across cultures." It must be free of personal or partisan concerns. Indeed, it must constrain them. And it must provide a way knowledge can be verified. Such grounds have included God, the material world, rationality, logic, eternal values, and the autonomous self.

Anti-foundationalism is, naturally enough, the opposite. "Questions of fact, truth, correctness, validity, and clarity can neither be posed nor answered in reference to some extracontextual, ahistorical, nonsituational reality, or rule, or law, or value." One can debate such questions only within the contexts or communities "that give them their local and changeable shape." We still name things like the world, language, and the self. We still assert various facts and values about them. But these things and what we say about them are inextricably entwined with the procedures we apply for understanding them and the communities and contexts in which we apply the procedures. Foundationalists claim to have found grounds, but in every case—and Fish is nothing if not down-to-earth—they turn out to be "functions of the local, the historical, the contingent, the variable, and the rhetorical." We have seen this relativizing, for example, with the "ground" of "meaning." It turns out to be Saussure's limited idea of signifying. (And someday my reliance on Chomsky's proofs, feedback, or constructive psychology will seem just as limited, although there is no way to know now what those limitations will turn out to be.)

Fish acknowledges various fears that his relativism arouses. But, he points out, anti-foundationalism is not an argument for unbridled subjectivity, for the absence of constraints on the individual. Just the opposite. "It is an argument for the situated subject, for the individual who is always constrained by the local or community standards and criteria of which his judgment is an extension."

By the same token, anti-foundationalism does not imply that texts can mean just anything at all. Nor that the text has "vanished." Nor that communication is impossible. Fish recognizes that these and other confused or spurious accounts of reader-response theory are simply unjustified fears. More exactly, they rest on a faith in "meaning" as one of the foundationalist absolutes that anti-foundationalists show again and again are relative.

> Literal meaning is not more stable (in the sense of being unchanging) than interpretations it supposedly authorizes. Literal meaning, rather than being independent of perspective, is a product of perspective (it is the meaning that, given a perspective, will immediately emerge); it is itself an interpretation and cannot therefore be the indisputable ground on which subsequent interpretations securely rest.

The same argument applies to the supposed power of the text to control response. Critics like Iser or Miller call on "grounds" like the "ethics of reading" or "constraints" to prevent readers from reading anything at all "into" a text. Yet these ethics or constraints are in the reader, not the text. It is not in human nature to have desires without constraints. The very desires that might lead someone to read "into" a text carry with them constraints on reading. The claim that there are no independent constraints and no literal meaning thus leads to a paradox. "Rather than leaving us in a world where the brakes are off, it situates us in a world where the brakes—in the form of the imperatives, urgencies, and prohibitions that come along with any point of view (and being in a point of view is not something one can avoid)— are always and already on."

"Does this mean, then, that we can never say 'what really happened'?" (This is a question constantly asked reader-response critics like me.) "Not at all," replies Fish. "Every description and account . . . is an attempt to say what really happened." But if someone disagrees with such a description, "it will not be contested by some view of the event independent of description but by a competing description." People will decide which is the better (more correct) description according to the norms and procedures "understood by the community to be appropriate to the determination of empirical fact." One could put that another way. Descriptions and hypotheses are not defeated by facts, but by other descriptions and hypotheses. Confusion arises

> only when one thinks that by "what really happened" is meant "what really happened after all the competing descriptions have been discounted or set aside?" But it's hard even to give *that* question a sense, since the fact of what happened, like any other fact, can only be said to exist relative to some characterization or description.

Fish summarizes his position this way. Anti-foundationalism "offers you nothing but the assurance that what it is unable to give you—knowledge, goals, purposes, strategies—is what you already have. And come to think of it, that may be an offer you can't refuse."

I have quoted and paraphrased Fish without commenting very much on his position. The reason is that in these statements, notably in that last splendidly Fishy paradox, as in many another, I find the views of Stanley Fish totally in harmony with my own. I write about individuals like Agnes, Ted, and Norm. I assume, often without writing much about it, that these individuals share cultural or professional ways of reading. Fish writes about professionals sharing cultural or professional ways of reading. He assumes, often without writing much about it, that there are individual styles within those professional norms. These norms (no pun intended!) Fish describes as "interpretive communities." I describe them as "canons" (as in chapter seven). Canons are my way of representing his "interpretive communities" as the schemata of cognitive psychology. I believe our views of reading coincide, although we differ in the way we present them. Fish tends to carry on philosophical argumentation (as with Iser). I resort to psychoanalysis, cognitive psychology, and feedback diagrams. Despite the different frameworks, however, I almost never find a statement by Fish with which I disagree. That, of course, has the unhappy result of leaving me much to applaud but little to say about him in a polemical discussion like this.

Lacan

By contrast, I have a great deal to say about Jacques Lacan. Of all the New Cryptics, Lacan is the most poetic, difficult, tantalizing, and exasperating. Yet, because he is psychoanalytic (as I am), he is the one I most have to I.

He is painfully obscure. Lacan limits his vocabulary to three fields. One, the elements of the oedipal stage: father, mother, phallus, vagina, or castration. Two, words out of the French philosophical stylebook that are emotionless, disembodied, either-or words: possibility, impossibility, absence, presence, lack, or desire (but without a desirer). Three, puns. Lacan delighted in word play, and he was marvelous at it.

In this limited lexicon Lacan discusses neurosis or psychosis (in just those global terms) or hysteria (which is back in fashion in Lacanian circles). One will look in vain to Lacan for the careful distinctions of the psychiatrists' DSM-III (the Diagnostic and Statistical Manual). Absent, too, is the everyday language with which we discuss, no matter how inadequately, love, sexuality, or gender. Instead we get essays that are dramatic, even titillating, but that present a real problem of decoding.

The obscurity of Lacan's language, François Roustang has pointed out, deflects our attention. We wear ourselves out trying to understand what Lacan has said, leaving little energy for assessing its worth. To save my strength in I-ing Lacan, then, I will often gratefully turn to explicators.

Whether we draw on Lacan himself or his explainers, there are three major troubles with Lacan: his linguistics, his psycholinguistics, and his idea of child development. Let me take them one by one.

To I Lacan is to write about Lacan's idea of the self, but for Lacan the self is closely linked to language. His proclaimed "return to Freud" meant remedying Freud's failure to use "modern" linguistics. "Modern" linguistics for Lacan, though, as for the other New Cryptics, means turn-of-the-century linguistics—specifically, Saussure's.

Lacan's most widely quoted dictum is, *The unconscious is structured like a language.* His idea of language rests on two of Saussure's basic principles. One, there is a process of signification in which a signifier generates a signified. Two, the relation between signifier and signified is arbitrary. Social forces determine that relation rather than any intrinsic properties of the words or signs.

Parenthetically, you can see how my problems in understanding Lacan begin right at the beginning. Freud explicitly dropped from his post–1923 thinking an independent system called "the" unconscious. Hence Lacan's account of unconscious processes seems backward to me, like the assumption that signifiers signify. Since I part company with Lacan at the very basis of his thought, I find it hard, impossible really, to trace out the intricate ramifications of his basic premises. Fortunately, to assess Lacan and the I, I can rely on an essay on just that topic by one of the clearest of Lacan's expositors: "Lacan and the Subject of Psychoanalysis" by William J. Richardson.

Lacan, Richardson reports, adopted Saussure's conception of a signifier signifying a signified. Where Saussure dealt with a whole language as two sides of one sheet of paper, however, Lacan returned to the individual sign. He treated it like a fraction that he could split into two parts. The signifier is the numerator, and the signified is the denominator. The two are separated by a bar. For Saussure, this bar indicated the irrational, non-logical, or "arbitrary" social relation between a word and its meaning. Lacan makes the "bar" much more important. He calls it a barrier to any one-to-one relationship between signifier and signified.

Indeed, says Lacan, any given signifier does not refer to some one signified. Rather, the signifier signifies some other signifiers and so on and on (that favorite picture of the New Cryptics). Each signifier refers to another signifier in a sequence or "chain" of signifiers that Lacan describes as being like "rings of a necklace that is a ring in another necklace made of rings." As Lacan says, the signifier slides.

Why does not the signifier signify a signified as with Saussure? Because that is how Lacan renders what he regards as Freud's essential discovery. Free associations have a "latent content." Some part of mental processing is repressed, therefore unconscious, therefore removed from the possibility of being spoken. The *barre* equals repression. A sign (a signified coupled to a given signifier by linguistics) will not, so to speak, tell the whole story. There will be unconscious, therefore unspoken dimensions to what the I who uses the signifier is talking about. As Lacan himself phrases it, "The unconscious is that part of the concrete discourse . . . that is not at the disposal of the subject in reestablishing the continuity of his conscious discourse." Ellie Ragland-Sullivan, in her fine study of Lacan, explains, "Lacan reduces language per se to the signifier and assigns to the signified the task of containing the subjective element in cognition."

We have already seen that Chomsky disproved this conception of language some thirty years ago. Lacan's version of psychoanalysis, however, remains firmly locked into it. That is the first "trouble with Lacan." Lacan goes wrong by relying (quite uncritically!) on Saussure's signifier-signified conception of language. It is understandable that Lacan, when he began to write in the 1930s, should learn Saussure's turn-of-the-century linguistics. But even at the end of his life he—and now his followers—write about signifiers and signifieds as though the Chomskyan revolution in linguistics had never happened.

Lacan apparently recognized that Saussure's model of language was a mere lexicon, for he borrowed from Roman Jakobson to account for sentence production. A sentence has, in effect, two directions: the axis of selection or substitution and the axis of combination or sequence. Lacan approximated Jakobson's metonymy or sequence or "syntagm" to Freud's "condensation." He approximated Jakobson's metaphor or substitution or "paradigm" to Freud's "displacement." Both moves are very approximate—and very old-fashioned. Lacan leaves himself only the image of a "chain" or "the signifying game" to represent our creating sentences.

As for a more powerful linguistics, in 1964 Lacan considered and dismissed Chomsky's 1957 book. Chomsky erred, he said, by "forgetting 'being' and its 'rift' for the sake of confining the subject in grammar." Syntactical linguistics was, he said, "a return to intuitionism." It is characteristic of Lacan to reject Chomsky's work, full of linguistic examples, on the most abstruse of philosophical grounds. He played "the card of Fregean logic, whose importance he had just discovered."

Interestingly, Lacan, in the fall of 1975, on one of his last trips to America, met Chomsky, and Lacan talked about their meeting in one of the last seminars he gave. Characteristically, Lacan took Chomsky's thought at its highest level of abstraction. "Language is itself an organ," is the way Lacan states Chomsky. Obviously, this does not fit Lacan's conception of language (nor is it a very happy statement of Chomsky's. According to their translator, Chomsky had said, "Language *is like* an organ"). In the seminar, Lacan insisted that language could not be an organ, because an organ is an object, and language is not an object but a hole (*un trou*) in the real. Lacan went on to develop topographic relations among the real, the imaginary (the pre-verbal), and the symbolic as a Borromean knot. From Lacan's point of view, because one can treat symptoms by language (in psychoanalysis), the symptom hangs from language (or "the symbolic"). By contrast, according to Lacan, Chomsky confounds the symptom and the real—and this is itself a symptom. "We do not believe in the object as such," he said in this seminar. "And we deny that the object can be seized by any organ . . . which is itself an object." That is how Lacan treats Chomsky's idea of language, as an object that apprehends objects. Their failure to understand each other was total. (So, at least, I was told by their translator on that occasion.) Their meeting left their linguistic positions completely opposed.

•

It will be said—it has been said to me—that this objection of mine to Lacan, that his linguistics is outmoded and false, does not count because Lacan only *uses* Saussure. Saussure is *only a metaphor* in Lacan's thinking. I find this justification unconvincing for two reasons.

First, it does not fit our use of metaphor. When we use a metaphor to understand something, we apply something we understand well to understand something we understand less well. We take an idea from a familiar "source domain" to understand a more puzzling "target domain." If I say "Life is a journey," I use something familiar and obvious, journeys, to understand something more removed and mysterious, life. I can then model difficulties in my life as obstacles in a path, choices as forks in a road, and so on.

This is not what Lacan does when he uses Saussure. He uses a still-mysterious subject, language, to understand a subject that Freud and many others have made relatively understandable, dreams, slips of the tongue, symptoms, and other unconscious processes. Rather than clarify something opaque in psychoanalysis, Lacan has tried to explain the clear by the unclear. That is yet another reason he is so obscure.

Furthermore, his account of his source domain, language, is wrong. What happens to our use of a metaphor to explore an unknown if the source term is an error or an illusion? For example, suppose we assumed, in our metaphor, that journeys are not along roads or toward destinations, but are all up and down, as in elevators. What happens then even to a familiar metaphor like life is a journey? It stops making sense. It does not help us understand life. The same is true of Lacan's use of Saussure. It does not help us understand unconscious processes.

•

In general, the whole question of unconscious processes leads me to my second difficulty with Lacan, his psycholinguistics. In effect, Lacan rewrites Saussure into a version of psychoanalysis. He makes Saussure's formal account of linguistics into a psychological account. Even if Chomsky were all wrong, even if Saussure's account of language were correct, this would still be a fundamental error.

As we have seen, Lacan approximates Jakobson's metonymy (roughly, sequence) and Jakobson's metaphor (roughly, substitution) to Freud's "condensation" and "displacement." That is, he converts linguistic concepts into psychological processes. Similarly, the *barre* Saussure posited between signifier and signified comes to equal the process of repression, a bar that signification cannot cross. The most important case where Lacan converts a linguistic entity to a psychological one is, of course, signifier and signified. Lacan more or less identifies Saussure's signifier with the conscious and the signified with Freud's unconscious.

In their excellent study of Lacan and language, Muller and Richardson summarize him this way: "The signifying game of metonymy and metaphor goes on without my awareness." In other words—and this follows from the principle of "signifying"—Lacan assumes that language combines and recombines itself apart from the speaking subject. "This signifying game," writes Lacan, " . . . is played until the match is called, there where I am not, because I cannot situate myself there."

Thus Lacan renders the *processes* Freud discovered by Saussure's *entities*. He eliminates the difference between E-language "out there" and I-language as a psychological process "in here."

Lacan substitutes this psychological signification for association, memory, learning, and ultimately all other psychological processes. This, he claims, is the essence of Freud's discovery.

> If what Freud discovered and rediscovers with a perpetually increasing sense of shock has a meaning, it is that the displacement of the signifier determines the subjects in their acts, in their destiny, in their refusals, their blind spots, their end and fate, their innate gifts and social acquisitions notwithstanding, without regard for character or sex, and that, willingly or not, everything that might be considered the stuff of psychology, kit and caboodle, will follow the path of the signifier.

Quite a role for a process that modern linguists doubt even exists!

The French title of Lacan's key essay on this theme begins, *L'instance de la lettre dans l'inconscient* (1957), and Lacan intends the full strength of *instance*. His translator, Alan Sheridan, says it is to be translated "agency," "acting upon," and even "insistence." Benvenuto and Kennedy, in their especially lucid explication of Lacan, render it as "a pressing solicitation, an insistent request, an urgent entreaty." "The 'instance of the letter' is therefore the authority of the letter." The signifier dominates over the subject. The subject is the slave of language, Benvenuto and Kennedy sum up. Freud's repetition compulsion (the human tendency to make the same mistake, or achievement, over and over again) is this "insistence of the signifying chain." "The letter marks the subject like a carved Egyptian inscription." For Lacan, language replaces either heredity or environment as the determining principle of character (which itself disappears as a concept). In effect, Lacan renders all psychic determinism as the single linguistic process of signification, much as Derrida renders all mental processes as "writing." The chain of signifiers, running along according to its own laws, determines the I, and the determinism is total. Lacan calls it "the dance of signifiers." Perhaps we should call it, as Raymond Tallis does, the "Lacan-can."

What is fascinating to me about Lacan's maneuver is that it quite reverses the assumption that Saussure had to make when he started out to build his linguistics. As we saw in chapter twenty-one, Saussure set out to model language in purely linguistic terms, free of psychology, sociology, or anthropology. That is, Saussure was trying precisely *not* to say what goes on in your or my mind when we understand a word or make up a sentence. Lacan, however, claims that Saussure's carefully apsychological theory describes just what it avoided describing, namely, what goes on in minds. Saussure was trying to de-psychologize linguistics. Then Lacan comes along and re-psychologizes Saussure. Lacan is using a *formal* theory of language to explain *empirical* events in the mind.

The result of this move is a behaviorist psychology. In 1964, Chomsky identified the structural linguistics that derives from Saussure as "radical behaviorist reductionism." Both behaviorists and structural linguists avoid the notion of the autonomous individual. So do the New Cryptics who follow Saussure's linguistics. So does Lacan.

Like Derrida, Lacan changes the signifiers-signified relation. What he does not change is the principle that the sign (or, as he calls it, the letter) *does* things. Despite the psychoanalytic claims of a "return to Freud," I see Lacan locked into stimulus-response thinking like the deconstructionists. Lacan's sliding signifiers correspond to Derrida's "freeplay of language" or Eco's "unlimited semiosis."

Nevertheless, Lacan is quite right to foreground the role of language (or, more accurately, perceptual schemata) in our experiencing. The fundamental truth psychoanalysis teaches us is: *It is not an event as such that affects our minds but how we process the event.* Surely one of the most important ways we process things is through language. Lacan, however, makes signifying replace a variety of basic psychoanalytic and biological principles. It takes over from Freud's repetition compulsion. It takes over from Fenichel's character. It takes over from such biologically based ideas as Lichtenstein's identity principle or the closely related biological principle of autopoiesis advanced by biologists Maturana and Varela. Lacanians react with horror to the idea that the brain determines psychic events, and they dismiss as irrelevant studies of infant behavior.

Incidentally, then, I have an idea of the reason Lacan has become so popular among some intellectuals. He converts both painful personal issues and the profoundest psychological and psychoanalytic puzzles into just the kind of language games that literary critics and philosophers feel comfortable with. Brain physiology and child observation, neither likely to be popular with highly verbal critics and philosophers, become irrelevant.

There may be other reasons. I once asked a graduate student why he liked Lacan so much. He replied: "It means I am not responsible for *anything,* not society, not my words, not me. Also, it helps me get girls." His "I" and "me" are the tip-off. Lacan divides the self into two parts. By rendering "the" unconscious as Other, opposed to the conscious I, he leaves an intellectual like himself free to dwell in that conscious, speaking, signifying self. The intellectual is free to write about, to philosophize, to decry the power of the Other, while never leaving the comfort of the surface self.

Indeed, as Ragland-Sullivan sums him up, "There is no whole 'self' in Lacan's epistemology; instead, there are sets of signifying chains and unities, which compose 'self' out of relational ensembles of meaning." One of Lacan's first American commentators, Anthony Wilden, noted "Lacan's logical view of the subject as the 'empty subject'—a subject defined only as a locus of relationships." Abracadabra, the self itself has vanished!

This is, of course, a familiar maneuver in behaviorist psychology. It is so astonishing a conclusion for a psychoanalyst, though, that it suggests how fundamental and far-reaching Lacan's errors are. Quite aside from Lacan's philosophical error of using Saussure's formal description of language psychology as if it were an empirical one, Lacan is also wrong on empirical grounds. That is, I cannot think of a serious psycholinguist who would agree with Saussure's or Lacan's account of the way we understand language. Words do not simply imprint meanings on our minds, as Saussure thought. Words require considerable processing, for example, through schemata and feedback loops. Any elementary textbook in the psychology of reading or the psychology of language would make this clear. The only justification for Saussure's and Lacan's idea that signifiers impose themselves on persons is the apparently compelling need of intellectuals to feel that the individual is not autonomous. Lacan's *linguisterie* is simply and unequivocally false by today's psycholinguistic standards.

•

I have concentrated on Lacan's use of a false and outmoded linguistics and a behaviorist psycholinguistics, because they seem to me central to his system. They also link his system to those of other New Cryptics. "If Derrida sees internal difference and the continual deferring of presence as constitutive of the literary text," notes Susan Suleiman, "that is precisely how Lacan sees the human subject." Derrida's "writing" corresponds to Lacan's "signifying." Both ontologize Saussure's signifier-signified.

Lacan, however, makes a third error in another fundamental concept, "the mirror stage." It is central to Lacan's notion of child development.

The child, says Lacan, identifies with its mirror image—and Lacan insists on an actual mirror, not some "mirroring behavior" from a parent. That is how the child forms an ego (the illusion of autonomy). Lacan claims a uniform or continuing process from six to eighteen months. During this time, says Lacan, the infant recognizes that the image in the mirror is an image of the infant himself. Lacan asserts "the jubilant interest shown by the infant over eight months at the sight of his own image in a mirror." Lacan goes on to explain this jubilation: "His joy is due to his imaginary triumph in anticipating a degree of muscular coordination which he has not yet actually achieved." In effect, Lacan is claiming that the infant makes a judgment, namely that this image is unified and coherent, and that he is in control of it. Finally, Lacan claims that it is before language, "at the *infans* stage," that the infant recognizes the image and makes the judgment that the image is more unified than he.

But what is the evidence for such a mirror stage? As usual, Lacan pays precious little attention to evidence. He cites a 1925 book by Wolfgang Köhler on the behavior of *chimpanzees*. He refers, without telling you what it is, to a philosopher, James Mark Baldwin's book on child development from 1903. He resorts to another author of that period, Wallon, who cites still others, Charlotte Bühler, Charles Darwin, Preyer, and P. Guillaume. All of them proceed the same way. They do not experiment. Instead they observe a child, usually a single child, in front of the mirror at various ages and "read" the child's interpretation of the image from the child's gestures, expressions, or sounds. The child thus created, I would say, is a very French child, reasoning its way logically (and amusingly) in the tradition of Descartes to its own existence.

Now this may be reasonable for Lacan. After all, he was inventing the mirror stage in 1936, and he may not have had access to any better data. But what about Lacanians of today? I have yet to see a Lacanian refer to the careful videotapes of infant behavior by Daniel Stern. Or Margaret Mahler's direct observation of nine infants' behavior with mirrors. Or indeed, the half-dozen or more articles on infants' behavior in front of mirrors that even a cursory search of *Psychological Abstracts* turns up.

When we look at these more sophisticated studies, we find that infants' behavior in front of mirrors is not a uniform process during the period from six to eighteen months, as Lacan claims. It is true that children uniformly show pleasure in playing with and responding to their own mirror images throughout the period from three to twenty-four months. What they respond pleasurably to is what psychologists call "contingent behavior." That is, the child enjoys making the image in the mirror move, just as it enjoys swatting a mobile over its crib to make it move. Babies enjoy demonstrating that kind of power to cause consequences, and there is nothing illusory about such an ability.

At age eight to nine months, the infant uses mirrors to reach for objects, for other people, and for itself. That is, the infant realizes that the image is an image, and it has some sense of the geometry of reflection.

Jeanne Brooks-Gunn's and Michael Lewis's work shows that at fifteen months and not before, children begin to identify the image in the mirror as themselves. Brooks-Gunn and Lewis have conducted precise experiments in which someone surreptitiously puts a vivid spot of rouge on the infant's nose. If the child touches its own nose when it sees the spot, then it knows the image in the mirror is an image of itself. (The same technique shows that some chimpanzees also know the image is of themselves.) At fifteen months, the babies then begin to exhibit self-conscious behavior, posing in front of the mirror, for example, not the jubilation Lacan claims. In short, up to fifteen months, few children pass the rouge test, and by twenty-four months, just about all normal children have passed the rouge test.

This is quite a different picture from Lacan's. By the time children can recognize their mirror image as themselves, most of them have already started using language. Hence, many of the children speak of the image as "me" or "I" or by their name. Children seem nervous and self-conscious in front of this recognized image, not jubilant as Lacan claims. There is no evidence whatsoever that the child makes a judgment that this image is unified or in some sense more powerful or otherwise different from the child's self. Indeed, how could there be evidence for this? How could you get in the child's head and prove that it was making such a judgment? Anyway, how could the child see the image in the mirror as different from its self? That is what the image is, after all, an image of the child.

As for Lacan's claim of a mirror stage, then, the evidence runs rather the other way. Perhaps Lacan knew no better in 1936, but why do present-day Lacanians go on quoting this mish-mash of conjecture and false evidence? The same question applies to Lacan's *linguisterie*. Why do Lacanians keep on talking about signifiers and signifieds and the system erected upon them? A simple look at the *Encyclopedia Brittannica* article on linguistics or any elementary textbook on linguistics or the psychology of reading would show that signifier-signified is outmoded and wrong.

•

My end in this book, however, is to assess Lacan's concept of the self, to I Lacan. Even if he arrived at it by false premises, his concept of the I might be, by other criteria, sound. Might be.

As I read him, Lacan offers a black-and-white, two-valued I. The bar that marks off signifier from signified in Saussure becomes, in Lacan, psychoanalytic repression, and it marks off two I's. One is a pseudo-I that does little more than designate the speaker. The imperfections of conscious speech, its gaps and slips, for example, evidence certain unconscious themes and so let us infer a realer, deeper I, *le sujet,* "the subject," an "ex-centric center."

Conscious and unconscious are thus *opposed* in Lacan's version of psychoanalysis. Sublimation is not part of this picture. Rather we all suffer alienation, and language equals repression. The mere fact that we humans use language makes us inwardly split and alienated, because language's translation of my deep needs or drives into speech introduces incompatibility into those needs. It makes them "pass through the defiles of the signifier." The speaking, conscious I becomes the victim of the linguistic processes we learned from parents and society.

Thus, in discussing a whole personality (his own), Lacan identifies it with a linguistic chain, a discourse. "This discourse . . . is the discourse of the circuit in which I am integrated. I am one of its links. It is the discourse of my father, for example, insofar as my father has committed faults that I am absolutely condemned to reproduce."

The same assumption governs Lacan's re-thinking of Freud's case history of the Rat Man. The Rat Man's individual myth is "the inaugural relationship between the father, the mother, and the friend" who in the distant past paid the Rat Man's father's gambling debt. In other words, events established the Rat Man's myth long before the Rat Man was even born. Lacan himself compares it to an astrologer's constellation.

There is, to be sure, a psychoanalytic truth to what Lacan

says. Our characters are affected by our parents' characters, therefore by their lives before we were born. Our characters are shaped in a culture and a language. Lacan, however, asserts these commonplaces in an exaggerated, bedazzling way. Signification *alone* determines personality and pathology.

Lacan's increasing commitment to this linguistic position led to a gradual change in his thinking about the I. Muller and Richardson call it "the ever more radical depersonalization of the subject." The I became a mere linguistic "shifter" who speaks "empty" language. Then who is the speaker? Muller and Richardson answer that Lacan's views changed over the decades.

> Since . . . words always say more than they pronounce, the speaker does not coincide with the conscious presence speaking, but appears in parapraxes ["Freudian slips"] as unaware of what is being said. The speaker, then, includes an "unconscious." In 1953 . . . it is the "unconscious of the subject," the *Kern unseres Wesens* [core of our being], who appears to utter "full" speech in distinction from the "empty" speech of the ego. This relatively straightforward duality is not so difficult to comprehend, but by 1960 . . . we no longer hear of the unconscious of the subject but rather of "the subject of the unconscious." This subject, like the "I" that fades from discourse, appears to be not a perduring, substantial entity, but rather a kind of intermittent presence caught between desire and discourse, subject to the laws of language and their impersonal processes. The subject becomes more and more "decentered," then, in these formulations as the consequences of Lacan's fundamental structuralism [i.e., his Saussurean linguistics—NNH] become more rigorously pursued.

Lacan's *sujet* or split I begins to flicker and disappear entirely, because the process of a signifier signifying a signified drops out the human factor. *The I drops out, not because of logic or of evidence, but solely because Saussure dropped it out.*

As we have seen, Saussure's assumption has no psychological basis at all. Nevertheless, it is from this linguistic platform that Lacan proclaims his famous split, alienated, and finally nullified self. I have to conclude that this vanishing I and the two-valued concept of an I it evolved from are forced, extreme, even bizarre.

•

I began by saying I was going to I Lacan. I was going to get at his idea of a self. When I do, I find that he has created a split, self-opposed I out of the idea that "the" unconscious and "the" conscious are opposed like signifier and signified. Every part of that idea is at least partly false.

If, however, we focus, not on Lacan's errors, but on his one undeniably correct assertion, that we must foreground the function of language in psychoanalysis, we can perhaps I him more profitably. We can recognize that he is doing something fine in recalling an older mode of psychoanalytic listening to language from classical and ego-psychology. It is a mode increasingly neglected in the psychiatric, DSM-III and -IV world of American psychoanalysis today.

We might also, in a spirit of reconciliation, compare his model of the self using and being used by language with the identity-governing-feedbacks, the codes-and-canons model of chapter nine. Interestingly, Lacan's model has some features in common with mine. Lacan's subject, *le sujet,* with its personal myth, corresponds roughly to my idea of identity. Lacan's order of signifiers, I take it, is the whole apparatus of language. His chains or order or "combinatory play" of signifiers thus corresponds roughly to my feedback loops.

Read that way, Lacan could be describing an identity governing feedback loops. He could be describing an I proposing hypotheses to the world and getting back the consequences. After all, I define the I precisely as what energizes feedback loops or Lacan's "order of signifiers." Without loops or signifiers, such an I cannot act, therefore cannot be a subject or evidence an identity.

In Lacan's version, language "writes" an inner I, *le sujet.* That unconscious I is implied by *language* (or more precisely, I would say, experiences as we render them to ourselves through the symbols and schemata described in modern psycholinguistics). That is the way I would translate Lacan into the language of cognitive science. This inner subject both speaks the loop and is spoken by the loop. The chain of signifiers insists on a subject, and the subject insists on a chain of signifiers. We achieve the paradoxes so dear to Lacanians.

By contrast with the model of chapter nine, though, Lacan makes a pervasive assumption that the feedback loops by which we speak and otherwise cope with the world are "the Other": frustrating, repressive, alien and alienating. Language is not mine or mind, but the language of the Other. The subject feels desire (like a drive), but its movement is shifted and shunted by "the play of displacement and condensation to which [the subject] is doomed in the exercise of his functions."

It seems to me that there is both a truth here and a distortion. Think, for a moment, of any kind of ability—ice-skating, say. I try out certain movements, and eventually I learn to propel myself on the surface of the ice. In one sense, of course, the skates limit me. I cannot walk or run in them. Moreover, I will never zip effortlessly across the ice like the skating stars I admire as they sweep and soar across my television screen. But I do manage to scuttle along. Knowing how to skate, that is, knowing the skating-code, makes something possible, but it also makes skating frustratingly less than I can imagine it. With skates on, I cannot do a lot of what I ordinarily can do with my feet. The ice-skating "code" both enables me and limits me.

So with language. I can articulate my needs and loves and angers. Even if I were a master poet, however, I would do so imperfectly, conflictedly, in T. S. Eliot's "raid on the inarticulate with shabby equipment always deteriorating." Language (or any feedback loop) enables us to express our desires, but limits us to those expressions the particular language or loop provides. So do the people I am involved with. So does my own body. It is this sense of being both enabled and limited that Lacan describes as the alienation of the subject.

Lacan, however, writes as though there were *only* the limitation, no enabling. Lacanians split off the feedback loops of any human ability, but language most of all, into something "other," something alienating, something repressing—and depressing. These are terms that appeal to moody youth, but they only tell half the story (if that!) of human functioning. Lacan's idea of the *barre* rules out sublimation.

If I compare Lacan's picture of the self with the model of chapter nine, his *barre* detaches the loops (his chains of signifiers) from the I. The I results from them, but has no control over them. By contrast, in my model the I (conscious and unconscious identity) is outside and beyond the signifying chain or feedback loops, *but* attached to them. The loops plus the I make up the whole person. The I is implied by the loops, since something must provide them a standard. In that sense the I is the governing agent of the loops. Yet the I is also the result of the loops' functioning, and in that sense it is the consequence. And the I can act only through the loops.

Lacan, however, cuts these loops off from the person who uses speech, body, or relationship. My ability to skate, my ability to speak, all my abilities—for Lacan they are "pure alterity." In my thinking, they are also part of me. I depend on them. I enjoy them. I own them. Obviously, others may own them, too. They may even be public property (like language). But the one owning does not cancel out the other (*pace* Culler).

I say the relation is not either-or but both-and, and the simple verb *use* allows us to say that both-and. We use language to express our conscious and unconscious desires as best we can. Partially we succeed, and partially we fail. It is this mixture of pain and pleasure that ego-psychology (especially its basic principle of multiple function) accounts for. It is this mixture of pain and pleasure that Lacan's two-valued thinking distorts and misrepresents, because Lacan describes the self wholly in the language of alienation and fragmentation.

In short, if we compare the Lacanian model to the identity-governing-feedback picture of chapter nine (or *The I*), there are some similarities but two differences. One, Lacan makes a one-way connection between personal identity and the codes, feedback loops, or chains of signifiers it governs. Language controls and is "Other." For me those loops are *both* "Other" *and* part of my being. For Lacan, they are *either* Other *or* part of one's being, and he chooses Other. Two, for Lacan, the I that governs the loops is trivial and superficial, a mere linguistic convenience. My I both governs and results from those loops. His deep-I is totally determined by these feedbacks, alienated from the governing I, and unknown to us. I would justify my claims by modern linguistics, psycholinguistics, and, in general, the "mind's new science." By contrast, *Lacan assumed his conclusions at the start. They rest only on the authority of Saussure.*

When Lacan adopted Saussure's idea of "signifying," designed to eliminate the human element in language, Lacan dropped all of us out. He dropped us out of speaking, out of understanding language, or out of experiencing a poem or a movie. He dropped us out of understanding one another, understanding ourselves, and out of psychoanalyzing and being psychoanalyzed. It is one thing for Saussure to omit the human element. He did not want to try to do psychology. But what are we to say of a psychoanalyst who does not want to do psychology? What can such a psychoanalysis contribute to literature, philosophy, or, quite simply, our understanding of the world around and within us? What, finally, do Lacan and the other neo-Saussureans offer us? I have to conclude, not much.

Conclusions I: Looking Backward

We have sampled a variety of distinguished New Cryptics: Miller, Johnson, Leitch, Barthes, Foucault, Derrida, Eco, Lacan. It would be a superhuman task to try to read all of contemporary literary theory, and it would be tedious beyond belief. These will have to do.

My argument has two conclusions, one negative and backward-looking (this chapter) and one positive and directed toward the future (the next chapter). In arriving at these conclusions, I have been I-ing audiences, critics, and, in part three, theorists. That is, I have been doing two things. First, I have tried to isolate what these different types demonstrate or say about the individual human being, the I. Second, I have been reading them against my own model of the I, the picture I proposed in chapter nine as a way of imaging how Agnes, Ted, and Norm responded to *The Story of O.*

Again and again, in part three, we have seen the New Cryptics reduce or attack the I. Again and again, they use the same argument. Language rests on a system of signifyings (or traces or interpretants) that are based wholly in language or culture. Indeed, Jonathan

Culler defines "theory" as "works that . . . offer novel and persuasive accounts of signification." Theory was "attractive because [it] offered richer conceptual frameworks than did the New Criticism for expounding the complexity of literary signification." Then, once the literary critic had got hold of signification, he or she could 'theorize' all fields—"fields as diverse as anthropology, psychoanalysis, and historiography," because theory "discovered an essential 'literariness' in nonliterary phenomena." (Note the "in" of a container metaphor).

Again and again, it all comes down to signification. Language determines its own meaning independently of the individual human beings using language. Again and again literary theorists proceed from this premise to talk of signifiers (or traces or words or interpretants) signifying or differing all by themselves. The theorists admit only two possibilities. Either humans control language or language controls and determines itself, and they opt for language. The conclusions that result are tricked out in a language of neologisms, parentheses, Greekisms, trope names, and inkhorn terms as though something drastically complicated and new were happening. All this entitles us to give up the idea of determinate meanings, coherent selves, or language that refers to anything outside itself. It leads to language signifying without beginning, end, boundary, or finality to make a vast sea of textuality.

The first thing to notice about these radical discoveries, however, is that they are quite traditional and conventional. They rest on a notion of language at least as old as the Renaissance, one that the twentieth century has seen disproved. Most intellectuals have not, for a long time, believed in absolute truth or objective knowledge. (Except, oddly, for literary critics with their belief in right readings.) Most intellectuals have recognized long ago that our linguistic categories do not reflect the necessary structure of the world. There needs no ghost come from the grave to tell us these wonders, and no deconstructionist.

The literary critics who have been banishing my I and yours to outer chaos like to claim that this is a marvelously daring and radical thing to do. Looked at from the point of view of modern psychology or linguistics, however, the literary criticism and theory of today that claims to be most radical has made no real break with the past. Most of today's literary theorists have lazily inherited the older critical modes they deplore. As we noted in chapter twelve, a New Critic of Theodore Spencer's era would also simply leave the I out. The poem defines its own proper response. The human reader simply has to be capable enough to pick it up. As we have seen in our sample, supposedly avant-garde critics of today are still saying that. The Lacanians and deconstructionists and miscellaneous postmodernists we have sampled proceed from the same premises as the literary theory, New Criticism, they claim to be overturning. That is, they assume that language has a meaning or meaning(s) in itself. They assume that texts impose these meaning(s) on an essentially passive I. People have to do something to "produce" meaning, but no theorist says what it is. It just isn't very important.

From a psychological point of view, many, perhaps all of these supposedly revolutionary theorists are reactionary. They keep repeating the stimulus-response psychology tacitly assumed by old-fashioned meaning-critics. The New Cryptics have failed to meet the deep questions posed by linguists and psycholinguistics and reader-response critics. They are simply perpetuating traditional meaning-criticism in new clothes, the Emperor's new clothes, perhaps. And, as Raymond Tallis cracks, when the Emperor shops for a new wardrobe, he generally shops in Paris.

I am by no means the first to point out this crypto-conventionality. "Deconstruction's major themes," notes John Ellis, "had been part of the critical scene long before its arrival." Frank Lentricchia states this conclusion this way:

> The work of deconstruction rests on the very vocabulary of knowledge-as-representation that it would subvert. . . . Deconstruction chooses to stay within the traditional paradigm of transcendental representation, finding its distinctive project in the necessarily endless demonstration that representations fail to do what they say they do.

The deconstructionists attacking traditional criticism use the very same model of meaning as the criticism that they seek to replace. (For Lentricchia's "representation," read Saussure's or Lacan's or Derrida's "signifying.")

It is in this context that I understand Lentricchia's view of

Paul de Man. De Man, predicts Lentricchia, "will be rediscovered as the most brilliant hero of traditionalism." Although there are differences between traditionalists and deconstructors, Lentricchia notes, "Both parties stand up for the notion of literary autonomy, however differently that autonomy may be defended, defined and located." The signifier signifies.

What Lentricchia is saying, and I agree, is that deconstruction is a conservative, not a radical movement. It is new only in that it is a new vocabulary for supporting the traditional games of the literary professoriate. Stanley Fish puts it this way:

> Deconstruction would have been literally unthinkable were it not already an article of faith that literary texts are characterized by a plurality of meanings and were it not already the established methodology of literary studies to produce for a supposedly "great text" as many meanings as possible. Deconstruction takes the additional step of attributing these meanings not to the text as a special kind of object, but to signification as a force untethered to any grounding origin . . . . Rather than something new which in its newness gives rise to revolutionary practices, deconstruction is a programmatic and tendentious focusing of ways of thinking and working that have already come to be regarded as commonplace and orthodox.

Being conservative is not *eo ipso* wrong (I guess). Nevertheless "commonplace" and "orthodox" do differ from the image that deconstructionists like to project of themselves daring to hover over a dizzy abyss. Yet the adjectives seem to me exact and just.

The "lit-crit" industry runs along much as it did when I entered the profession thirty years ago. Literary critics have a method which they apply with dogged persistence. Basically, for deconstruction, it is, If I am picky enough, I can show that this or any text is self-contradictory. Patrick Hogan has spelled the method out in detail and quite accurately. (Check him against Ade's or Bee's comments on "Thirty days.")

> Begin by isolating contradictions; this may be done by uncovering ambiguities in the text (for which we are all well-trained, of course) or by wordplay or by ignoring historical meanings or by overlooking literary conventions. (If stuck, attend to any discussions of writing, speech, books, letters, postcards—that sort of thing.) From one of the contradictions, establish a hierarchy. Identify this hierarchy with writing/speech. Return to the text and elaborate along similar lines, etc.

The method has become as routine as the explications churned out by New Critics. "Deconstruction, as popularly understood and practiced," concludes Hogan, "is a godsend for the market; it is no wonder that deconstruction has achieved such phenomenal popularity—it is, in a sense, the assembly line of literary studies."

Today's literary theorists also like to claim that they are saying or even doing something *politically* daring, radical, even revolutionary, by their acts of interpretation. A politically active critic himself, Hogan describes such a move by a deconstructionist,

> Recently, I attended a convention in which deconstruction was lauded for its revolutionary and liberatory 'gestures' in roughly the following words: "Deconstruction is an ideology which valorizes the fragment, the discontinuous, the differe/ant, and thus supports, on the theoretical plane, the struggles of women and minorities in the face of white, patriarchal power structures of homogeneity and organicity." I found it a bit difficult to isolate precisely what the speaker was trying to get at. For example, was he trying to say that those who analyze, in this case, *Ulysses* as a discontinuous and unsynthesizable play of differance were more likely to support bussing, preferential hiring for minorities and women, and the ERA, whereas those who sought to uncover synthetic unities in the work were more likely to be organizing anti-bussing protests, filing reverse discrimination suits, and enthusiastically promoting the "Family Protection Act"? Or was he trying to say that if the bulk of literary criticism were deconstructive, and, thus, fragment-valorizing, that most people in the United States would support gay liberation and thus institute non-prejudicial policies with regard to non-heterosexuals?

Yes, it is hard to believe, as Andrew Gordon likes to say, that the president of General Motors trembles when Derrida turns to his word processor. What current literary theory badly needs is less theory, more irony.

Although literary theorists claim that their abstruse theories are politically "radical," it seems to me that just the opposite is true. As my Lacanian student pointed out, the text-active model leaves you free of any responsibility at all.

Yet, many literary critics do claim we ought to be political, and many, notably feminists, actually try to be political in action. I feel they (and I—I am a feminist, too) are hamstrung by this dreary, unconvincing theory. Political action loses its way in the mazes of an asocial, anti-political "signification." Feminism should not, need not, rest its just claims on false theories. The impersonal free play of signifers, the easy positing of an automatic "intertextuality," the assumption that one is not responsible for one's codes or canons, all these claims sidestep the vital personal interests, the human-ness that is feminism at its best.

Indeed, signifying sidesteps real persons altogether. Literary critics (even so-called "cultural critics") don't talk about society as we see it in people's lives. They talk about society as we see it in texts, more exactly in their interpretations of texts. They maintain that real responses by real people come "from" the poem, the story, or the television commercial. They thus divorce literary criticism from the real world beyond the text. There is nothing, they tell us, *hors de texte.*

If one really cares what happens to the poor, the homeless, women, gays, and minorities, it is an idle, even pernicious, fiction to prattle on about signifying. The insistence that texts mean on their own, independent of any interpreter, all too easily serves profoundly anti-political, even inhuman and inhumane ends. In this context, the counterclaim, that literary critics' interpretations exert political power, seems simply silly, particularly when the critics are interpreting language that has already deconstructed itself or fixed its own meaning. But the claim, loudly voiced, does make literary critics seem *very* important people.

The *New York Times* quoted some portentous statements from literary critics in solemn conclave assembled. For example, "Terrorism is a way of wounding the body of a dominant discourse." Tell it to the people blown up on Flight 103. Or this one justifying the funny word "postcoloniality."

> I mean, if you just use the word "postcolonial," you have to specify a postcolonial this or a postcolonial that. But if you use *postcoloniality* you give substance to that formerly abstract, helping term. Now, it is empowered as a word. It gains independence, clout all by itself.

Talk about the active text! A mere -ality gives substance, even clout. It is hard to imagine what kind of political action can come from people who think suffixes are actions in themselves. I have heard of a bumper sticker, "Help Stamp Out Nouns." I want one.

I have to admit at this point to an occupational tic. As a psychoanalytic critic, when I am confronted with this kind of professional irrationality, it is hard for me to resist psychoanalyzing the profession in question. Every occupation has its psychological basis, of course. The body-ness of the actor, the sadism of the surgeon, or the de-sexualized curiosity of the scientist are familiar examples. We literary critics, and I happily acknowledge my membership in the group, are people who at some point chose to focus our lives on poems and stories and plays and movies. We put books—language, really—before people. We share with lawyers an occupational tendency to endow language with magical powers. We believe it has "force," "impact," or "strength."

This mental move is what psychoanalysts term "the omnipotence of thoughts" or "magical thinking." That is, we attribute to thoughts (or language or symbols) the powers of real things or people. We sometimes exaggerate those powers to magical proportions. Think of the way people get agitated about flags, logos, or sexual pictures. Think of the power or eroticism or emotion they attribute to these symbols, although they are, after all, only inanimate objects that need us to supply the emotions in question. Superpatriots and politicians attribute magical properties to flags, ayatollahs to novels, and fundamentalists to the Bible. In the same way, literary critics and philosophers attribute magical powers to language, and literary theorists to "signifying."

Magical thinking is an error we all easily stumble into, but that is no reason to dive into it headfirst. Armed with their deep understanding of signification, literary critics like Culler are entitled to pronounce on language, mind, history, and culture. They can proclaim to the anthropologist, the psychoanalyst, and the historian what they are actually doing. What power! What intellect! What pretension!

It is as though, in the psyche of the theorist, language does what people do. A literary historian, trying to understand the grandeur of, say, *King Lear,* will turn to English history, to the particular details of Shakespeare's London, the customs of his stage, the intellectual trends of his day, or the politics or manners of Jacobean England—all embodied in one or another piece of language. A theoretical critic will turn to philosophy, religion, ethics, aesthetics, or metaphysics—all texts again. The formalist critic will focus on the language of the play. But few indeed are the critics who will turn to the people experiencing the play. Who will ask audience members what they are experiencing? Who will try to find out why they are experiencing greatness? Language substitutes for persons. Language and persons become, finally, opposites, and Saussurean linguistics thrives, long after its demise among real students of language.

Literary critics turn readily enough to history or philosophy, to claims of political or metaphysical power, to texts, sub-texts, and pre-texts, but not to psychology. Humanists, but especially literary people, tend to attribute great "force" to language. I have suggested two reasons for this: an occupational choice of books over people and a tendency to magical thinking. There may be others. For example, Saussure's linguistics is easier to understand than Chomsky's or the linguistics that has evolved after Chomsky. Chomsky can be forbiddingly mathematical, and humanists can feel ignorant or afraid in the face of science and mathematics. Teachers of literature often seek and observe in their classrooms a uniformity of response. How can one explain it? By the "constraint" of the text. Because words mean. That explains uniformity in a much more satisfying way than by the social situation of a literature class and the power of the professor.

Whatever the reasons, few are the critics who will explore the grandeur of the experience of *King Lear* psychologically. That is unfortunate. Paradoxically, by ignoring psychology in favor of Saussure and philosophy, by assuming language has power, many critics have made their own language powerless. They have developed a criticism and theory that has little relevance to the real world. Fewer and fewer people have reason to listen to us. David Lodge, a humorous and knowledgeable observer of the lit-crit scene, notes

> the tragic irony that English and literary studies have reached a point in their theoretical development when they've become almost incapable of communicating to the layman at the very historical moment when they've most needed to justify their existence.
> The brightest and most innovative people in literary criticism are as impenetrable as nuclear physicists. The left-wing intelligentsia is trapped in a kind of ghetto that only they understand, and so can't bring any leverage on the body politic.

This opaque literary thought rests on Saussure's assumption that a signifier (or something like a signifier) imposes willy-nilly a signified (or something like a signified) on the mind of a hearer. The idea that a signifier can simply evoke a signified is just plain wrong, however.

There has been a half-effort to correct this deficiency on the part of some literary theorists. Eco, Iser, Derrida, among others, have brought back the person in a bi-active model. Language generates meanings, but people have to do something (not specified) to actually produce them. But this is literally only half. These theorists cling to the idea of a psychologically active language. They do not seem to be able to cope with the idea that, when we use language, linguistic rules and our human creativity *combine*. Neither functions without the other. The bi-active model looks like a compromise, but it simply perpetuates the old error.

One reason this literary formalism persists is a general pattern of either-or thinking common among literary critics. *Either* the text controls response *or* the reader does. *Either* there is a fixed meaning *or* meaning can be anything at all. *Either* there is an objective text *or* subjectivity rules. Given such alternatives the literary critic who values language above people plumps for the text. There are variations, of course. The differencing of Derrida is more sophisticated than the either-or of Culler or Lacan. Nevertheless, measured against even a simple psychological model of an I, differencing is no better than either-or. Both are clumsy ways to think about human psychology compared to modern systems theories or information-processing models (like that of chapter nine) or the multi-valued logics of modern philosophy.

Considered in this more abstract way, the problem is that literary theorists are trying to solve an empirical problem with logic (or choplogic, really). Today's theorists are trying to use philosophy to answer what are essentially psychological questions. Now, philosophy can point out the hidden assumptions, the weaknesses if you will, in any position. Philosophy can phrase the questions science can answer. But philosophy cannot substitute for science. Even the Lacanians, although they claim to be psychoanalytic, reason their psychology out of Saussure and philosophy, not the experience of couch and clinic. How you and I use codes, whether we can ever escape our codes, how we are related to our codes— these are questions that require the methods of psychological research. The formal methods of philosophy are not going to help answer them at all. Neither will Saussure's weak and discredited linguistics.

Some of the New Cryptics' difficulties come about because of this either-or tactic. Others arise because, in describing a process like reading, we all customarily use nouns that suggest separable things: text, reader, form, content, subjectivity, competence. Nouns lend themselves well to either-or reasoning, but they serve only clumsily to describe processes. With nouns, something has to be here or there, so or not so, this or that, objective or subjective, and none of these dichotomies will make sense of a complex or even a simple feedback process. For Jonathan Culler, for example, either conventional codes make meaning or people do. Lacan is more sophisticated: either the ego makes meaning or the chain of signifiers does. Derrida is still more sophisticated: either a text has an organizing center or it doesn't. But all these either-ors and nouns (*meaning, chain, center*) exclude the verbs. They replace human actions with -alities. They ignore the processing of feedback that the psychologists tell us is basic to human thinking.

The errors all derive from Saussure's easy dichotomies into signifier and signified. Saussure's signifying differences keep up the either-or, and they allow the literary theorist to make great claims for the "force," "power," or "impact" of words—as we have seen. Derrida and his followers will claim that they have overturned the whole western philsophical tradition by foregrounding the power of language.

By contrast, I will be accused of lapsing into metaphysics myself, of proclaiming the I, that bourgeois, capitalist fiction, as a transcendental signifier, as a god-term. Again, I think the situation is actually the other way round. It may look as though I ("liberal," "humanistic," and otherwise unenlightened) have simply substituted for the stable text of the traditional critic a stable, centered person (or reader). Not so. I have substituted for the fashionably flickering text of the deconstructionist a fashionably flickering reader (as we shall see in the next chapter).

The deconstructors and other theorists, inevitably, have introduced their own god-term. Theirs is some version of signifying. A text-active model justifies ideas like the free play of language or the sea of intertextuality that has no shores, only islands. Literary theorists like Derrida, Eco, Barthes, or Lacan imagine the hypothesis-loops not as loops but as language referring to language referring to language. They make a world without end out of intertextuality. Referring, deferring, signifying, these are their god-terms, their basic assumptions, despite the theorists' claims that they have got rid of such things.

A closely related assumption, the one that underlies the bi-active models of Eco, Iser, or Derrida, is that one can separate a response into an important part determined by language and a lesser part determined by a person. All the theories, argues William Ray, rest on one dichotomy, "between what 'I mean' and what 'the word means.'" I would go further. All the theories rest on the assumption that that *is* a dichotomy. They rest, in other words, on the belief that words can mean otherwise than by a psychological process.

In short, I think the literary theorists' god-term is language as it makes meaning. No one escapes *some* term which is axiomatic. I have my god-term, like everybody else, although I would like to make it as minimal an assumption as possible. Mine is some kind of construction by some kind of self as the in here acts toward the out there and the out there acts toward the in here. In other words, I am positing as my basic assumption a process by which people interpret the world, including language. Less minimally, it is the process described in chapter nine. I think my god-term is endlessly interlocking transactions of the self as the self acts outward through its various feedbacks. I would point to an endless field of human relations, persons relating to persons relating to persons through various cultural codes. It is a field very like the endless sea of intertextuality, but the players on my field are not texts but people. Imperfectly, flickeringly perceived, but people nevertheless.

I can therefore put the negative part of my argument briefly and bluntly. When you hear someone drop the person out and announce that a text *does* something, reads itself, supplies a meaning or a context, invites a certain kind of reading, deconstructs itself, and at the root of it all "signifies," you can be sure that you have found one weak point in the argument. At that point the critic or theorist is assuming something that is simply not true of language. More importantly, he or she is assuming a psychology of the human being that is profoundly misleading. At

that point you can proceed in perfect confidence to ignore, con-
tradict, or demolish whatever follows from that premise of a signifying text.

In particular, you can dismiss the idea that some imaginary
power of language has eliminated the self. You and I have not
been driven from existence by these arguments that show more
cleverness than wisdom. You and I really are here in this time and
space. We really are functioning human beings who organize the
world so as to meet our basic interests and needs. We can even
read books of literary theory or anti-theory and make something
profitable out of them for ourselves.

Conclusions II:
Looking Forward

In part three, I have been examining closely what to-day's literary theorists claim about the I. I—and I use that pronoun calculatingly—have been aiming at two conclusions. My first and negative conclusion looks backward. I say that the claim by today's literary theo-rists that the self has disappeared rests on a variety of false premises. My second and positive conclusion looks forward. There is a better way. We can do what we want to do without the signifier-signified model (and its variations). I propose a more useful model, that of chapter nine. This is the model I developed in *The I* in 1985 and in *The Brain of Robert Frost* in 1988.

A psychological model, if it works, lets us under-stand what we are doing when we read literature, whether we choose to play such old-fashioned critical games as Spencer's New Criticism or such newfangled ones as Ben Bee's deconstructionism. Such a model purports to be a description of what is going on in our heads when we read and interpret. It does not tell us how to read. It neither forbids Spencer's quest for unity or advocates Derrida's quest for disunity. The model describes. It does not prescribe.

I would claim it is value-neutral, although I know that is, strictly speaking, impossible. Let me put my claim this way. The model rests on the conclusions of cognitive and psychoanalytic psychologists. As a group, they can fairly say, I think, that they arrive at their conclusions by rules that suspend their personal desires more than the rules by which philosophically inclined literary critics or literarily inclined philosophers play. Scientists play their games by different rules from literary critics. In that sense, this model is more likely to provide useful feedback about a literary transaction than the invented or imagined processes put forward by "theory."

Even if it seeks to be value-neutral, can the model nevertheless help us to read better? Will cognitive science help us write better essays on Shakespeare? No, of course not. A psychological model will help us to understand better what we are doing when we write essays on Shakespeare. It will also help us not to make fantastic claims for our theories—if we are willing to let it help us. Finally, though, the model tells us that how we read and how we theorize (and how we build models) is up to us. Whether we do these things well or badly depends entirely on us. The model only says *how* we do what we do. It cannot tell us *what* to do.

•

As we saw in chapter nine, the model consists of an identity governing a hierarchy of feedback loops, each providing the standard for the loop below it. It consists of—

> at the highest level, a unique identity interpreted as a theme and variations;
> at intermediate levels, loops internalized from culture, of two kinds: canon-loops, rules about which different "interpretive communities" regularly differ;
> code-loops: "No member of this culture would normally believe the rule is otherwise;"
> at the lowest level, physiological loops the human species shares.

With this model, we can explain people's reactions to *The Story of O*, the Kuleshov experiment, or "Thirty days hath September." With it, you can test the claims made for language by Derrida, Lacan, and the other disciples of Saussure.

It is a fairly simple feedback model, but it seems to me to meet the needs of literary theory. The model accounts for the various phenomena people want to account for, the phenomena we have seen in this book, for example. How the similarities in literary response can be both collective and individual. How culture and individuality co-act. How traditional psychoanalytic theory meshes with contemporary cognitive science. How language can be a cultural code but used in an individual way. The relative standings of readings by Ade, Bee, Cee, Dee, Ede, and the Fays.

Although it is a rather simple feedback model, it avoids the either-or error. It does not require such pseudo-issues as, *Either* the movie controls Ted *or* Ted determines the movie. *Either* I control language *or* language controls me (and if language controls me, I don't exist). *Either* the poem means *or* Spencer can interpret it any way he wishes. *Either* I am an individual subject *or* I am the result of systems of signs. *Either* I operate through language *or* language operates through me. *Either* you agree that the text signifies *or* you are saying the text doesn't exist.

Instead, this model enables us to visualize a both-and. The model simply says, I *use* codes and canons. I use them just the way I play a violin or drive a screw with a screwdriver. What results from violin, screwdriver, or code comes *both* from the violin, screwdriver, or code *and* from the human being using them. One cannot divide what results into a part from the instrument and a part from the human.

The codes in the model both enable and limit me, as a violin or a screwdriver does. They enable me to do something I could not otherwise do. They limit me, because they only let me do what violins or screwdrivers can do. Yet in no sense need we assume that they make the I disappear. Just the opposite. Codes and canons require an I to work them just as the violin or the screwdriver does.

Moreover, I can use whatever canons I choose. I can deconstruct the text or psychoanalyze it. I can look for themes or inconsistencies. I can read for gender, colonialism, social justice, or historical background. The model purports only to say what we are doing without attributing it to some activity of the text.

Such a model allows us to account for the samenesses and differences in readings, but not by falsely dividing the reading into part from the text and part from the reader. Consider our seven readings of "Thirty days hath September." Some similarities run through these seven readings. We all talked about months. We all saw February as salient. Ede and I both recalled a domineering teacher. Theodore Spencer personified February much as I did, as a striving male. Dee was brought to aggression, envy, and apprehensions about women, and Ade and Bee and Fay also began to think about women.

Don't we have to assume these similarities "come from the poem"? Don't they show that the poem determines at least "part of" Spencer's and Ede's and my responses? No. Those are false metaphors. "Thirty days" did not deliver some message or "signify" anything about women. We read it. We interpreted it, sometimes alike and sometimes differently. The poem did not "contain" something about women that the readers "got out of it." A text does not "force" a response (Derrida) or "foresee" one (Eco) or "constrain" one (Iser). Nor do the various readings answer to metaphors of "part of" or "This has more to do with my feelings than the poem."

The term to keep in mind is "use." How can one separate a performance into part coming from the violinist and part from the violin? Or the driving of a screw into a part from the carpenter and part from the screwdriver? The musician and the carpenter *use* their respective codes and instruments to make a performance compounded of both.

•

An individual uses language and is thereby both freed and constrained. Chapter nine's model lets us see the relation between Spencer's and Holland's and Dee's and Ede's readings. In the same way, in part one, the model showed how Agnes, Ted, and Norm's interpretations of *The Story of O* could be both communal and individual. So in part two, it shows that the similarities between Spencer's reading of "Thirty Days" and mine do not come from a core of "content" undeniably "there." That is what Spencer would have thought: that we shared a "content" that constrained us to certain reponses, although we could add our personal variations. That is what the New Cryptics think.

Today, however, we know that what similarities Spencer and I discover "in" the poem come from reading the same thing only if we read it similarly. We have to constitute "Thirty days" the same way. We have to use similar processes to read it. Even then the individual identities governing the processes are necessarily different. Even if those two different identities try out the same guesses on the text, they will hear differently the way the text reinforces or defeats the various hypotheses they try out. Hence the poem as experienced, parodied, interpreted, even described, will be, in every instance, different. Even if Spencer and Holland used the same interpretive strategies, they would apply them differently, individually. (As Ede and I did.) Otherwise all skilled critics would sound alike.

Of course, one may *feel* controlled by the text or the image on the screen. The Kuleshov audience automatically identified a bowl of soup or supplied a connection between two shots. They did so instantly, unquestioningly, unanimously. Nevertheless, stimulus-response does not adequately model what is happening. Cognitive science tells us that the Kuleshov effect does not come from the stimulus-response model used by the New Critics and the New Cryptics of part three. Rather, such responses come from low-level physiological loops or cultural codes, rapid, unthinking, and unconscious.

In the 1980s, a number of new ideas about these low-level processes arose in cognitive science. It may be, according to Jerry Fodor, that some of these low-level loops are "modular," only loosely involved with identity. According to Ulric Neisser, we may have evolved two modes of perception. One, "direct," may have evolved earlier for the kind of fast, automatic, or "direct" perception of space, like a cat's. It may be separated from personal identity or largely unaffected by personal differences. The other, more complex modes, would be associated with our primate brains and serve for all kinds of perception and cognition except for spatial relations. These low-level loops, David Rumelhart suggests, may be connected for "parallel processing" rather than sequential. If so, one such loop may determine another's processing rather than both answering to one central controlling identity. All these are possible future developments in cognitive science.

For the time being, though, literary critics will not go wrong by assuming that low-level automatic loops serve personal identity through a hierarchy of feedbacks. For our purposes it is enough for us to recognize that I used the cross-cutting in *The Graduate* to serve my moralistic reading of the movie. It is enough for us to know how the kind of themes that concerned Agnes, Ted, and Norm, relationship, domination, or rules, built on and directed our perception of the film through low-level codes. What exactly those codes are in a psychological sense, we had best leave to the psychologists. One thing we can be sure of, however. They are codes in our heads, not "significations" in the movie.

In contemporary literary theory much of the confusion comes from trying to apply to higher-level processes the feeling we have about lower level processes. That is we *feel* controlled when we recognize a letter or a word. We *feel* controlled when we sense a rhyme-scheme or when a film cuts to another plot line. Critics tend to assume this kind of control is the norm. Iser's *Rezeptionsästhetik,* for example, assumes that there is a lower-level in which the text controls, the way a stimulus controls a response. Then there is a higher level in which the reader is independent, filling in gaps left at the level of control. Basically, though, *Rezeptionsästhetik* treats the feeling of being controlled as the root of literary response, and the application of hypotheses the exception, variation, or sophistication. Cognitive science shows, however, that the person is applying hypotheses at basic physiological levels: color, shape, pitch, or texture.

If so, then we are saying that interpreters of books and movies (and of dreams and identities) are always engaging their selves, their identities, de-centered, deconstructed, and systematically elusive though those identities may be. Sometimes the responder will feel as though he or she is being controlled or like a mere response to a stimulus. In fact, though, response is always a feedback process, even if it "could not be otherwise." By contrast, the idea that films (or texts) signify puts the film in the active role. It is a stimulus-response model.

To use the automatic process to model the personal one is like doing psychoanalysis without acknowledging transference and countertransference. It is to try and do criticism, be it of fiction or film, without acknowledging the way critics re-create the text. It is to resort to the older model (of the New Critics) of an "objective" world "out there" independent of the fluctuating, "subjective" world in here that knows that outer world. We need instead, in the language of cognitive linguistics, an "experientialist" account.

•

When I read the New Cryptics against a feedback model, I see the same strategy over and over. The theorist disconnects whatever governs the feedback loops from the loops and imagines the loops as running along by themselves. In reading or writing, the theorist imagines the I, if at all, as something inchoate, not much worth talking about, a mere "act of production."

In this book, I have advanced, by no means for the first time, my personal counter to these positions. I want you to hear "I" against the picture of the mind as an identity governing a hierarchy of feedbacks. In the book as a whole, I have asked you to join me in using that model as a lens with which to look at people's experiences and our theories about those experiences. In part one, we used that lens to look at Agnes, Ted, and Norm looking at *The Story of O* and to reconsider the Kuleshov experiment. In part two, we used it to interpret Spencer's and Ade's, Bee's, Cee's, Dee's, Ede's, the Fays', and my readings of "Thirty days hath September." In part three, we have used the model to explore the obscure assertions of literary theorists. That is what I want you to carry away from this book, the picture of an I governing a hierarchy of feedbacks. And I want you to use it as a code, to listen to the claims of literary critics and theorists through it.

It is only fair, then, that we use that model to look at my own assertions, at the model itself. One thing is immediately obvious, according to the model. You are using a code or a canon to listen to my model as well. And you direct your listening to serve your personal goals.

If you have this picture of an I in your mind when you think about the I, then you will recognize that the New Cryptics, for all their errors, are right to question the idea of a simple, straightforward, organically unified I. Jonathan Culler, who has been one of the chief offenders in my writ, writes:

> As the self is broken down into component systems, deprived of its status as source and master of meaning, it comes to seem more and more like a construct: a result of systems of convention. Even the

idea of personal identity emerges through the discourse of a culture: the 'I' is not something given but comes to exist as that which is addressed by and relates to others.

If we balance Culler's claim against the picture of an identity governing feedbacks, we have to agree. Yes, we *can* only perceive a self through the ways that selves perceive things. Yes, of course, the self is a construct. It is the way we construe one another. No doubt Japanese or Bantus or Eskimos construe people differently than Americans do. Yes, constructs emerge, as we have seen, through the codes and canons of a culture as well as the physiology of the human body. The I "comes to exist as [it] relates to others." Yes. In that sense the self is as real as tables and chairs, for we perceive them, too, as a result of systems of convention.

One cannot know the self apart from the processes by which the self knows things, and they are subject to both conscious and unconscious biases. The self in that sense is systematically elusive or, if you prefer, fashionably flickering. When I read your self, or my own for that matter, I do so through exactly the same type of interpretive process by which Agnes and Ted and Norm saw *The Story of O*. I use codes, language, systems of psychology, the systems of my language and my culture, "systems of convention" in Culler's term, and personal systems, "not otherwise" codes, and all the rest, to build a picture of you. You do the same with me. I do that when I think of myself—to the extent I can know myself, and that (we know from psychoanalysis) is sharply limited. I cannot interpret anything except through the interpretive systems by which I interpret things. An I, any I, is always a product of intepretation by an I. The I will not serve as some axiomatic presence. I cannot know it absolutely. There is no God's-eye (or God's I) view of the self or of a chair or anything else.

But it does not follow that there is no I. Nor does it follow that the self (or a chair) is *only* a result of systems of convention. That follows only if you assume there is *either* self *or* convention. The I does not disappear. Rather, the self emerges as selves perform the discourse of a culture. The self (or the chair) is what the identity-governing-feedback system perceives. We have simply said that the I is always a construction by another I and subject to all the limitations that that implies.

What I find interesting is that the identity-governing-feedback model enables us to be somewhat more precise about those limitations. We become able to visualize what we can and cannot know about ourselves, and why. We can, so to speak, look down the model, but not up. We can know the loops we use, but our vision is obscured when we look up toward identity. That is, we can perceive (as the model says we do) the codes and canons we use to perceive. We can be very knowledgeable about them, because we can use one code or canon to check another. Literary critics, for example, make very perceptive interpretations of our cultural codes and canons. On the other hand, we cannot look upward through the model. Only in the most limited way can we use our identity-governing-feedbacks to understand our own identity. Why? Because we cannot change our identity, as we can change codes or canons, to perceive our identity.

That is why the self-understanding of psychoanalysis is so laborious and imperfect. If my identity has a certain blind spot (an unconscious block), there is no way I can get round it and see through it (except psychotherapy). There is no way we can simply change codes to get a fuller view of ourselves, free of the identity that colors our view. And when I say that, when I to that extent deconstruct myself, I see we have come to closure and a final question. What next?

·

What we literary theorists need is a turn toward contemporary psychology. What we have got is a new scholasticism. Like the last scholasticism, that of the seventeenth century, it has isolated itself from the science of its day. It has thereby doomed itself to become no more than a somewhat laughable pedantry.

Let us begin again, then. We can get beyond the balks and confusions of abstract either-ors. We can do so by turning to psychology instead of logic for an account of human-ness. Once we do so, a new synthesis awaits the literary theorist. A new way of thinking about the relation between persons and books is emerging from a cluster of theorists in widely diverse fields.

In one direction I would point to the remarkable achievements of today's cognitive science, the new psychologies of perception, knowing, and remembering, as summarized, for example, in Howard Gardner's excellent introduction, *The Mind's New Science*. Particularly relevant to the book you are reading is the idea of scripts put forward by theorists of artificial intelligence, notably Roger Schank and Robert Abelson. We organize our experience by carrying in our heads things like the restaurant script, the baseball script, and, I suppose, the lit-crit script. Scripts must be another source of hypotheses alongside the codes and canons I pointed to in chapter seven.

In another direction, I would point to the way feminist literary critics have made us aware of the ways our preconceptions about gender (but about many other things as well) structure our experience. In literary theory, I would point to the way Jane Tompkins has called into question our traditional values in reading literature. Traditionally, we label texts masterpieces if they transcend their time and place (like "Thirty days"). She suggests another way of reading literary texts: "as a blueprint for survival under a specific set of political, economic, social, or religious conditions." In effect, Tompkins has introduced a powerful new canon (in my sense, as well as her own).

Among linguists and philosophers, I would single out the school of "cognitive linguistics" as developed by George Lakoff, Mark Johnson, and Mark Turner. They give us ways of understanding how our body metaphors and our ways of categorizing things structure the world for us. These metaphors provide yet another source of hypotheses alongside codes and canons. I am thinking, too, of Heinz Lichtenstein's theme-and-variations concept of identity which gives us a rigorous way of thinking about the individual who governs those metaphors and other cognitive processes. I am thinking of the principle of *autopoiesis* as developed by the biologists Umberto Maturana and Francisco Varela. Although they are unaware of Lichtenstein's theme-and-variations concept of identity, they provide a basis for it in cybernetics and biology. They develop a system of identity-governing-feedbacks that applies from the most primitive animals to the most complex human communities. Among theorists, I have pointed to a theorist of history, Richard Harvey Brown, whose notion of "symbolic realism" corresponds exactly to the idea I am putting forward here, that we always interpret texts through a personal and social system of symbols.

In short, from a variety of disciplines come the makings of a world-view that would serve literary theorists far better than the outmoded linguistics of Saussure. I believe the identity-governing-feedbacks model represents that knowledge in a manageable form. It provides a model of the I against which to read claims about literary experiences or the human beings who have them. We do not have to divide our experiences into an objective part and a subjective part. Rather, we can think of a subject *using* objective things, things-out-there, things widely shared like the words on the page, the image on the screen, the codes by which we read or see movies, the canons of our interpretive communities, and the prevailing scripts and metaphors of our culture.

To think this way, we need ideas based on systems and process instead of scholastic categories. We need to think in the verbs and participles of feedback. (Surely those who can pick their way through the thickets of Lacanian prose should not find that difficult.) Then we can attune literary thought to what we are beginning to discover about the architecture of the brain and the extraordinarily subtle way that humans know things and know that they know them.

This book asks you to begin that change. What I am suggesting is that we are moving, in this century, into a new transactive paradigm of the person. Not all at once, of course. As we have seen in parts two and three, we still encounter some very popular ways of thinking that rest on that older subjective-objective paradigm: formalist or structuralist criticism; stimulus-response psychology; the sender-message-receiver model for communication; signifier-signified and Lacanian and Derridian theories that rely on "signifying." We can see that these popular modes of thought are not adequate to explain the way Agnes, Ted, and Norm saw *The Story of O*. They will not explain the Kuleshov experiment. Nor will they account for the ever so various readings of "Thirty days hath September."

In short, for the old stimulus-response, signifying model, we can substitute a richer, more flexible picture of language and the process of meaning. We can better our ideas about poems and stories and plays if we use a stronger model of the I, an I testing the world through a hierarchy of hypotheses. We can recognize that humans do respond to stimuli, but as a part of a continuing process of control and self-creation. We respond to poems and stories and movies both individually and culturally, not either one way or the other. We can understand that we do have codes and systems of belief. These codes and canons do speak through us, but their presence does not require that we disappear. Rather they require us to run them. These codes both enable and limit us as we live imperfectly in this imperfect world. They enable us to do some things, but our very doing limits us from other things.

In short, we need not lock ourselves into the stifling either-ors of today's literary theory. We can have it both ways, several ways, indeed many ways. So let's.

Notes

shows how identical answers to a questionnaire express different identities.

41 *kinds of theories,* Polan 1986: 98.

42 *exactly the same.* Pudovkin 1929: 140.

42 *of half-naked actresses.* Hill 1967: 8.

44 *scientists tell us* See Gardner 1985, ch. 10, or Holland 1985, ch. 5.

45 *"eyeballs are blind."* Hanson 1958, 9.

48 *"mind's new science."* Gardner 1985.

48 *and Edward Branigan.* Bordwell 1985, 1989a, 1989b; Branigan 1984, 1986.

48 *widely read spokesman.* Gombrich 1960, 1982.

48 *in earlier works,* Holland 1982, 1988, 1989.

48 *by literary critics).* Crowder 1982; Flynn and Schweickart 1986; Smith 1988; Spiro, Bruce, and Brewer 1980; Taylor and Taylor 1983.

49 *"track of it."* Bordwell 1989b: 11.

54 *the Kuleshov effect.* For a more detailed discussion of text-active film theories and how this model rebuts them, see Holland 1989.

55 *not just movies.* For a popular account of today's psychology of perception, see Gardner 1985. For more technical accounts, see Neisser 1967, Sternberg 1985, or Carver and Scheier 1981.

56 *we call identity.* Barnes 1986; Restak 1986: 19, 55–57, 68–70, and especially 92; Blakeslee 1986.

56 *Maturana and Varela* Maturana and Varela 1980, 1987.

65 *and eighteenth centuries.* See Bartlett 1855; Northall 1892; Apperson 1929; Cohen and Cohen 1960; Stevenson 1967.

66 *industrial nation-state.* Ohmann 1976.

66 *true for undergraduates.* In this account, I am gratefully and heavily relying on Graff 1987.

69 *of the best.* Spencer 1943; Spencer 1966 includes a biographical sketch.

73 *date it earlier.* Among the many surveys and collections of current literary theory, I have gotten particular help from reading Beaugrande 1988; Davis 1986; Eagleton 1983; Graff and Gibbons 1985; Lentricchia 1980; Selden 1985; and Todorov 1984, and I am much indebted to them in what follows.

75 *and philosophical basis.* Crane 1953.

75 *New Critical Picture.* Frye 1957.

75 *and immediately experienced.* A particularly fine example of phenomenological criticism is Miller 1966.

75 *the postmodern challenges.* Macksey and Donato 1970.

76 *came German Rezeptionsästhetik.* Iser 1976; Jauss 1970; Segers 1975.

83 *their living room.* For a collection and memoir, see Manheim and Manheim 1966.

84   *of Bernard Paris.* Paris 1974.
84   *one before it.* Holland 1978; 1983.
85   *compulsion to repeat.* See Waelder 1930; Nunberg 1931.
85   *a psychological defense.* Holland 1968, chs. 4–5.
86   *had become "postmodern."* Holland 1983.
86   *"Where is literature?"* Schwartz 1975.
87   *needs and defenses.* Holland 1975.
99   *commonplace-book or "promptuary"* Holland 1975: 285–287.
101 *readings are misreadings.* Bloom 1975.
107 *book called* The I, Holland 1985.
107 *"point de départ."* Miller 1976a: 345.
107 *"effect of language."* Miller 1977: 440.
107 *"construction—a metalepsis."* Miller 1976b: 60n.
108 *"the concept 'self.' "* Leitch 1983: 277.
108 *"a new form."* Foucault 1966: 14–15.
108 *"dissimulation, and deferment."* Johnson 1984: 279.
109 *"within the text."* Johnson 1978: 3.
109 *"desires, and fatigue."* Johnson 1980: 14.
109 *"power of language . . ."* Miller 1987, 291.
109 *"text on itself."* Miller 1975: 31.
109 *"or her students."* Miller 1986: 2b.
110 *"own rhetorical mode . . ."* De Man 1979: 17.
110 *"logical-metaphysical postulate—"* Nietzsche 1901, sect. 484.
110 *"only a fiction."* Nietzsche 1901, sect. 370.
110 *"fiction, much follows."* Nietzsche 1901, sect. 552.
110 *"medley of sensations."* Nietzsche 1901, sect. 552.
110 *"as an affect."* Nietzsche 1901, sect. 556.
111 *"through concrete particulars."* Brooks and Warren 1960: 268.
111 *"apparently discordant elements."* Brooks and Warren 1960: 561.
111 *"fabric of meaning."* Richards 1934: 219.
111 *"that contains meaning."* Frye 1963: 65.
111 *a "signifying practice."* Culler 1982a: 22.
112 *"literary competence."* Culler 1980.
112 *"pursue historical scholarship."* Hirsch 1984: 203.
112 *"indeterminacy of meaning."* Hartman 1979: vii-viii.
114 *linguist Michael Reddy.* Reddy 1979.
114 *cluster of metaphors.* Lakoff and Johnson 1980: 10–12. See also
     Lakoff 1987: 450.
115 *then at Yale)* Brown 1981: 345–346.
116 *"less vital ones,"* Miller 1975: 24.
117 *"always be* interpreted." Barthes 1957; 1972: 132.
117 *"origin is lost."* Barthes 1970: 16–17; 1974: 10.
119 *"identical to itself."* Derrida 1967b: 42. My translation is adapted
     from Culler 1982a: 133.
120 *"the unthinkable itself."* Derrida 1970: 247–248. Derrida 1978:
     278–279, offers a slightly different translation.

121 *"not the center. . . ."* Derrida 1970: 248.
121 *"signification ad infinitum."* Derrida 1970: 249.
121 *"of the center."* Derrida 1970: 249.
122 *prescribed by* langue. Saussure 1915, Engl: 11–15; Fr: 27–32.
122 *"center is passive."* Saussure 1915, Engl: 13; Fr: 29.
122 *"minds of speakers."* Saussure 1915, Engl: 13; Fr: 30.
123 *unimportant or secondary.* Saussure 1915, Engl: 13–14; Fr: 29–31.
123 *"properties of water."* Saussure 1915, Engl: 103; Fr: 145.
124 *as "grossly misleading."* Saussure 1915, Engl: 113; Fr: 157.
124 *"associated with it."* Saussure 1915, Engl: 12; Fr: 29.
124 *generally more abstract.* Saussure 1915, Engl: 66; Fr: 98.
124 *most famous statement.* Saussure 1915, Engl: 120; Fr: 166.
125 *"that surround it."* Saussure 1915, Engl: 120–121; Fr: 166–167.
125 *the linguistic institution.* Saussure 1915, Engl: 120–121; Fr: 166–167.
126 *thought from sound.* Saussure 1915, Engl: 113; Fr: 157.
126 *"de nos sens").* Saussure 1915, Engl: 66; Fr: 98.
127 *"knowledge in general."* Lenneberg 1976, 206.
127 *understand the phonemes.* Smith and Holmes 1971.
127 *a passive hearer.* See, for example, Gibson and Levin 1975: 117–125; Goodman 1968: 15–26; Perfetti 1985; Luria 1980: 114–116; Moskowitz 1978: 130–131; Rumelhart 1977: 169; Smith 1971: 105–122; Smith and Holmes 1971; Spiro, Bruce, and Brewer 1980; Taylor and Taylor 1983: 355–368; Woods 1980. For a relevant study within the new model of "parallel distributed processing," see Rumelhart and Zipser 1986.
128 *"are only differences."* Saussure 1915, Engl: 120; Fr: 166.
128 *"that surround it."* Saussure 1915, Engl: 120; Fr: 166.
128 *"within each sign."* Saussure 1915, Engl: 120; Fr: 166.
129 *and many another.* Meek 1983; Grant 1986; Smith 1978; Anderson, Spiro, and Montague 1977; Applebee 1978.
129 *that it does.* Saussure 1915, Engl: 113; Fr: 157.
129 *"and for itself."* Saussure 1915, Engl: 232; Fr: 317.
129 *"manifestations of speech."* Saussure 1915, Engl: 9; Fr: 25.
130 *psychology of perception.* Saussure 1915, Engl:29–31, 98–99, 121, 157, and 317.
131 *"radical behaviorist reductionism."* Chomsky 1964: 25.
131 *"to each individual."* Saussure 1915, Engl: 19; Fr: 38.
131 *ninety-eight different senses.* Sweetser 1990.
132 *elephant folio pages.* Shenker 1989: 89.
132 *of* Paradise Lost. Kenner 1989: 26–27.
133 *a "real result."* Chomsky 1988b.
134 *"being ignored elsewhere."* Ellis 1989: 83.
134 *in nonlinguistic terms.* Chomsky 1988a: 37.
135 *are sufficiently similar.* Chomsky 1988a: 36.

135   *particular rule system).* Chomsky 1986: 27–28.
135   *epiphenomenon at best."* Chomsky 1986: 25.
136   *corresponding real-world object."* Chomsky 1986: 27.
136   *of our minds.* Saussure 1915, Engl: 19; Fr: 38.
136   *grasp at all.* Saussure 1915 discusses sentences at Engl: 127–139; Fr: 176–192. I am grateful to Gary Miller for expounding to me the linguistics of Saussure's contemporaries and Chomsky's recent work.
137   *"be a mistake."* Saussure 1915, Engl: 139; Fr: 191.
137   *"to language [langue]."* Saussure 1915, Engl: 124; Fr: 172.
137   *"without any explanation."* Chomsky 1986, 19, 32.
138   *"immediately preceding elements."* In this and the next paragraph, I am drawing on John Lyons' excellent introduction to Chomsky's work. Lyons 1978: 45. Chomsky 1957, ch. 3.
138   *left to right.* Lyons 1978: 48–49; Chomsky 1957: 22–23.
140   *just bad shots.* Lyons 1978: 52; Chomsky 1957: 36–37.
140   *therefore, more powerful.* Lyons 1977: 58–59; Chomsky 1957, ch. 5.
141   *"to my knowledge."* Marcus 1984: 254–55.
141   *according to Chomsky.* Chomsky 1972: 20.
141   *Turner calls it,* Turner 1987: 6.
142   *just painfully accurate.* Chomsky 1972: 20.
142   *"use of language."* Chomsky 1964: 23.
142   *"a language system."* Chomsky 1964: 23.
142   *"a certain concept,"* Saussure 1915, Engl: 104; Fr: 146.
143   *"previously unheard sentences."* Chomsky 1964: 111 and 111n.
143   *of stimulus-response chains.* Chomsky 1959.
144   *"interpretation and action."* Chomsky 1986: 5.
144   *from the world.* Anderson et al. 1977. I have been asked where does existing knowledge originate. What rules start the feedback? They may be genetic. We are apparently hard-wired with knowledge for understanding language, for children in the last six weeks of pregnancy can recognize speech as such, and at fifty hours after birth can distinguish one spoken passage from another. DeCasper and Spence 1986.
145   *"what we hear."* Chomsky 1986: 261. Pylyshyn 1984. I extended Pylyshyn's notion to literary codes in Holland 1988: 103.
145   *"free and indeterminate."* Chomsky 1986: 261.
145   *for various emotions.* Fodor and Pylyshyn 1981: 171–172.
145   *"of speech production."* Chomsky 1986: 261–262.
146   *"mechanism of language."* Saussure 1915, Engl: 111; Fr: 154.
147   *"underlies actual performance."* Chomsky 1965: 140, emphasis mine.
148   *the other way.* See, for example, Dillon 1978.
149   *well-known literary theorist).* Culler 1982b.
149   *"relation to his."* Lyons 1983: 995–96.

151 *"only in signs."* Derrida 1967a; 1976: 50.
152 *"from its signified."* Derrida 1970: 250.
152 *it outside itself.* Derrida 1970: 250–251.
152 *"play of differences."* Derrida 1973: 140.
152 *"thought and experience."* Derrida 1976: xvii.
153 *"appearance and signification."* Derrida 1967a; 1976: 64.
153 *"not simply present."* Derrida 1981: 26.
153 *"chain or system."* Derrida 1981: 26.
153 *"keep disrupting it."* Rajnath 1989: 74.
154 *"of the signified."* Derrida 1970: 260–261, also 262–263.
154 *"is being said."* Ellis 1989: 53.
155 *"experience at all."* Eagleton 1983: 130.
155 *"systems and logics."* Eagleton 1983: 134.
156 *"which produce interpretations."* Kearns and Newton 1980: 21–22.
156 *"reading should* produce." Derrida 1967a; 1976: 158.
157 *"text in question."* Miller 1988: 820.
158 *"are symbolically constructed."* Brown 1978: 5.
159 *"pas de hors-texte."* Derrida 1967a; 1976: 158.
160 *"of differential marks."* Derrida 1977: 183.
160 *"an* extra-linguistic *reality."* Tallis 1988: 17.
160 *the language system?* Tallis 1988, 69–70.
161 *between the phonemes?* Tallis 1988: 58–59.
161 *"what it is."* Derrida 1978: 27.
162 *"musical, sculptural 'writing.' "* Derrida 1967a; 1976: 9.
162 *"of its horizon."* Derrida 1967a; 1976: 44.
163 *"within the text."* Derrida 1967a; 1976: 159.
163 *"redo a text."* Derrida 1976: lxxvii.
163 *"in another way."* Derrida 1976: lxxv.
163 *"is yet reading."* Derrida 1967a; 1976: 159.
163 *"is historically articulated."* Derrida 1967a; 1976: 159.
164 *"force of rupture."* Derrida 1977, 182.
164 *"determined textual system."* Derrida 1967a; 1976: 160.
164 (Rezeptionsästhetik, *for example),* See my discussion of *Rezeptionsästhetik* in Holland 1988, chs. 4 and 7, and in ch. 28 of this book.
165 *and Johnson, experiential.* Lakoff and Johnson 1980, chs. 25–30.
165 *own term, transactive.* Holland 1976.
165 *"God's Eye view."* Putnam 1981: 54–55.
165 *"embodied imaginative understanding."* Johnson 1987: 212.
168 *"operate through it."* Culler 1981: 32–33.
168 *of my utterance.* Tallis 1988: 275.
170 *of their "creators."* Culler 1981: 159–60.
170 *"play of signifiers."* Leitch 1983: 111.
171 *"attempt to split."* Barthes 1971b: 271; Harari 1979a: 30.
172 *"no more sentence)."* Barthes 1973, Engl: 30–31.

172   *"explosion, a dissemination."* Barthes 1971a; Harari 1979b: 76–77.
172   *subsequent quotations come),* Barthes 1981.
172   *"typology of significations . . ."* Barthes 1981: 36.
172   *"in the work-as-product."* Barthes 1981: 37.
173   *call the "signifiance."* Barthes 1981: 37.
173   *"possible meanings intersect."* Barthes 1981: 37.
173   *"operation, a labour . . ."* Barthes 1981: 36.
173   *"able to approach."* Barthes 1981: 36.
173   *"the combinative play . . ."* Barthes 1981: 36–37.
174   *"or the consumer."* Barthes 1981: 37.
174   *"the Cartesian 'cogito.' "* Barthes 1981: 38, 36.
175   *"signifier upon itself) . . ."* Barthes 1981: 40.
175   *"field of language . . ."* Barthes 1981: 38.
175   *"a generalised metonymy . . ."* Barthes 1981: 40.
176   *"that we practice."* Foucault 1969: 150.
177   *"literature," in 1898.* Foucault 1969: 144.
177   *"recomposition of fiction."* Foucault 1969: 158.
177   *"proliferation of meaning."* Foucault 1969: 157.
177   *"within a society."* Foucault 1969: 147.
177   *"unity of Discourse?"* Foucault 1966, Engl: 385–86; Fr: 397.
178   *expert on Foucault.* Hacking 1986: 32.
178   *his central topic.* Hoy 1986a: 2–3.
178   *his own action.* Hoy 1986a: 4. Rorty 1986: 42. Dreyfus and Rabinow 1983: 237–8.
179   *"own Model Reader."* Eco 1979: 10.
180   *"their Model Reader."* Eco 1979: 24.
180   *"expression and content."* Eco 1975: 15.
180   *"multiple readings proposed,"* Eco 1976: 276.
180   *"codes to apply."* Eco 1976: 39.
181   *"in its development."* Eco 1976: 276.
181   *"or psychologistic theory."* Eco 1979: 196.
181   *(as I would).* Eco 1976: 315.
181   *the Greek text.* Eco 1979: 197–198.
181   *"of the content."* Eco 1979: 197.
181   *"of the other."* Eco 1979: 197.
182   *"of unlimited semiosis."* Eco 1976: 68.
182   *"condition of signification."* Eco 1979: 198.
183   *"place for study."* Todorov 1980: 77–78.
183   *dozens of them.* My own sample would include Crowder 1982; Flynn and Schweickart 1986; Smith 1988; Spiro, Bruce, and Brewer 1980; Taylor and Taylor 1983.
184   *"of the recipient."* Iser 1976: 34.
185   *"grasp the text."* Iser 1976: 34.
185   *"grasping and comprehending."* Iser 1976: 37.
185   *"schemata are aspects."* Iser 1976: 227.

185 *"has to apprehend."* Iser 1976: 109.
185 *"reader's constitutive activity."* Iser 1980: 118.
185 *"not been conscious."* Iser 1976: 158.
186 *the identity-governing-feedbacks model.* See Holland 1986 or 1988, ch. 4.
186 *"theorists in America."* Mailloux 1981.
187 *could possibly have.* Fish 1981: 10.
188 *the autonomous self.* Fish 1989: 342–343.
189 *"and the rhetorical."* Fish 1989: 344–45.
189 *"is an extension."* Fish 1989: 323.
189 *"interpretations securely rest."* Fish 1989: 185.
190 *"and already on."* Fish 1989: 12.
190 *"characterization or description."* Fish 1989: 158.
190 *"you can't refuse."* Fish 1989: 355.
193 *deflects our attention.* Roustang 1986, 1990.
193 *called "the" unconscious.* Strachey 1961.
193 *William J. Richardson.* Richardson 1983.
194 *"made of rings."* Richardson 1983: 54.
194 *"his conscious discourse."* Lacan 1966, Engl: 49.
194 *"element in cognition."* Ragland-Sullivan 1986: 196.
195 *"had just discovered."* The phrasings quoted are those of Elisabeth Roudinesco's English translator. Roudinesco 1990, 401. The seminar in which Lacan rejected Chomskyan linguistics is as yet unpublished and was unavailable to me. *Problèmes cruciaux pour la psychanalyse,* session of December 2, 1964.
195 *seminars he gave.* Lacan 1975. These seminars are, at the time I am writing, unpublished and untranslated. I am grateful to my colleague Daniel Moors for providing me a copy.
196 *on that occasion).* Turkle, Sherry. Personal communication, May 10, 1976. See also Turkle 1978: 244–45.
197 *"without my awareness."* Muller and Richardson 1982: 179.
197 *"situate myself there."* Lacan 1966, Engl: 166.
197 *"of the signifier."* Lacan 1956, Engl: 60.
198 *and even "insistence."* Sheridan 1977: vii-viii.
198 *"of the letter."* Benvenuto and Kennedy 1986: 107.
198 *slave of language,* Benvenuto and Kennedy 1986: 108.
198 *"the signifying chain."* Benvenuto and Kennedy 1986: 91.
198 *"carved Egyptian inscription."* Benvenuto and Kennedy 1986: 107.
198 *determinism is total.* Ragland-Sullivan 1986: 128, 145.
198 *does, the "Lacan-can."* Tallis 1988: 153.
198 *"radical behaviorist reductionism."* Chomsky 1964: 25.
199 *like the deconstructionists.* Holland 1985a.
199 *from Fenichel's character.* Fenichel 1945: 467.
199 *Lichtenstein's identity principle,* Lichtenstein 1961; 1977: 49–122.

199 *Maturana and Varela.* Maturana and Varela 1980; 1987.
200 *"ensembles of meaning."* Ragland-Sullivan 1986: 147.
200 *"locus of relationships."* Wilden 1968: 182.
200 *make this clear.* For a sample of the literature in this field see Crowder 1982; Dillon 1978; Flynn and Schweickart 1986; Kintgen 1983; Kolers 1972; Laberge and Samuels 1977; Meek 1983; Smith 1988; Spiro, Bruce, and Brewer 1980; Taylor and Taylor 1983.
200 *"the human subject."* Suleiman 1980: 41.
201 *"yet actually achieved."* Lacan 1953: 14–15.
201 *unified than he.* Lacan 1977: 1–2.
201 *development from 1903.* Baldwin 1903.
201 *its own existence.* Wallon 1934: 171–77.
201 *by Daniel Stern.* Stern 1971, 1974, 1977.
201 *behavior with mirrors.* Mahler 1982.
201 Abstracts *turns up.* See Amsterdam 1969, 1972; Lewis 1977; Lewis et al. 1985; Dixon 1957; Gallup 1979; Brooks-Gunn and Lewis 1975; Lewis and Brooks-Gunn 1984; Kronen 1982.
203 *designate the speaker.* Richardson 1983.
203 *"condemned to reproduce."* Lacan 1954–55: 112.
203 *the Rat Man.* Lacan 1953.
204 *"more rigorously pursued."* Muller and Richardson 1982: 416–417.
205 *common with mine.* I am grateful to Robert Silhol for helping me see the parallels.
206 *"of his functions."* Lacan 1966, Engl: 287; Fr: 692.
207 *function) accounts for.* Waelder 1930.
210 *"in nonliterary phenomena."* Culler 1987: 168.
211 *"before its arrival."* Ellis 1989: 153.
211 *"say they do."* Lentricchia 1983: 50.
212 *"defined and located."* Lentricchia 1983: 39.
212 *"commonplace and orthodox."* Fish 1987: 438; Fish 1989: 154–155.
213 *"of literary studies."* Hogan 1985: 183–84.
213 *"regard to non-heterosexuals?"* Hogan 1987: 85–86.
214 *"all by itself."* Bernstein 1990: 16.
216 *"the body politic."* Nightingale 1989.
219 *" 'the word means.' "* Ray 1984: 2.
225 *involved with identity.* Fodor 1983.
225 *for spatial relations.* Neisser 1988, 1989.
225 *central controlling identity.* Rumelhart et al. 1986.
227 *an "experientialist" account.* See Lakoff and Johnson 1980, especially chs. 25–30; Lakoff 1987; Johnson 1987.
228 *"relates to others."* Culler 1981: 33.
230 Mind's New Science. Gardner 1985.
230 *idea of scripts* Schank and Abelson 1977.

230   *structure our experience.* Flynn and Schweickart 1986. See especially the essays by Schweickart, Flynn, and Crawford and Chaffin.

230   *"or religious conditions."* Tompkins 1985, xvii.

230   *of "cognitive linguistics"* Lakoff and Johnson 1980; Lakoff 1987; Johnson 1987; Turner 1987; Lakoff and Turner 1989.

230   *other cognitive processes.* Lichtenstein 1977.

230   *and Francisco Varela.* Maturana and Varela 1987.

230   *system of symbols.* Brown 1978.

231   *new transactive paradigm* Holland 1976.

References

Abbreviations: P = Press, Presses
                U = University, Universities

Amsterdam, B. K. 1969. "Mirror-behavior in Children Under Two Years of Age." Ph. D. diss. U of North Carolina.

Amsterdam, B. K. 1972. "Mirror Self-image Reactions Before Age Two." *Developmental Psychobiology* 5:297–305.

Anderson, Richard C., Rand J. Spiro, and William E. Montague, eds. 1977. *Schooling and the Acquisition of Knowledge*. Hillsdale NJ: Lawrence Erlbaum.

Apperson, G. L., comp. 1929. *English Proverbs and Proverbial Phrases: A Historical Dictionary*. London and Toronto: J. M. Dent.

Applebee, Arthur N. 1978. *The Child's Concept of Story: Ages Two to Seventeen*. Chicago and London: U of Chicago P.

Baldwin, James Mark. 1903. *Mental Development in the Child and the Race: Methods and Processes*. 2d ed. New York and London: Macmillan.

Barnes, Deborah M. 1986. "Brain Architecture: Beyond Genes." Research News. *Science* 253 (July 11):155–56. Report of a conference, "Brain Beyond Genes," New York, June 2–4, 1986, Institute for Child Development Research, 330 Madison Ave., New York NY 10017.

Barthes, Roland. 1957. *Mythologies*. Paris: Éditions du Seuil. Trans. Annette Lavers. New York: Hill and Wang, 1972.

Barthes, Roland. 1970. *S/Z*. Paris: Éditions du Seuil. Trans. Richard Miller. New York: Hill and Wang, 1974.

Barthes, Roland. 1971a. Interview with Raymond Bellour. *Le Livre des autres*. Paris: L'Herne. Quoted and translated in Harari 1979b, 30.

Barthes, Roland. 1971b. "De l'oeuvre au texte." *Revue d'Esthétique* 24.3:225–32. "From Work to Text." Trans. Josué V. Harari. In Harari 1979b, 73–81.

Barthes, Roland. 1973. *Le Plaisir du texte*. Paris: Éditions de Seuil. *The Pleasure of the Text*. Trans. Richard Miller. New York: Hill and Wang, 1975.

Barthes, Roland. 1981. "Theory of the Text." In Robert Young, ed., *Untying the Text: A Post-Structuralist Reader*, 31–47. Boston and London: Routledge and Kegan Paul.

Bartlett, F. C. 1932. *Remembering: A Study in Experimental and Social Psychology*. Cambridge: Cambridge UP.

Bartlett, John, compiler. 1855. *Familiar Quotations: A Collection of Passages, Phrases, and Proverbs Traced to Their Sources in Ancient and Modern Literature*. 13th and Centennial Ed. Boston: Little, Brown, 1955.

Beaugrande, Robert de. 1988. *Critical Discourse: A Survey of Literary Theorists*. Norwood NJ: Ablex.

Benvenuto, Bice and Roger Kennedy. 1986. *The Works of Jacques Lacan: An Introduction*. New York: St. Martin's P.

Bernstein, Richard. 1990. "On Language: When Parentheses Are Transgressive." *New York Times Magazine* July 29:16.

Blakeslee, Sandra. 1986. "Rapid Changes Seen in Young Brain." Science Times, *New York Times* June 24: C1, C10.

Bloom, Harold. 1975. *A Map of Misreading*. New York: Oxford UP.

Bordwell, David. 1985. *Narration in the Fiction Film*. Madison: U of Wisconsin P.

Bordwell, David. 1989a. *Making Meaning: Inference and Rhetoric in the Interpretation of Cinema*. Cambridge: Harvard UP.

Bordwell, David. 1989b. "A Case for Cognitivism." *Iris* 9 (Spring):11–40.

Branigan, Edward. 1984. *Point of View in the Cinema: A Theory of Narration and Subjectivity in Classical Film*. Berlin and New York: Springer Verlag.

Branigan, Edward. 1986. " 'Here is a Picture of No Revolver!': The Negation of Images and Methods for Analyzing the Structure of Pictorial Statements." *Wide Angle* 8.3–4:8–17.

Brooks, Cleanth and Robert Penn Warren. 1960. *Understanding Poetry*. 3rd ed. New York: Holt, Rinehart, and Winston.

Brooks-Gunn, Jeanne and Michael Lewis. 1975. "Mirror-image Stimulation and Self-recognition in Infancy." ERIC ED no. 114 193.

Brooks-Gunn, Jeanne and Michael Lewis. 1984. "The Development of Early Visual Self-Recognition in Infancy." *Developmental Review* 4:215–39.

Brown, Homer Obed. 1981. "Ordinary Readers, Extraordinary Texts, and Ludmilla." *Criticism* 23:335–48.

Brown, Richard Harvey. 1978. "Symbolic Realism and Sociological Thought: Beyond the Positivist-Romantic Debate." In Richard Harvey

Brown and Stanford M. Lyman, eds., *Structure, Consciousness, and History*, 13–37. Cambridge: Cambridge UP.

Carver, Charles S. and Michael F. Scheier. 1981. *Attention and Self-Regulation: A Control-Theory Approach to Human Behavior.* New York and Berlin: Springer-Verlag.

Chomsky, Noam. 1957. *Syntactic Structures.* The Hague: Mouton.

Chomsky, Noam. 1959. "A Review of B. F. Skinner's *Verbal Behavior.*" *Language* 35:26–58. Reprinted in Jerry A. Fodor and Jerrold J. Katz, eds., *The Structure of Language: Readings in the Philosophy of Language*, 547–78. Englewood Cliffs NJ: Prentice-Hall, 1964.

Chomsky, Noam. 1964. *Current Issues in Linguistic Theory.* The Hague: Mouton.

Chomsky, Noam. 1965. *Aspects of the Theory of Syntax.* Cambridge: MIT P.

Chomsky, Noam. 1972. *Language and Mind.* Enlarged edition. New York: Harcourt Brace Jovanovich.

Chomsky, Noam. 1986. *Knowledge of Language: Its Nature, Origin, and Use.* New York: Praeger.

Chomsky, Noam. 1988a. *Language and Problems of Knowledge.* The Managua Lectures. Cambridge: MIT P.

Chomsky, Noam. 1988b. *Language in a Psychological Setting.* Lectures recorded at UCLA. 160 minutes, audiotape. 1814 Spruce, Boulder CO 80302: David Barsamian / Alternative Radio.

Cohen, J. M. and M. J. Cohen, comps. 1960. *The Penguin Dictionary of Quotations.* London: Allen Lane.

Crane, R. S. 1953. *The Languages of Criticism and the Structure of Poetry.* Toronto: U of Toronto P.

Crowder, Robert G. 1982. *The Psychology of Reading: An Introduction.* New York: Oxford UP.

Culler, Jonathan. 1980. "Prolegomena to a Theory of Reading." In Suleiman and Crosman 1980, 46–66.

Culler, Jonathan. 1981. *The Pursuit of Signs: Semiotics, Literature, Deconstruction.* Ithaca: Cornell UP.

Culler, Jonathan. 1982a. *On Deconstruction: Theory and Criticism after Structuralism.* Ithaca: Cornell UP.

Culler, Jonathan. 1982b. "Literature and Linguistics." In Jean-Pierre Barricelli and Joseph Gibaldi, eds., *Interrelations of Literature*, 1–24. New York: Modern Language Association of America.

Culler, Jonathan. 1987. "Poststructuralist Criticism." *Style* 21.2:167–80.

Davis, Robert Con, ed. 1986. *Contemporary Literary Criticism: Modernism Through Poststructuralism.* 1st ed. New York: Longman.

DeCasper, Anthony J. and Melanie J. Spence. 1986. "Prenatal Maternal Speech Influences Newborns' Perception of Speech Sounds." *Infant Behavior and Development* 9:133–50.

De Man, Paul. 1979. *Allegories of Reading: Figural Language in Rousseau, Nietzsche, Rilke, and Proust.* New Haven and London: Yale UP.

Derrida, Jacques. 1967a. *De la Grammatologie.* Paris: Minuit.

Derrida, Jacques. 1967b. *L'Écriture et la différence*. Collection *Tel Quel*. Philippe Sollers, ed. Paris: Éditions du Seuil.

Derrida, Jacques. 1970. "Structure, Sign, and Play in the Discourse of the Human Sciences." In Richard Macksey and Eugenio Donato, eds., *The Languages of Criticism and the Sciences of Man: The Structuralist Controversy*, 247–65. Baltimore and London: Johns Hopkins UP.

Derrida, Jacques. 1973. "Speech and Phenomena: Introduction to the Problem of Signs in Husserl's Phenomenology." In *Speech and Phenomena and Other Essays on Husserl's Theory of Signs*, 3–16. Trans. David B. Allison. Evanston: Northwestern UP.

Derrida, Jacques. 1976. *Of Grammatology*. Trans. Gayatri Chakravorty Spivak. Baltimore and London: Johns Hopkins UP.

Derrida, Jacques. 1977. "Signature Event Context." *Glyph* 1:172–97.

Derrida, Jacques. 1978. *Writing and Difference*. Trans. Alan Bass. Chicago: U of Chicago P.

Derrida, Jacques. 1981. *Positions*. Trans. Alan Bass. Chicago: U of Chicago P.

Deutsch, Helene. 1945. *The Psychology of Women*. 2 vols. New York: Grune and Stratton.

Dillon, George L. 1978. *Language Processing and the Reading of Literature: Toward a Model of Comprehension*. Bloomington and London: Indiana UP.

Dixon, J. C. 1957. "Development of Self-recognition." *Journal of Genetic Psychology* 91:251–56.

Dreyfus, Hubert L. and Paul Rabinow. 1983. *Michel Foucault: Beyond Structuralism and Hermeneutics*. 2d ed. Chicago: U of Chicago P.

Eagleton, Terry. 1983. *Literary Theory: An Introduction*. Minneapolis: U of Minnesota P.

Eco, Umberto. 1975. "Looking for a Logic of Culture." In Thomas A. Sebeok, ed., *The Tell-Tale Sign: A Survey of Semiotics*, 9–17. Lisse: Peter de Ridder P.

Eco, Umberto. 1976. *A Theory of Semiotics*. Bloomington: Indiana UP.

Eco, Umberto. 1979. *The Role of the Reader: Explorations in the Semiotics of Texts*. Bloomington: Indiana UP.

Ellis, John M. 1989. *Against Deconstruction*. Princeton: Princeton UP.

Fenichel, Otto. 1945. *The Psychoanalytic Theory of Neurosis*. New York: Norton.

Fish, Stanley. 1980. *Is There a Text in This Class? The Authority of Interpretive Communities*. Cambridge: Harvard UP.

Fish, Stanley. 1981. "Why No One's Afraid of Wolfgang Iser." *Diacritics* 11:2–13.

Fish, Stanley. 1987. "Change." *South Atlantic Quarterly* 86.4 (Fall):423–44.

Fish, Stanley. 1989. *Doing What Comes Naturally: Change, Rhetoric, and the Practice of Theory in Literary and Legal Studies*. Durham and London: Duke UP.

Flynn, Elizabeth A. and Patrocinio P. Schweickart, eds. 1986. *Gender and Reading: Essays on Readers, Texts, and Contexts.* Baltimore and London: Johns Hopkins UP.

Fodor, Jerry A. 1983. *Modularity of Mind: An Essay on Faculty Psychology.* Cambridge: MIT P.

Fodor, Jerry A. and Zenon W. Pylyshyn. 1981. "How Direct is Visual Perception? Some Reflections on Gibson's 'Ecological Approach.'" *Cognition* 9:139–96.

Foucault, Michel. 1966. *Les Mots et les choses.* Paris: Gallimard.

Foucault, Michel. 1969. "What Is an Author?" Trans. Josué V. Harari. In Harari 1979b, 141–60.

Foucault, Michel. 1970. *The Order of Things: An Archaeology of the Human Sciences.* New York: Pantheon Books, 1970.

Frye, Northrop. 1957. *Anatomy of Criticism.* Princeton: Princeton UP.

Frye, Northrop. 1963. "Literary Criticism." In James Thorpe, ed., *The Aims and Methods of Scholarship in Modern Languages and Literatures,* 57–69. New York: Modern Language Association.

Gallup, G. G., Jr. 1979. "Self-recognition in Chimpanzees and Man: A Developmental and Comparative Perspective." In Lewis and Rosenblum 1979, 2:107–26.

Gardner, Howard. 1985. *The Mind's New Science: A History of the Cognitive Revolution.* New York: Basic Books.

Gibson, Eleanor J. and Harry Levin. 1975. *The Psychology of Reading.* Cambridge and London: MIT P.

Gombrich, Ernst. 1960. *Art and Illusion: A Study in the Psychology of Pictorial Representation.* Princeton: Princeton UP.

Gombrich, Ernst. 1982. *The Image and the Eye: Further Studies in the Psychology of Pictorial Representation.* Ithaca: Cornell UP.

Goodman, Kenneth S. 1968. "The Psycholinguistic Nature of the Reading Process." In Kenneth S. Goodman, ed., *The Psycholinguistic Nature of the Reading Process,* 15–26. Detroit: Wayne State UP.

Graff, Gerald. 1987. *Professing Literature: An Institutional History.* Chicago and London: U of Chicago P.

Graff, Gerald and Reginald Gibbons, eds. 1985. *Criticism in the University.* *TriQuarterly* Series on Criticism and Culture, No. 1. Evanston IL: Northwestern UP.

Hacking, I. 1986. "The Archaeology of Foucault." In Hoy 1986b, 27–40.

Hanson, Norwood R. 1958. *Patterns of Discovery.* Cambridge: Cambridge UP.

Harari, Josué V. 1979a. "Critical Factions/Critical Fictions." In Harari 1979b, 17–72.

Harari, Josué V., ed. 1979b. *Textual Strategies: Perspectives in Post-Structuralist Criticism.* Ithaca: Cornell UP.

Hartman, Geoffrey H. 1979. Preface. Harold Bloom, Paul De Man, Jacques Derrida, Geoffrey H. Hartman, and J. Hillis Miller. *Deconstruction and Criticism.* New York: Seabury P.

Hill, Steven P. 1967. "Kuleshov—Prophet without Honor?" *Film Culture* 44 (Spring):2–16.

Hirsch, E. D., Jr. 1984. "Meaning and Significance Reinterpreted." *Critical Inquiry* 11:202–25.

Hogan, Patrick Colm. 1985. "The Political Economy of Criticism." In Graff and Gibbons 1985, 178–86.

Hogan, Patrick Colm. 1987. "Argumentation, Truth, and the Political Morality of Literary Theory." *Restant* 15.1:85–106.

Holland, Norman N. 1968. *The Dynamics of Literary Response.* New York: Oxford UP. New York: Columbia UP, 1989.

Holland, Norman N. 1975. *5 Readers Reading.* New Haven and London: Yale UP.

Holland, Norman N. 1976. "The New Paradigm: Subjective or Transactive?" *New Literary History* 7:335–46.

Holland, Norman N. 1978. "Literary Interpretation and Three Phases of Psychoanalysis." In Alan Roland, ed., *Psychoanalysis, Creativity, and Literature: A French-American Inquiry,* 233–47. New York: Columbia UP.

Holland, Norman N. 1982. *Laughing: A Psychology of Humor.* Ithaca and London: Cornell UP.

Holland, Norman N. 1983. "Postmodern Psychoanalysis." In Ihab Hassan and Sally Hassan, eds., *Innovation/Renovation: New Perspectives on the Humanities,* 291–309. Madison WI: U of Wisconsin P.

Holland, Norman N. 1985a. "Speaking Figuratively, I . . . '' Keynote address, Fourteenth Annual Twentieth-Century Literature Conference: Self and Other. U of Louisville, February 22.

Holland, Norman N. 1985b. *The I.* New Haven and London: Yale UP.

Holland, Norman N. 1986. "The Miller's Wife and the Professors: Questions about the Transactive Theory of Reading." *New Literary History* 17:423–47.

Holland, Norman N. 1988. *The Brain of Robert Frost.* New York and London: Routledge.

Holland, Norman N. 1989. "Film Response from Eye to I: The Kuleshov Experiment." *South Atlantic Quarterly* 88 (Spring): 415–42.

Holland, Norman N. and Murray Schwartz. 1975. "The Delphi Seminar." *College English* 36:789–800.

Hoy, David C. 1986a. Introduction. In Hoy 1986b, 1–25.

Hoy, David C., ed. 1986b. *Foucault: A Critical Reader.* Oxford: Basil Blackwell.

Iser, Wolfgang. 1976. *Der Akt des Lesens: Theorie ästhetischer Wirkung.* Munich: Wilhelm Frink. *The Act of Reading: A Theory of Aesthetic Response.* Baltimore and London: Johns Hopkins UP, 1978.

Iser, Wolfgang. 1980. "Interaction between Text and Reader." In Suleiman and Crosman 1980, 106–19.

Jauss, Hans Robert. 1970. *Literaturgeschichte als Provokation der Literaturwissenschaft.* Frankfurt: Suhrkamp.

Johnson, Barbara. 1978. "The Critical Difference." *Diacritics* 8/2:2–9.
Johnson, Barbara. 1980. "Nothing Fails like Success." *Society for Critical Exchange Reports* 8:7–16.
Johnson, Barbara. 1984. "Rigorous Unreliability." *Critical Inquiry* 11:278–85.
Johnson, Mark. 1987. *The Body in the Mind: The Bodily Basis of Meaning, Imagination and Reason.* Chicago and London: U of Chicago P.
Kearns, James and Ken Newton. 1980. "An Interview with Jacques Derrida." *The Literary Review* 14 (April 18-May 1):21–22.
Kenner, Hugh. 1989. "Ode on an OED." *New York Times Book Review* April 16:26–27.
Kintgen, Eugene R. 1983. *The Perception of Poetry.* Bloomington: Indiana UP.
Kolers, Paul A. 1972. "Experiments in Reading." *Scientific American* (July):84–91.
Kronen, Jerilyn. 1982. "Maternal Facial Mirroring at Four Months." *Dissertation Abstracts International* 43 (October):1237-B. Dissertation, Yeshiva U.
Laberge, David and S. Jay Samuels, eds. 1977. *Basic Processes in Reading: Perception and Comprehension.* New York: Lawrence Erlbaum.
Lacan, Jacques. 1953. "Le mythe individuel du nevrosé ou 'Poésie et Verité' dans la nevrose." *Ornicar?*, No. 17. "The Neurotic's Individual Myth." Trans. Jacques-Alain Miller. *Psychoanalytic Quarterly* 48 (1979):405–25.
Lacan, Jacques. 1954–55. *Le Séminaire: Livre II. Le moi dans la théorie de Freud et dans la technique de la psychanalyse.* Paris: Éditions du Seuil, 1978.
Lacan, Jacques. 1956. "Le séminaire sur 'La lettre volée.'" *La Psychanalyse* 2:1–44. "Seminar on 'The Purloined Letter.'" Trans. Jeffrey Mehlman. *Yale French Studies* 48 (1972): 38–72.
Lacan, Jacques. 1966. *Écrits.* Paris: Éditions du Seuil. *Écrits: A Selection.* Trans. Alan Sheridan. New York: Norton, 1977.
Lacan, Jacques. 1975. "Le Sinthome." Unpublished photocopy of transcript. Séminaire du 9 décembre 1975. Paris.
Lakoff, George. 1987. *Women, Fire, and Dangerous Things: What Categories Reveal About the Mind.* Chicago and London: U of Chicago P.
Lakoff, George and Mark Johnson. 1980. *Metaphors We Live By.* Chicago and London: U of Chicago P.
Lakoff, George and Mark Turner. 1989. *More than Cool Reason: A Field Guide to Poetic Metaphor.* Chicago and London: U of Chicago P.
Leitch, Vincent B. 1983. *Deconstructive Criticism: An Advanced Introduction.* New York: Columbia UP.
Lenneberg, Eric H. 1976. "Problems in the Comparative Study of Language." In Bruce Masterton, William Hodos, and Harry Jerison, eds., *Evolution, Brain, and Behavior: Persistent Problems*, 199–213. Hillsdale NJ: Lawrence Erlbaum.

Lentricchia, Frank. 1980. *After the New Criticism*. Chicago: U of Chicago P.

Lentricchia, Frank. 1983. *Criticism and Social Change*. Chicago and London: U of Chicago P.

Lewis, Michael. 1977. "The Busy, Purposeful World of a Baby." *Psychology Today* 10.9:53–56.

Lewis, Michael and Jeanne Brooks. 1975. "Infants' Social Perception: A Constructivist View." In Leslie B. Cohen and Philip Salapatek, eds., *Infant Perception: From Sensation to Cognition*. 2 vols. 2:101–48. New York: Academic P.

Lewis, Michael, Jeanne Brooks-Gunn, and John Jaskir. 1985. "Individual Differences in Visual Self-Recognition as a Function of Mother-infant Attachment Relationship." *Developmental Psychobiology* 21.6:1181–87.

Lewis, Michael and Leonard A. Rosenblum, eds. 1974. *The Effect of the Infant on Its Caregiver*. New York: Wiley.

Lewis, Michael and L. Rosenblum, eds. 1979. *The Child and Its Family; The Genesis of Behavior*. 2 vols. New York: Plenum P.

Lichtenstein, Heinz. 1961. "Identity and Sexuality: A Study of Their Interrelationship in Man." *Journal of the American Psychoanalytic Association* 9:179–260.

Lichtenstein, Heinz. 1977. *The Dilemma of Human Identity*. New York: Jason Aronson.

Luria, Aleksandr Romanovich. 1980. *Higher Cortical Functions in Man*. 2d ed. Trans. Basil Haigh. New York: Basic Books.

Lyons, John. 1978. *Noam Chomsky*. Rev. ed. Penguin Modern Masters. Harmondsworth: Penguin.

Lyons, John. 1983. "Linguistics." *Encyclopedia Britannica*. 1983 ed.

Macksey, Richard and Eugenio Donato, eds. 1970. *The Languages of Criticism and the Sciences of Man*. Baltimore: Johns Hopkins UP.

Mahler, Margaret and John B. McDevitt. 1982. "Thoughts on the Emergence of the Sense of Self, with Particular Emphasis on the Body Self." *Journal of the American Psychoanalytic Association* 30:827–48.

Mailloux, Steven. 1981. "How to Be Persuasive in Literary Theory: The Case of Wolfgang Iser." *Centrum* n.s., 1.1 (Spring):65–73.

Manheim, Leonard and Eleanor Manheim, eds. 1966. *Hidden Patterns: Studies in Psychoanalytic Literary Criticism*. New York and London: Macmillan.

Marcus, Mitchell. 1984. "Some Inadequate Theories of Human Language Processing." In Thomas G. Bever, John M. Carroll, and Lance A. Miller, eds., *Talking Minds: The Study of Language in Cognitive Science*, 253–77. Cambridge: MIT P.

Maturana, Humberto R. and Francisco J. Varela. 1980. *Autopoiesis and Cognition: The Realization of the Living*. Dordrecht, Boston, and London: D. Reidel.

Maturana, Humberto R. and Francisco J. Varela. 1987. *The Tree of Knowl-*

edge: The Biological Roots of Human Understanding, Boston and London: New Science Library.

Meek, Margaret. 1983. With Stephen Armstrong, Vicky Austerfield, Judith Graham, and Elizabeth Plackett. *Achieving Literacy: Longitudinal Studies of Adolescents Learning to Read.* London: Routledge and Kegan Paul.

Miller, J. Hillis. 1966. *Poets of Reality: Six Twentieth-Century Writers.* Cambridge: Harvard UP.

Miller, J. Hillis. 1975. "Deconstructing the Deconstructors." Review of *The Inverted Bell* by Joseph Riddel. *Diacritics* 5:24–31.

Miller, J. Hillis. 1976a. "Stevens' Rock and Criticism as Cure, II." *Georgia Review* 30:330–48.

Miller, J. Hillis. 1976b. "The Linguistic Moment in 'The Wreck of the Deutschland.' " In Thomas Daniel Young, ed., *The New Criticism and After,* 47–60. Charlottesville: U of Virginia P.

Miller, J. Hillis. 1977. "Nature and the Linguistic Moment." In U. C. Knoepflmacher and G. B. Tennyson, eds., *Nature and the Victorian Imagination,* 440–51. Berkeley: U of California P.

Miller, J. Hillis. 1986. "President's Column: Responsibility and the Joy (?) of Teaching." *MLA Newsletter* (Summer):2.

Miller, J. Hillis. 1987. "Presidential Address 1986: The Triumph of Theory, the Resistance to Reading, and the Question of the Material Base." *PMLA* 102:281–91.

Miller, J. Hillis. 1988. Forum. *PMLA* 103:820–21.

Moskowitz, Breye Arlene. 1978. "The Acquisition of Language." In William S-Y. Wang, ed., *Human Communication: Language and Its Psychobiological Bases,* 121–31. San Francisco: W. H. Freeman, 1982.

Muller, John P. and William J. Richardson. 1982. *Lacan and Language: A Reader's Guide to Écrits.* New York: International UP.

Neisser, Ulric. 1967. *Cognitive Psychology.* New York: Appleton-Century-Crofts.

Neisser, Ulric. 1976. *Cognition and Reality: Principles and Implications of Cognitive Psychology.* San Francisco: W. H. Freeman.

Neisser, Ulric. 1988. "Five Kinds of Self-Knowledge." *Philosophical Psychology* 1:35–59.

Neisser, Ulric. 1989. "Direct Perception and Recognition as Distinct Perceptual Systems." Department of Psychology, U of Florida. October 12.

Nietzsche, Friedrich. 1901. *The Will to Power.* Trans. and ed. Walter Kaufmann and R. J. Hollingdale. New York: Random House, 1967.

Nightingale, Benedict. 1989. "The Tools an English Writer Used For Building an Industrial Novel." (Interview with David Lodge.) *New York Times* October 16, The Living Arts.

Northall, G. F., compiler. 1892. *English Folk-Rhymes: A Collection of Traditional Verses Relating to Places and Persons, Customs, Superstititions, etc.* London: Kegan Paul, Trench, Truebner. Nunberg, Henry. 1931. "The Synthetic Function of the Ego." *International Journal of Psychoanalysis* 12:123–40.

Ohmann, Richard. 1976. *English in America: A Radical View of the Profession.* New York: Oxford UP.

Paris, Bernard J. 1974. *A Psychological Approach to Fiction: Studies in Thackeray, Stendhal, George Eliot, Dostoevsky, and Conrad.* Bloomington: Indiana UP.

Perfetti, Charles A. 1985. "Reading Ability." In Sternberg 1985, 59–82.

Polan, Dana. 1986. "The 'Kuleshov Effect' Effect." *Iris* 4.1 (sp. issue: L'effet Koulechov/The Kuleshov Effect): 95–105.

Powers, William T. 1973. *Behavior: The Control of Perception.* Chicago: Aldine.

Powers, William T. 1978. "Quantitative Analysis of Purposive Systems: Some Spadework at the Foundations of Scientific Psychology." *Psychological Review* 85:417–35.

Pudovkin, Vsevelod I. 1929. *Film Technique and Film Acting: The Cinema Writings of V. I. Pudovkin.* Trans. Ivor Montague. London: Vision, 1944.

Putnam, Hilary. 1981. *Reason, Truth, and History.* Cambridge: Harvard UP.

Pylyshyn, Zenon W. 1984. *Computation and Cognition: Toward a Foundation for Cognitive Science.* Cambridge: MIT P.

Ragland-Sullivan, Ellie. 1986. *Jacques Lacan and the Philosophy of Psychoanalysis.* Urbana and Chicago: U of Illinois P.

Rajnath. 1989. "The New Criticism and Deconstruction: Attitudes to Language and Literature." In Rajnath, ed., *Deconstruction: A Critique.* London: Macmillan.

Ray, William. 1984. *Literary Meaning: From Phenomenology to Deconstruction.* Oxford: Blackwell.

Reddy, Michael. 1979. "The Conduit Metaphor—A Case of Frame Conflict in Our Language about Language." In Andrew Ortony, ed., *Metaphor and Thought,* 284–324. Cambridge: Cambridge UP.

Restak, Richard M. 1986. *The Infant Mind.* Garden City NY: Doubleday.

Richards, I. A. 1934. *Coleridge on Imagination.* Bloomington: Indiana UP, 1960.

Richardson, William J. 1983. "Lacan and the Subject of Psychoanalysis." In Joseph H. Smith and William Kerrigan, eds., *Interpreting Lacan,* 51–74. Psychiatry and the Humanities, vol. 6. New Haven and London: Yale UP.

Rorty, Richard. 1986. "Foucault and Epistemology." In Hoy 1986b, 41–49.

Roudinesco, Elisabeth. *Jacques Lacan & Co.: A History of Psychoanalysis in France, 1925–1985.* Trans. Jeffrey Mehlman. Chicago: University of

Chicago Press, 1990. *La bataille de cent ans: Histoire de la psychanalyse en France, 2.* Paris: Éditions du Seuil, 1986.

Roustang, François. 1986. *Lacan de l'équivoque à l'impasse.* Paris: Éditions de Minuit.

Roustang, François. 1990. *The Lacanian Delusion.* New York: Oxford UP.

Rumelhart, David E. 1977. *Introduction to Human Information Processing.* New York: Wiley.

Rumelhart, David. E. and D. Zipser. 1986. "Feature Discovery by Competitive Learning." In Rumelhart et al. 1986, 1:151–94.

Rumelhart, David E., James L. McClelland, and the PDP Research Group. 1986. *Parallel Distributed Processing: Explorations in the Microstructure of Cognition.* 2 vols. A Bradford Book. Cambridge: MIT P.

Saussure, Ferdinand de. 1915. *Cours de Linguistique Générale.* Charles Bally, Albert Sechehaye, and Albert Reidlinger, eds. 3d ed. Paris: Payot, 1955. *Course in General Linguistics.* Trans. Wade Baskin. New York: Philosophical Library, 1959.

Schank, Roger and Robert P. Abelson. 1977. *Scripts, Plans, Goals, and Understanding: An Inquiry into Human Knowledge Structures.* Hillsdale NJ: Lawrence Erlbaum.

Schwartz, Murray M. 1975. "Where is Literature?" *College English* 36: 756–65.

Segers, Rien T. 1975. "Readers, Text and Author: Some Implications of *Rezeptionsästhetik.*" *Yearbook of Comparative and General Literature* 24:15–23.

Selden, Raman. 1985. *A Reader's Guide to Contemporary Literary Theory.* Lexington: UP of Kentucky.

Shenker, Israel. 1989. "Annals of Lexicography (O.E.D.)." *New Yorker* April 3:86–100.

Sheridan, Alan. 1977. "Translator's Note." Jacques Lacan. *Écrits: A Selection.* vii-xii. New York: Norton.

Smith, Frank. 1971. *Understanding Reading: A Psycholinguistic Analysis of Reading and Learning to Read.* 3d ed. New York: Holt, Rinehart and Winston.

Smith, Frank. 1978. *Reading.* Cambridge: Cambridge UP.

Smith, Frank. 1988. *Understanding Reading: A Psycholinguistic Analysis of Reading and Learning to Read.* 4th ed. New York: Holt, Rinehart, and Winston.

Smith, Frank and D. L. Holmes. 1971. "The Independence of Letter, Word, and Meaning Identification in Reading." *Reading Research Quarterly* 6:394–415.

Spencer, Theodore. 1943. "How To Criticize a Poem (In the Manner of Certain Contemporary Critics)." *The New Republic* 109:816–18.

Spencer, Theodore. 1966. "How to Criticize a Poem." *Selected Essays.* Alan C. Purves, ed. 352–55. New Brunswick: Rutgers UP.

Spiro, Rand J., Bertram C. Bruce, and William F. Brewer, eds. 1980. "Introduction." *Theoretical Issues in Reading Comprehension: Perspectives from Cognitive Psychology, Linguistics, Artificial Intelligence, and Education.* 7–9. Hillsdale NJ: Erlbaum.

Stern, Daniel N. 1971. "A Micro-analysis of Mother-infant Interaction: Behaviors Regulating Social Contact Between a Mother and Her Three-and-a-half-month-old Twins." *Journal of American Academy of Child Psychiatry* 10:501–07.

Stern, Daniel N. 1974. "Mother and Infant at Play: The Dyadic Interaction Involving Facial, Vocal, and Gaze Behaviors." In Lewis and Rosenblum 1974, 187–213.

Stern, Daniel N. 1977. *The First Relationship: Infant and Mother.* The Developing Child. Cambridge: Harvard UP.

Sternberg, Robert J., ed. 1985. *Human Abilities: An Information-Processing Approach.* New York: W. H. Freeman.

Stevenson, Burton, comp. 1967. *The Home Book of Quotations: Classical and Modern.* 10th ed. New York: Dodd and Mead.

Strachey, James. 1961. "Editor's Introduction" to *The Ego and the Id. The Standard Edition of the Complete Psychological Works of Sigmund Freud.* Trans. and ed. James Strachey, Anna Freud, Alix Strachey, and Alan Tyson. 24 vols. 19:3–11. London: Hogarth P, 1953–1974.

Suleiman, Susan R. 1980. Introduction. In Suleiman and Crosman, 1980, 3–45.

Suleiman, Susan R. and Inge Crosman, eds. 1980. *The Reader in the Text: Essays on Audience and Interpretation.* Princeton: Princeton UP.

Sweetser, Eve. 1990. *From Etymology to Pragmatics: The Mind-as-Body Metaphor in Semantic Structure and Semantic Change.* Cambridge: Cambridge UP.

Tallis, Raymond. 1988. *Not Saussure: A Critique of Post-Saussurean Literary Theory.* London: Macmillan.

Taylor, Insup and Martin M. Taylor. 1983. *The Psychology of Reading.* New York: Academic P.

Todorov, Tzvetan. 1980. "Reading as Construction." Trans. Inge Crosman and Thekla Zachrau. In Suleiman and Crosman 1980, 67–105.

Tompkins, Jane. 1985. *Sensational Designs: The Cultural Work of American Fiction 1790–1860.* New York: Oxford UP.

Turkle, Sherry. 1978. *Psychoanalytic Politics: Freud's French Revolution.* New York: Basic Books.

Turner, Mark. 1987. *Death is the Mother of Beauty: Mind, Metaphor, Criticism.* Chicago and London: U of Chicago P.

Waelder, Robert. 1930. "Das Prinzip der Mehrfachen Funktion." *Internationale Zeitschrift für Psychanalyse* 16:286–300. "The Principle of Multiple Function: Observations on Over-Determination." *Psychoanalytic Quarterly* 5 (1936):45–62.

Wallon, Henri. 1934. *Les Origines du Caractère chez l'Enfant: Les Préludes du sentiment de personnalité.* 3d ed. Paris: Presses Universitaires de France, 1954.

Wilden, Anthony. 1968. "Lacan and the Discourse of the Other." Jacques
    Lacan. *The Language of the Self*. Baltimore: Johns Hopkins UP. 159–
    311.
Woods, William A. 1980. "Multiple Theory Formation in Speech and Read-
    ing." In Spiro, Bruce, and Brewer, 1980, 59–82.

Index